BACKSTREETS

BACKSTREETS

SPRINGSTEEN: THE MAN AND HIS MUSIC

Charles R. Cross and the editors of **Backstreets** *Magazine*

. . . . .

With Contributions by Erik Flannigan, Robert Santelli, Robert Hilburn,

Mary Schuh, Andy Reid, Ed Sciaky, Paul Williams, Arlen Schumer,

Ken Viola, Marcello Villella, Chuck Bauerlein, Ruth Atherly, Steven Allan,

and the Asbury Park Rock 'n' Roll Museum

. . . . .

Design by John Fontana

HARMONY BOOKS
. . . . .
New York

Photographs by Phil Ceccola, Lynn Goldsmith, David Gahr, Eric Meola, Barbara Pyle, Joel Bernstein, David DuBois, Debra L. Rothenberg, David Denenberg, Rex Rystedt, James Shive, Watt M. Casey, Jr., A.J. Pantsios, Mike D'Adamo, Kathie Maniaci, Steve Zuckerman, Jeff Albertson, Paul Johnson, Robert Minkin, Kenny Barr, the Asbury Park Rock 'n' Roll Museum, Steven Allan, Ron Delany, Vinnie Zuffante, Brooks Kraft, Chuck Jackson, Franck Stromme, Joanne Jefferson, John C. DeSantis, Marty Perez, Jim O'Loughlin, Kathleen M. Gammon, Mark Greenberg, and Todd Kaplan.

Production by Dale Yarger · Type by RocketType

Most of the contents of this book were originally published in *Backstreets* magazine. The following articles are reprinted by permission of the authors:

"Glory Days: I Played Baseball Against the Boss and Won (Sort of) by Chuck Bauerlein. Copyright © 1985 by Charles R. Bauerlein. Originally published in *Sports Illustrated*, October 14, 1985.

"Out in the Streets" by Robert Hilburn. Originally published in the *Los Angeles Times*.

"Lost in the Flood" by Paul Williams. Copyright © 1988 by Paul Williams.

"Bruce Has the Fever" by Ed Sciaky. Copyright © 1978 by Ed Sciaky.

Published by Harmony Books, a division of Crown Publishers, Inc., 201 East 50th Street, New York, New York 10022

HARMONY and colophon are trademarks of Crown Publishers, Inc.

Manufactured in Japan

Library of Congress Cataloging-in-Publication Data

Backstreets: Springsteen • The Man and His Music/Charles Cross and the editors of *Backstreets,* with Erik Flannigan, Mary Schuh, and Robert Santelli; contributions by Andy Reid...[et al.].
p.   cm.
Discography: p.
1. Springsteen, Bruce.   2. Springsteen, Bruce—Interviews.
3. Rock musicians—United States—Interviews.   I. Cross, Charles.
II. Backstreets.
ML420.S77S7   1989
784.5'4'00924—dc19   89-1882

ISBN 0-517-57399-7

10 9 8 7 6 5 4 3 2 1
First Edition

CONTENTS

REASON TO BELIEVE

An Introduction to Backstreets Magazine and This Book

GROWIN' UP

Asbury Park, Freehold, and the Jersey Shore Music Scene

TALK TO ME

Interviews with the Man and the Band

CONTENTS
. . . .

THE TIES THAT BIND
Fans Behind the Scenes

YOU CAN LOOK (BUT YOU BETTER NOT TOUCH)
Springsteen Collectibles

SPARE PARTS
Springsteen's Studio Sessions, 1966-88

PROVE IT ALL NIGHT
Springsteen's Performances, 1965-89

RESOURCES AND PHOTO CREDITS

ACKNOWLEDGMENTS
Tramps Like Us . . .

REASON TO BELIEVE

Have You Heard the News?

Running into the Darkness: Seattle, Wash., December 20, 1978.

REASON TO BELIEVE
. . . .

An Introduction to Backstreets *Magazine and This Book*

"**H**ave you heard the news? There's good rockin' tonight." That's the line I thought I heard Bruce Springsteen shout out at ten minutes before eight on October 24, 1980, and hearing it sent panic through my bones. Listening now to tapes of that night, I'm sure that's what Springsteen said — but at the time I could barely make out Springsteen's gruff mumble before the E Street Band kicked in behind him. Though there was a front-row-center seat inside the hall with my name on it, I was still standing outside the coliseum when those first chords came pounding out.

Now, almost ten years later, you hold in your hands one culmination of that tardiness. Rather than hear the news that night, I was outside passing out my own version of the news — the very first issue of my own Springsteen fanzine, a four-page tab called *Backstreets*. Little did I know at the time that a decade later the damn thing would still be around as a quarterly magazine and be called by some "the world's greatest fanzine." As I write this, more than 30 issues of *Backstreets* have been published, and in the magazine industry (where 90 percent of all new titles fail within the first three years) that's a lifetime. Add all those issues together and you get over 1,000 pages of Bruce Springsteen news and comment, making *Backstreets* the single largest source for Springsteen information anywhere — bigger, more complete, and, perhaps, with even more continuing impact than any of the many biographies written about the Boss.

Backstreets was, is, and probably always will be a nutty idea: an entire magazine devoted exclusively to one performer. While there have been numerous other fanzines about popular performers through the years, most have been either photocopied labors of love devoted to cult artists or publications created by performers' press agents as vehicles for pin-up pictures. *Backstreets* has never sought to be a pin-up forum, nor have we ever been photocopied. Our timing has been such that we never had the opportunity to write about Springsteen as a cult figure; by the time we began, he was already a certified superstar.

We did have one model, a Springsteen fanzine called *Thunder Road* that broke some ground when it first appeared in 1978, while Bruce was still a cult artist. It had its problems, though. Only six issues were published in seven years, and its mix — half official and approved of, and half fan-oriented — didn't take. But following that lead, and fueled by a desire to spread the gospel of Bruce Springsteen, I decided to publish my own Springsteen fanzine. I had already written numerous stories about Springsteen for my college newspaper, of which I was the editor, but undertaking my own magazine called for a leap of faith. And I think a leap of faith was exactly what I was looking for.

Getting ready for that jump meant dropping the objective, distanced stance taught me by my college journalism instructors. I had never felt that the Associated Press inverted-pyramid style of news reporting was appropriate for rock 'n' roll, and it certainly made no sense as applied to Bruce Springsteen. That's not to say one *can't* be objective about Springsteen, as I once wrote an objective, AP-style story about Springsteen with little of my personal emotion in it. This was back in 1975, when Springsteen performed his Seattle debut only a week after the *Time* and *Newsweek* Springsteen covers hit newsstands. I wrote a factual piece that described Springsteen's background, listed the songs played and the manner in which they were performed, and left the hyperbole out. I turned the article in to the paper's editor, who completely ignored my story (though he used my background facts) and wrote his own "rip job" illustrated by the word "HYPE," which he'd spelled out by cutting those letters from the *Time* and *Newsweek* covers. The headline read, in part, "Bruce Springsteen, 'the biggest hype since Frankie Avalon.'" So much for the virtues of objectivity. I get a little satisfaction by looking at that clipping and realizing that collectors pay upwards of $100 for a mint *Time* or *Newsweek* from that week. That editor not only made one of the biggest critical miscues in history, but he also cut up a $400 nest egg in the process.

I'd first seen Bruce Springsteen play in the summer of 1974 at the Bottom Line in New York City. Though it was a legendary show, it's hard for me to remember too much about it, as I was completely unfamiliar with him or his music that night. Springsteen ended up playing a guitar solo standing atop my table, and as he dripped sweat on me that hot summer night, I imagine I was baptized in some alien way. I came out of the theater a changed sixteen-year-old (I'd snuck in on a fake ID). I lived on the East Coast at the time, so I caught as many Bruce shows as I could after that, seeing some incendiary shows at halls like the Mosque in Richmond, Virginia, my hometown.

Those were early days of wild romance, late-night drives, summers at the beach — both for me in my life, and in Springsteen's songs at the time. I enjoyed seeing Bruce live more than any other performer. But you couldn't have called me a Bruce Tramp yet. That happened on December 20, 1978, at the show I chose to write about in the first issue of *Backstreets*.

The hall was the Seattle Center Arena, which held about 5,000 spectators. The Seattle date was less than a week after the legendary Winterland concerts and broadcasts, but for my taste it was an infinitely better show. Springsteen performed "Pretty Flamingo" for the first time in years, and unreleased versions of songs like "The Ties That Bind," "Rendezvous" and "The Fever." "Prove It All Night" ripped like a chainsaw from hell, and during the guitar solo Bruce broke two strings, yet he never hesitated or changed guitars, he simply continued playing, and what the song lacked in dynamic range he made up in dynamite. He did both his "Mona/She's the One/Gloria" medley and the touching "Backstreets/Drive All Night" segue. There was also an early version of "Independence Day" and the classic romantic barn-burner "Fire." Of the 26 songs played that night, 15 were either entirely unavailable on record or not available in the versions performed that night.

Yeah, it was great; it was magic; it was *something*. When Springsteen ended his third and seemingly final encore with "Quarter to Three," declaring himself "just a prisoner of rock 'n' roll," I remember distinctly thinking to myself, "This is the best concert I've ever seen in my life." By three encores I don't mean three *songs* as part of an encore set, I mean he left the stage on three separate occasions, only to be drawn back out by the applause. For the Winterland broadcast, Springsteen had also stunned the crowd, the announcers, and the radio audience by doing three encores (stunned them so completely that the final song "Quarter to Three" was cut off the broadcast). In Seattle, "Quarter to Three" ended about one in the morning, with Bruce stomping on my fingers while Clarence dripped about a gallon of sweat onto my already sopping head. If I'd gone to Clarence's house that night, I'm sure his dogs would have greeted me like family.

I was sitting in my chair completely exhausted. (It wasn't my chair, but I'd rushed the stage about three hours earlier and hadn't seen my chair since then, so who cared?) I'd been on 20-mile runs that had left me with more energy. My knuckles were bleeding, my ears were ringing like an errant auto alarm, and I was so hoarse from shouting that I sounded like Sally Kellerman with a head cold. I wasn't doing too much talking, though — my friends and I just sat there staring at each other, and there was nothing to say. There were about 200 people left in the hall at this point, and all of us seemed too confused or too tired to know what to do with the rest of the evening, maybe with the rest of our lives. I imagine we were all asking the same questions of ourselves: Just what do you do to follow this experience? Is there an encore in life that matches what we'd just seen Bruce Springsteen accomplish? We sat and pondered the answers while the roadies ripped down the speakers. I was lucky enough to grab the set list from the front of Springsteen's monitor — the set he'd drawn up had ended about two hours earlier, and the rest had been uncharted. The hall was silent as I read, since all the applause had ended ten full minutes earlier. Those of us who remained were just too tired to leave, so we sat and watched fat guys rip wires out of sockets and drop speaker cabinets.

Then it happened. It was such a strange thing to see that I at first actually wiped my eyes to make

Holmdel, N.J., 1978 ▶

Tacoma Dome, Tacoma, Wash., October 19, 1984.

sure it wasn't some apparition. From stage left, with a towel around his neck and carrying a guitar, Bruce Springsteen was running onstage. When I said before that there was no applause left, I meant there was absolutely no applause at all (almost everyone had left) when Springsteen came running onstage. He wasn't walking or sauntering, either, the way most performers would go onstage for an encore; he ran as if in some mad dash, like the character in the movie *D.O.A.* in a desperate search to locate an antidote that would be the only thing to save him from certain death. Not only did the sight of him stun me, but the whole audience watched in disbelief. I think they, like myself, were half expecting him to go up to the mike and announce that some horrible national tragedy had occurred, or that maybe he'd say, "The building is on fire, get the hell out of here!" But when he ran up to the only remaining mike stand, the one usually reserved for Steve Van Zandt, he started yelling and strumming his guitar. He wasn't yelling anything about a fire, though. He was unamplified, but I could hear him yell "Rave on!"

Around this time the rest of the band started to waltz back onstage, and maybe 20 people in the crowd started politely clapping. Springsteen was already into the second verse at this point, which was a little strange since he had no amp for his guitar and "Rave On" is not exactly "This Land Is Your Land" when it comes to intimacy. Finally, Bruce pulled up and waited as the roadies madly dashed to get equipment plugged back in. Everyone — the band, the audience, the roadies — just sort of stood there for a while, looking at Bruce. And there he was, with a big grin. After three years of nasty lawsuits; after a time he described even ten years later as his own season of hell; after a three-hour concert that had exhausted even the hot-dog vendors; after it seemed he'd already said everything that could or should be said about rock 'n' roll; after all that, Bruce Springsteen just stood there with that stupid gap between his teeth, looking for all the world like the Cheshire Cat. It was one of the handful of times in your life — like your first kiss with the woman you'll eventually marry — when you know you are experiencing a moment that you will never forget. I've never forgotten that grin. I never will.

Springsteen played "Rave On" and "Twist and Shout" and finished it up. There had been about

200 people left in the hall, but when the sound became amplified, anyone within hearing distance charged back into the arena and maybe another 200 made it, knocking over security guards in the process. When Springsteen finished "Twist and Shout" and left the stage again, it was with confusion as much as appreciation that the crowd responded. The tape I have of the show is fascinating — you can hear the remaining members of the crowd trying to come to terms with what they'd just seen (and you can hear me in the background, shouting "BROOOOOCE!" like a loon). "I thought it was all over," says one guy standing right next to the tape recorder. "I kind of got caught off guard. Half the people had already left." "Yeah," chirps in another. "Wild, isn't it?" Wild and innocent.

At this point, nobody was leaving the building until the security guards threw us out — I mean, who was to say that Bruce wouldn't come back one more time? Finally, all the lights were turned off, which meant that the remaining crowd had to find their way out in the dark.

When we did leave the building, we found a chilly December night and a full moon. The temperature had dropped a good 20 degrees in the five hours since we'd entered the hall, and it was so late that the Monorail (the main method of transportation between the Seattle Center and downtown) had shut down. With my friends, I walked the 20 blocks to the core of the city in silence, and it actually started to snow — a rare occurrence in Seattle, even in December. I made it home at 15 minutes after four on the morning of December 21. It had never felt more like Christmas.

· · · · ·

That December 20 show may not be the single best Springsteen concert ever (that honor may be held by Berkeley Community Theater 1978 or L.A. Sports Arena 1981 or maybe the Main Point 1973) but it was surely the best show *I* ever saw, and it planted a seed that urged me to start *Backstreets*. I felt like a man on a mission, and when Springsteen came around two years later with the *River* tour, I was ready to ride.

I persuaded a local radio station to pay for some of the printing costs in exchange for an ad; a friend of mine donated typesetting; another offered photos from the Arena show; I put up a couple of hundred bucks and soon I had 10,000 copies of a four-page tabloid. I called it *Backstreets* after my

favorite song, and subtitled it "Seattle's Bruce Springsteen Fanzine." The front-page story was about the December 20 show, illustrated by some great pictures from that night. The center spread was a poster, and there were three small stories on the back page about collecting. My girlfriend, her sister, and I spent the two hours before the show handing them out free to everyone standing in line, which was why I missed "Good Rockin' Tonight." I never gave any thought to charging for the magazine — do the Gideons charge for hotel Bibles? — though I was a bit disappointed after the show to see so many copies trashed beneath people's seats. Anyone who trashed the mag made a mistake, but I made the biggest mistake of all by not saving a few thousand; I now own only one copy albeit an autographed one.

Serious collectors now will pay upwards of $100 for copies of that first issue of *Backstreets*. And though there are probably not 10,000 people who would put out that sort of dough for something so small, if there *were*, you could say I gave away a million dollars' worth of fanzine that night. It was worth every cent, no matter what it cost me, because it has paid off with friends, with the ties that bind over the years. That was the genesis of the magazine, and from that point it has grown into something far greater than it was that night, something far greater than I could ever have imagined it becoming. And finally, when we realized we'd written about five books' worth of material about Bruce Springsteen, we decided to create this book.

Our growth was slow, however. The magazine was around for four years before the number of subscribers passed 1,000, and even today more people see Springsteen at a single coliseum-sized concert than subscribe to *Backstreets*. Eventually we added color printing, slick paper, and the sort of graphics that make us look like any other magazine on the newsstand. But it was seven years before the magazine could afford to move the office out of my basement, and it has never been a financial success (I've always worked other full-time jobs to support myself). But remember — since the magazine was fueled by passion rather than entrepreneurial drive, we don't judge our success on a business scale.

The major impact of the magazine has been on the hearts and minds of the people who read it. Every day we get letters from Bruce Tramps (many in far-off places around the globe) who tell us they

thought they were "the only one in the world" who felt this way about Springsteen, until they read *Backstreets*. Every subscriber I've ever spoken with has admitted to reading the magazine from cover to cover on the day it arrives, which is not something you can say about *Rolling Stone* or *Time*.

Considering that *Backstreets* has always counted my personal fanaticism as its major (and sometimes its only) resource, we have accomplished some surprising things. It was in an interview with *Backstreets* that Steve Van Zandt first announced he was leaving the E Street Band for his solo career; it was *Backstreets* that dug up Suki Lahav, former E Street Band violinist, for her first interview with the press in more than ten years; and it was *Backstreets* that led the pack in first reporting on the upcoming releases of the *Born in the USA* and *Live* records. That's all in addition to having the most complete coverage of the *Born in the USA* and *Tunnel of Love* tours anywhere, including *Backstreets'* tradition of running song lists from every Springsteen performance. We've also tracked and reported on every individual Springsteen record release from the United Kingdom to Uruguay. At least two couples have met and married through the pen-pal classifieds in the back of the magazine (probably to the tune of Bruce's "I Wanna Marry You").

If you're noticing that I'm not boasting about *Backstreets* being the first to break the news of Springsteen's marriage (or divorce) or any of the other developments in his personal life, there's a good reason for that; *Backstreets* is about Bruce Springsteen's performing and recording career, *not* about his personal life. We surely would have sold more copies of the magazine if we covered that stuff (Bruce's personal life has been hot copy these past few years), but that idea is contradictory to everything we are about. When I saw Bruce that night in December of 1978, it wasn't who he was sleeping with that impressed me. Reporters are constantly asking me questions about Springsteen's life, and when I choose to tell them nothing but the obvious, they seem offended; it is as if, in this celebrity-driven media circus, my neutral position offends people. They seem to think that all public figures deserve to be dragged through the lion's den, and anyone who doesn't agree with that concept is some sort of heretic. Springsteen fans, for the most part, are concerned with who Spanish

◀ *The Stone Pony, Asbury Park, N.J., April 22, 1984.*

Johnny is sleeping with, but not Bruce himself.

In this respect, *Backstreets* might seem to take the company line on Bruce Springsteen. But before you start thinking of this magazine as some extension of a publicity machine, consider that the magazine has also been highly critical of some of Springsteen's career moves (playing stadiums, doing funk remixes, and, in general, the gross overcommercialization of his career around the time of *Born in the USA*). Though I have yet to hear a Springsteen song I dislike, many of the machinations that go on around those songs are open to debate in *Backstreets*. This occasional criticism, and the very fact that we have an independent viewpoint on Springsteen that doesn't have anything to do with selling his records, has led to mixed relations with his management company.

As I've said many times before in the magazine, *Backstreets* is not so much a magazine *about* Bruce Springsteen as it is *for* Bruce Springsteen *fans*. That may sound like a minor point, but it is indeed a large distinction. *Backstreets* does not even necessarily have a whole hell of a lot to do with Springsteen *the man*, while it has everything to do with Springsteen's *work*.

It's ironic to consider that Springsteen himself doesn't examine his own work as closely as his fans do. He's very aware of his image and he considers his art carefully. (He said prior to the *Tunnel of Love* tour that that album was his personal favorite. He says that every time he starts a tour, but you get the feeling he really means it.) I think he finds fans like me, who collect and catalog all his work, including unreleased studio outtakes and rare one-time-only concert performances, to be a little off the deep end. As I understand his composition process, it's the material he's currently writing, the new songs for the *next* record, that concerns him — not the unreleased version of "Loose Ends" recorded in 1979 that I think stands as his best unreleased work. He probably hasn't listened to that song in years.

So what does Bruce Springsteen think about *Backstreets*? I've asked him on more than one occasion, and the best I've ever gotten out of him was a response like, "Everybody's sure talking about it." Even if he liked it, I couldn't much imagine him saying so publicly, since he's very careful with any sort of public endorsement. He reads it, I know, since on at least two occasions in concert he's referred to information only published in *Backstreets*. And I know he read my review of *Born in the USA* because in 1984 he autographed my copy of it and said he thought my discussion of western imagery was more appropriate for *Nebraska*. That autograph on my review in that *Backstreets* is my most prized possession — owning Elvis's gold lame suit wouldn't mean more to me.

When I was younger and caught up in the hysteria surrounding the *Born in the USA* tour, I probably was guilty of being a pain-in-the-ass fan. Whenever I ran into him I bugged him about playing some unreleased song or I tried to gain some B-side release info. A typical exchange follows:

Cross: Bruce, when are you going to release 'Roulette'? It's your best song.

Springsteen: We don't know that one.

Cross: Yeah, you know it. I'll even write down the words for you.

Springsteen: Nah, the band doesn't know it.

Cross: They do, they told me they want to play it.

Springsteen: Ah, Charley, could you just leave me alone? Can't you see I'm trying to swim laps here?

Springsteen did finally release "Roulette" in 1988 as a B-side, but one would have to figure it was be-

cause he ran out of finished studio outtakes from *Tunnel of Love* and not out of a desire to see my wish finally come true. Nonetheless, when it was first announced that it would be the new B-side, there was more screaming in our office than you'd hear if the actual incident the song is about (the Three Mile Island nuclear accident) was happening right across the street.

Despite being an unofficial publication, and without the benefit of late-night phone calls from Bruce himself (Bruce: you can call collect), *Backstreets* has continued to exist because there are many people within the organization, within the band, and within the music business who believe in the concept of a magazine that is nonexploitative and who basically think *Backstreets* is an honor to Bruce Springsteen, whether he sees it that way or not. Occasionally we've made the wrong call or

gotten information wrong, but considering our situation we've done better than one might have expected. On the last two tours, *Backstreets* covered the shows more extensively than any historian could have, listing sets from every single stop, be it Indianapolis, Indiana, or New Delhi, India. We have our sources, but again they are people who provide us with information on songs and shows and the like, not personal dirt.

We make an effort to make sure that everything we do in *Backstreets* magazine, and everything we've done in this book, reflects the enthusiasm we feel every time those opening chords to "Rosalita" come cranking out. Though we cater to the collector mentality, we try not to be elitist — many of Springsteen's present fans didn't have a chance to see him in small clubs like I did. Still, this is probably not the book for the casual Springsteen fan. The other contributors and I are the type of fans who find almost every bit of information about Springsteen's work important and illuminating. For example, how many people who bought the *Born to Run* album would care to know that nine different titles were considered for the album — including *Sometimes at Night* and *War and Roses* — and that "Thunder Road" was at one point planned to open and close the record? Probably not many, but for those people, *Backstreets* is the *Encyclopedia Britannica* of the Boss. It's an obsession and a passion, and after you look through the concert listings here (detailing every single public performance known to have been played by Springsteen in the last 20 years), you might agree.

This book collects the best pieces we've run in the magazine over the years — interviews, history, behind-the-scenes details about what goes into making Springsteen's music. Also, we've assembled some of the raw data we've collected over the years — on collecting, on Springsteen's recording sessions, and on the aforementioned concert listing. It's a lot, and it's my hope that you'll find every bit of it useful or entertaining.

When reading this material, do consider the time frame; *Backstreets* didn't even begin until after *The River* was released, so most of these stories center around the recent part of Springsteen's career. Though we have included plenty of historical articles, we didn't have the opportunity to review *The Wild, the Innocent and the E Street Shuffle* when it came out. (If we had reviewed it, I'd have given it 11 on a scale of 10 — it's my favorite Springsteen

Philadelphia, Pa., July 19, 1981.

record.) We've also compiled exclusive original material that even hard-core *Backstreets* subscribers will find enlightening and new.

Back during the early years of Springsteen's career, when he was doing lots of interviews (Springsteen even spent his birthday in 1979 driving around all day with a reporter from an obscure New Jersey tabloid), one of the questions he was most frequently asked concerned what drove him to perform with the intensity he exhibits onstage. I think most reporters asked this because sometimes onstage Springsteen is positively otherworldly, and describing even that can get difficult. And, of course, Bruce had no answer for them. He has always been the way he is. Like the heir to a royal throne, he was born the King.

So Bruce usually took the question and turned it around to talk about what he thought about on-

stage and where he directed his show. His line was that he put the show on, played the guitar solos, wrote the songs, did the whole thing for "that kid in the tenth row." "I go out every night," he once said, "and I try to think about that kid in the tenth row. If I can reach him, then I know I've done my job."

Ironically, when I walked into the Seattle Center Arena in December of 1978, my seat was nowhere near the tenth row; I was in the rafters, since I'd been out of town when tickets first went on sale. But it didn't matter where I sat, because the tenth row Bruce Springsteen was playing to that night wasn't a physical place — it was a state of mind.

This book is about sitting in that tenth row, and if you can find that place inside yourself, perhaps one day you'll see four encores, one of them ten minutes after all the applause has ended.

—*Charles R. Cross*

GROWIN' UP

*Asbury Park, Freehold,
and the Jersey Shore
Music Scene*

Wasted in the Heat: Child, Long Branch, N.J., June 1969.

TWENTY YEARS BURNING DOWN THE ROAD

The Complete History of Jersey Shore Rock 'n' Roll

Mention the English city of Liverpool to the average soul on the street, and chances are the first vision that will pass through his or her mind is that of four mop-topped lads called the Beatles. Try it sometime. Ask your mom or dad, or your boss. Ask the postperson, or the middle-aged woman in the supermarket.

Liverpool isn't known or remembered as an important prewar seaport, which it was, or for its soccer team. It's known to the world as the city where the Beatles originated. It's practically impossible to separate this glum, working-class city from the legacy of the Beatles, and vice versa.

Mention Asbury Park, New Jersey, to that same person, and it's a good bet that they'll say something like "Asbury Park? Yeah, that's the place where Bruce Springsteen comes from." Granted, that's not entirely accurate, because Springsteen was, of course, born and raised in nearby Freehold (although at times in the late sixties and early seventies, he did reside in Asbury Park, and he certainly spent much time playing the city's clubs and bars).

Nonetheless, because of Bruce Springsteen, Asbury Park has earned a secure place in rock history books. The city's rich past as a prewar seaside resort, with once-beautiful beaches and a bustling boardwalk, and the nationally reported race riots that tore through the city and devastated its downtown shopping district in 1970 are both, historically speaking, secondary to the city's relationship to the man they call the Boss. The fact is, Asbury Park is inextricably linked with Bruce Springsteen, and vice versa.

There are other similarities that, in a way, make Liverpool and Asbury Park sister cities. Each is a city whose past is brighter than its present. In each, unemployment remains high, decay is dominant, and the landscape can best be painted in shades of gray. True, there is much talk about a renaissance or rebirth of Asbury Park. And over the past couple of years the city has striven hard to initiate a massive facelift and implement a more positive image. Yet, sadly, Asbury Park largely remains the same Asbury Park that Bruce Springsteen pinpointed so forcefully in his early music.

Interestingly, ever since Springsteen came to prominence, the media have possessed a somewhat morbid fascination with Asbury Park. To many journalists, photographers, TV reporters and filmmakers, Asbury Park has routinely symbolized a particular slice of America's underbelly, a place just brimming with the kinds of stark, gloomy images from which great works of art, literature — and music — originate.

The idea was always that if you could understand the environment (Asbury Park and the rest of the Jersey Shore) of the artist (Springsteen) — namely, the seaside bars and blue-collar beer joints, the boardwalk amusements and pizza parlors, the lonely streets and broken dreams — then you'd appreciate more fully the artist's art (Springsteen's songs). To a large degree, this is true. Few American songwriters have been able to take such detailed images of the American Dream, as well as the tales of hardship and disappointment that accompany them, and imbue them with the universality that Bruce Springsteen has. Springsteen took from all around him. He transformed the characters that hung out in Asbury Park's bars and boardwalk into song personalities that symbolized life's struggle. He worked his impressions of Asbury Park and the rest of the Jersey Shore into his lyrics in such a way that the songs weren't about Asbury or Jersey, but about America and about you and me.

"It was natural right from the beginning that when people wanted to learn more about Bruce, that they came to Asbury," said one local. "It's not much to look at, I know, but for rock 'n' roll it's a

Widner College, Chester, Pa., February 6, 1975 with Suki Lahav on violin.

great place. It's a rock 'n' roll town if there ever was one. And it's really pretty spiritual. I mean, you don't go visiting the town where Jackson Browne came from, do you?''

Actually, the media fascination with Asbury Park began more than a decade ago — in 1975, to be precise. And it started with the biggest of bangs. What longtime Springsteen fan can ever forget that amazing week in October when the covers of both *Time* and *Newsweek* were graced with the face of Bruce Springsteen? Before that came the cover story on Bruce in the now defunct but at the time critically praised magazine *Crawdaddy*. And there were others. It was part hype and part intrigue, but all of a sudden Asbury Park was being touted the same way Liverpool was some ten years earlier.

"It was really weird," said Southside Johnny in an interview a few years ago. "You had photographers and reporters poking their heads into clubs and looking for God knows what. Nobody ever paid attention to Asbury Park or the musicians who played there and lived there before. Some people never got the hang of it."

The world found out about Bruce Springsteen's roots and about Asbury Park. And in the process, some of the more astute observers discovered a music scene that was vibrant and rich with bands. There was Southside Johnny and the Asbury Jukes. There was Cahoots. There was Lord Gunner, the Shakes, and Cold, Blast, and Steel. They were the local stars in the local clubs. Few of them had ever ventured beyond the Jersey Shore with their guitars and amps. It was strictly a home-grown rock scene. While popular music in the mid-seventies began flirting with disco, and rock was caught with a bad case of the blahs, the music heard in Asbury Park clubs — like the Stone Pony — revolved around rhythm and blues and sixties soul. Outside the scene, such influences were considered dated and passe. But in Asbury Park, R&B-based rock was hot and sassy.

Also, blues was big, especially in the late sixties, just as it was in San Francisco and England. It was an easily adaptable style of music, and it lent itself to jamming. Jamming was what Asbury Park's legendary club, the Upstage, was all about. In fact, if any one element was (and still is) most representative of the Jersey Shore music scene in general and Asbury Park's in particular, it was the concept of late-night jams and sitting in. It began at house parties, moved to the Upstage in the late sixties and later to the Stone Pony as well as a whole slew of other clubs such as the Student Prince, the Fast Lane, Mrs. Jay's, and the High Tide Cafe.

Right from the very beginning, there were some bands that began overshadowing the others. Down around Asbury Park, Sonny and the Starfires ruled. Sonny Kenn, a guitarist influenced by the likes of Link Wray and Lonnie Mack, was the bandleader and frontman. The Starfires' backbeat was kept by a self-taught drummer named Vini Lopez. Out in the Freehold area, it was the Motifs, the band that came closest to turning professional and reaching beyond the Jersey Shore, and the Castiles, which included two respected guitarists, George Theiss and Bruce Springsteen. Up in Red Bank, The Source, led by Steve Van Zandt, was making itself known by playing in local battle-of-the-bands contests and playing high school dances.

To take advantage of the wealth of young rock talent at the Shore in the mid-sixties and of the seemingly insatiable appetite of kids there for live rock 'n' roll, a host of nonalcoholic teen clubs sprouted throughout the area. The Hullabaloo chain of teen clubs was especially popular. Sonny and the Starfires became regulars at the Asbury Park Hullabaloo club. Here is how Sonny Kenn remembers those days:

"We wore gold lame suits and fancy boots, and we had Ampeg and Fender amplifiers. We'd get up there onstage at around 8 P.M., and we'd play 55 minutes with a five-minute break. Then we'd go back and play again. It was just enough time to have a cigarette and a soda. We played there all summer and gained a tremendous amount of experience. By this time Vini [Lopez] had introduced me to this kid from Garden Grove, Johnny Lyon [later known as Southside Johnny], and he started coming to all our gigs and practice sessions. Whenever we played at Hullabaloo or a school dance or something, he'd go out in the audience to make sure our amps were turned up high enough."

The competition between bands at the Jersey Shore in the mid-sixties was certainly keen, but it was not cutthroat. Instead, there was a subtle yet strong bond between musicians that later made the Upstage experience such a valuable one for them.

Despite the occasional squabble, such camaraderie allowed for the frequent trading of ideas and riffs, and enabled musicians and bands to grow.

Even though the mid-sixties saw the rise of a large number of bands at the Shore, few groups played anywhere but the Shore. What with teen clubs, high school and CYO dances, and battles of the bands, of which there were many, there were plenty of places to perform locally without having to venture to New York.

One group, the Castiles, had more drive than most. It also had a manager, Tex Vinyard, who took it upon himself to push the group musically and force it to seek brighter horizons. Because of him, the Castiles were one of the few mid-sixties Shore bands to make a record (a self-produced, self-recorded single, "That's What You Get" backed with "Baby I"). Vinyard also worked the Castiles into a regular set of gigs at New York's legendary club, the Cafe Wha?, where groups like the Blues Project and artists such as Jimi Hendrix and Bill Cosby got their start.

"Tex was a big ego builder," George Theiss remembers. "He would sit there and tell you how the girls were going crazy over you. At 16 or 17, that's just what you wanted to hear. He made sure we were confident."

Confidence. That's the key word. Vinyard instilled a sense of sureness in the Castiles, especially Springsteen, that never really left them. Vinyard also exposed the group to a whole new level of rock in New York City that most other Shore bands missed during this era. Such things enabled Springsteen to leave the Castiles when the Jersey Shore music scene was about to enter a new stage in the late sixties and to form his own bands fueled by his own rock visions.

From this point on, it was Springsteen who set the pace, who broke the most new ground, and, as Theiss says, who acted "as if he already had a plan ...and knew exactly where he was heading."

· · · ·

Much has been written about the Upstage. "It was really a unique place, the Upstage," said Van Zandt. "I've never ever run across another club like it anywhere else in the world."

"Everybody went there 'cause it was open later than the regular clubs and because between one and five in the morning you could play pretty much whatever you wanted, and if you were good enough, you could choose the guys you wanted to play with," wrote Springsteen in the liner notes for *I Don't Want to Go Home*, the debut album of Southside Johnny and the Asbury Jukes.

"It was like going to school," recalled Sonny Kenn a few years ago. "Upstage, when you think about it, really was a school. Better yet, for those of us who used to play at Hullabaloo and the teen clubs, it was almost a college of sorts."

The entire Jersey Shore music scene revolved around the Upstage for the two years or so in the late sixties that it was open. Run by Tom and Margaret Potter, it was a meeting place, a proving ground, and a musical laboratory all in one. More groups were formed there, and more groups broke up there, than anywhere else.

Musicians at the Upstage were part of a large pecking order. The best — Springsteen, Van Zandt, and other guitar players like Billy Ryan, Ricky DeSarno, and Sonny Kenn, drummers such as Vini Lopez and Big Bobby Williams, harp players like Southside Johnny, and keyboard players such as David Sancious — had first dibs on stage time. Other musicians worked their way onstage when they were good enough to play with the first team.

The Upstage acted as a springboard for what was to follow at the Jersey Shore in the 1970s. No one could ever have deliberately planned a club so crucial to the development of so many musicians. The incredible thing is that it worked. The informality, the competition, Tom Potter's zany, slapstick-like organizational skills, and the madness that never really surfaced long enough to blow the whole thing out of control, all created an atmosphere of intense apprenticeship.

It was during this time that Bill Chinnock's Downtown Tangiers Band gained notoriety and respect as far north as New York, that Maelstrom (Southside on bass and harp, Kenn on guitar, and Ronnie Romano on drums) practically became the house band at the downstairs coffeehouse section of the Upstage, and that Steel Mill, the first of the truly great Shore bands, was born.

· · · · ·

Steel Mill's best lineup was Springsteen on guitar and vocals, Steve Van Zandt on bass, Danny Federici on organ, and Vini Lopez on drums. On a bad night Steel Mill was still the best outfit on the Shore, perhaps in all of Jersey. On a good night, the band was, well, simply amazing.

I remember going to see the band in concert at Ocean County College in Toms River, New Jersey. It was a typically hot and humid night at the Shore. I think it was August 1970. The gymnasium was packed with sweaty, anxious souls. The word had spread about Steel Mill. Anticipation filled the air. Even though Springsteen had briefly attended Ocean County College, and Toms River is part of the Jersey Shore, it wasn't part of Steel Mill's true stomping grounds. Many people in the audience that night had only heard about how good the band was supposed to be.

For the two hours or so that Steel Mill played, Springsteen and company simply overwhelmed everyone on the other side of the stage. Had his brand of blues-rock been available on record at the time, or had that concert been somehow made into a live album and rushed to radio stations and record stores, it would have rivaled Led Zeppelin's best, I swear.

People who had seen Steel Mill for the first time walked out of that show as if they had participated in a mystical musical experience. Springsteen's manager, Jon Landau, saw the future of rock 'n' roll four years later in 1974. A lot of us at the Shore saw it that night.

There were other fine bands at the Shore during this time. Southern Conspiracy was one. Sunny Jim was another. Both opened for Steel Mill on a regular basis. It was an era of shared apartments and skimpy meals, and of free outdoor concerts at local parks and at Monmouth College in West Long Branch, when the weather was good.

It was also an era of restlessness. Steel Mill made a trip to California and played the Fillmore West. Afterwards, rock impresario Bill Graham offered the band free recording time. They recorded three songs for him but turned down his contract offer. Back in Jersey a few months later, Springsteen formed Dr. Zoom and the Sonic Boom, which represented a classic case of musical absurdity and was the result of wild experimentation never before seen at the Shore.

Musicians came and went. Garry Tallent, David Sancious, Southside Johnny, and others left Asbury Park and headed to Richmond, Virginia, a town that became a home away from home for Asbury Park players. Others split for California, Colorado, and New England. Springsteen's restlessness is well documented. He broke up Steel Mill. He formed the Bruce Springsteen Band. He broke up the Bruce Springsteen Band. He became a folk-

The E Street Band, August 1973 (L to R): Danny, Vini, Bruce, Garry, Clarence, and David Sancious.

singer. He commuted to New York's Greenwich Village and played the clubs there. And then he got a recording contract.

. . . . .

Springsteen's signing with Columbia Records was enough of an event to bring most everyone back to Asbury Park in 1972 and 1973. The scene, which had become disjointed and lost its purpose, was about to be righted.

"Bruce needed a band to make *Greetings from Asbury Park, N.J.* with," recalled Garry Tallent. "So the word went out and people came home." A new version of the Bruce Springsteen Band was formed, the record was made, and the boys hit the road to promote it.

"It was an interesting time," remembers Big Danny Gallagher, who acted as the band's road manager. "We played all these weird places and drove hundreds of miles to do it again the next

night. Nobody saw much in the way of money. We practically starved."

Back home, musicians, caught up in the enthusiasm of one of their own actually making a record and going on tour, formed new bands and hoped to follow in Springsteen's footsteps. One such group was the Blackberry Booze Band.

"The kind of music we played was blues," says David Meyers, the Booze Band's bass player. "Steve [Van Zandt] was in the band and so was Southside. We played the kind of stuff that might have been heard during the Upstage days, but we did it with more polish, I think. We also played a lot of material that no one else had ever heard before. We were a band rather than a bunch of musicians that simply showed up and jammed, although at times that did happen when friends asked to sit in."

By this time a new club had opened up on Ocean

Avenue in Asbury Park, called the Stone Pony. Its owners were looking for a house band that would draw locals to the club on a regular basis. Using some of the ideas worked out in the Blackberry Booze Band, Miami Steve Van Zandt and Southside Johnny formed just the group the Pony was searching for, Southside Johnny and the Asbury Jukes.

Van Zandt, who had toured with the Dovells after Steel Mill broke up, and who had always been infatuated with black music, formed the Asbury Jukes around a horn section and a pepper-hot rhythm section. Not prepared to take center stage himself, he gave that task to Southside. Armed with a blazing harp and an encyclopedic knowledge of blues and R&B, Johnny sang and moved like his heroes — Jackie Wilson, Otis Redding, Sam Cooke, and Ray Charles — and the Pony began to fill up.

When Springsteen and his band came off the road, they found the Stone Pony the place to hang out. Gradually, the club became the unofficial meeting place of Jersey Shore musicians, especially those with strong links to Asbury Park.

"It filled a gap," says Kevin Kavanaugh, an original member of the Asbury Jukes who still plays keyboards in the band. "When the Upstage closed, there was really no place where you knew you could go on a given night and find plenty of musicians. The Pony became that place."

· · · · ·

It was in 1976 that the music scene of the Jersey Shore, particularly in Asbury Park, had matured into one worthy of national attention. Springsteen's *Born to Run*, released the year before, had been critically acclaimed in virtually every nook and cranny of the rock media. The *Time* and *Newsweek* stories had introduced him to mainstream America. All the hype that surrounded Springsteen nearly destroyed his career, but it did wonders for Asbury Park and the Stone Pony.

When record company executives came looking for another Springsteen in the back alleys and beer joints of Asbury, they almost certainly wound up at the Pony, where they were introduced to the Asbury Jukes. Springsteen praised the band and helped open important doors at Epic Records. Soon Southside and the Jukes had a record deal. On Memorial Day 1976 they celebrated the release of *I*

Don't Want to Go Home with a Stone Pony concert broadcast live on the radio.

David Sancious, who had left the E Street Band, along with drummer Boom Carter, to start a solo career as a jazz-rock fusion artist, also scored a record deal. His album, *Forest of Feelings*, although not nearly as commercially popular as *I Don't Want to Go Home*, scored high critical marks nonetheless.

Other Asbury Park-based bands such as the Shakes, Cold, Blast and Steel, Lord Gunner and the Cahoots scrambled to be the next in line. None ever did land a contract, but they came close. All this added up to what many locals consider the heyday of Jersey Shore music. Asbury Park was, in a word, music-rich. It was primarily a rock-R&B blend that one heard echoing out of area clubs, flavored with the sounds of a saxophone and the gritty vocals of a lead singer well versed in soul and Motown. Black leather jackets, newsboy caps, and earrings were in. Bands like Paul Whistler and the Wheels and the Shots kept the musical momentum strong.

Eventually the scene diversified enough to allow bands such as Kinderhook Creek, with deep-seated ties to country and Southern rock; Salty Dog, the Shore's answer to heavy metal; and Sam the Band, perhaps the area's best Top 40 bar band, to develop large, devoted followings.

One would have thought, though, that with all the musical energy coming out of the Shore and with the large number of bands — and good bands at that — vying for a chance at stardom, at least one or two other outfits would have signed their names on record contracts.

"You have to take into consideration the 'Springsteen curse,'" says one prominent Shore musician who asked to remain anonymous. "As much as Bruce was good for the local scene, he was also bad for it. Every band that was worthy of a recording contract in the late seventies was branded a Springsteen clone, it seemed. That's why nobody got signed in those years. Record companies heard you were from Asbury Park and right away they shut their doors. The hype was over. A lot of good bands were denied their chance to get a deal because of the whole Springsteen bit. Now don't get me wrong. I ain't saying it was his fault. It just happened that way."

Consider the case of Billy Chinnock. An Upstage veteran and longtime member of the Shore music scene, it was Chinnock's bad luck to be

◀ *Atlantic Highlands, N.J., September 11, 1970.*

Bryn Mawr, Pa., February 26, 1974.

labeled an Asbury Park artist with an R&B-styled sound that closely resembled Springsteen's. Chinnock even looked and sounded like Springsteen at times. But worse, even though he was one of the precious few to sign a recording contract in the late seventies (with Atlantic), what did he call his debut album? *Badlands.*

"I had no idea Bruce had a song with the same name," said Chinnock in an interview. "I couldn't help it that I sort of have the same features as he does. And we came from the same roots, so why should my music sound all that different from his?

"It was like no matter what I did or where I turned, there was this Bruce-ghost following me. I knew I'd never get the proper attention in Jersey, so I moved to New York, then Maine, then back to Jersey, and finally to Nashville. It was there that I got a record company (CBS Associates) to take another look at my songs. It took a long time and a lot of running."

Gradually, disappointment and frustration began to take a toll in Asbury Park. Bands broke up. Some musicians turned away from music altogether. Disco was hot elsewhere in America, so many club owners sought out DJs or Top 40 dance bands to fill the dance floors on the Shore. Even the Stone Pony began booking cover bands.

What saved the scene was the opening of a new club in Asbury Park, the Fast Lane. Its booking agent and manager, Jim Giantonio, sought out national acts when no one else would, and hired local bands which played original music to open for them. Almost overnight it became the Shore's premier club. Not only did acts like Joe Jackson, the Ramones, Robert Gordon, and seemingly countless New Wave bands from Britain play the club in the early eighties, but "honorary" Shore groups such as Beaver Brown and Norman Nardini and the Tigers developed strong followings.

Giantonio actively encouraged area bands to

focus on original music. He was, for example, responsible for pushing a band called The Rest, which included a lead singer named John Bongiovi (later to be known as Jon Bon Jovi), to deal seriously with its image and stage presence as well as its original songs. The result? The Rest became the best on the Shore in the early eighties.

The success of the Fast Lane prompted the Stone Pony to change gears and revert to its old policy of featuring original music bands. Another club, Big Man's West, owned by E Street band member Clarence Clemons, opened in nearby Red Bank. A whole new generation of Shore bands filled these clubs: Clarence Clemons and the Red Bank Rockers, Sonny Kenn and the Wild Ideas, Hot Romance, Cats on a Smooth Surface, Junior Smoots and the Disturbers. At the Pony, E Street Band members were back hanging out, and Springsteen would routinely show up on Sunday nights to sit in with Cats on a Smooth Surface. Suddenly the Shore music scene was back on its feet.

. . . . .

Sidenote: While all this was happening in Asbury Park and Red Bank, a hardcore punk offshoot of the Shore music scene sprouted in nearby Long Branch. The host club was the Brighton Bar. It permitted slamdancing and gave the rowdiest punk bands a place to perform.

"Hardcore at the Shore is just a violent reaction to all the hype that surrounds Asbury Park and the bands that play there," said The Mutha, owner of Long Branch's Mutha Records and a leader of the local punk movement a couple of years ago. "We don't want any part of that crap." Brighton bands openly resented bands that played the Asbury Park/Red Bank circuit and repudiated the R&B roots of the area in grand fashion.

Yet there were ties. John Eddie played the Brighton as much as he played Big Man's West. So did Sonny Kenn. Little Steven was even known to sign in at the Brighton when he was at the Shore. And some very good bands came out of the scene, bands that, with the proper guidance, could have gone much farther than they did. One such group was Secret Syde. Another was the Wallbangers.

. . . . .

All this brings us to the present. The Fast Lane is gone, as is Big Man's West. The Stone Pony has reclaimed its right to be called the Shore's most prestigious rock club, though redevelopment plans for Asbury Park will probably mean the demolition

Bryn Mawr, Pa., October 31, 1973.

of the club's Ocean Avenue site. The Brighton Bar lives on. And there are some new clubs — the Deck House in Asbury Park, the Green Parrot in Neptune, Jasons in South Belmar — that regularly book the best local bands and carry on the tradition of the Jersey Shore music scene.

There is yet another generation of artists and bands worth noting, too. John Eddie is at the top of the list, and right behind him is Glen Burtnick. Then there are the Cruisers and LaBamba and the Hubcaps, two bands with strong links to R&B; the Fairlanes, the Shore's best blues act; and new entries like Mike Wells and the Wage, Big Danny and the Boppers, Beyond the Blue, Baby Boom, and the World.

"The Shore music scene is still something special," says Stone Pony DJ Lee Mrowicki. "Overall, the quality of bands is quite good, and you'll never know who might jam on any given night. It's a tight scene, too, just like it's always been. Maybe that's what makes it so special. If you play in a Shore band, I think you feel like you belong to something bigger than the three or four guys in your group. You feel like you're part of a legacy or a tradition. Few other scenes have that. And I know most of us are pretty proud of it."

—Robert Santelli

RESEARCH: ASBURY PARK ROCK 'N ROLL MUSEUM
ARTWORK: ANDY REID © 1988 BACKSTREETS MAG.

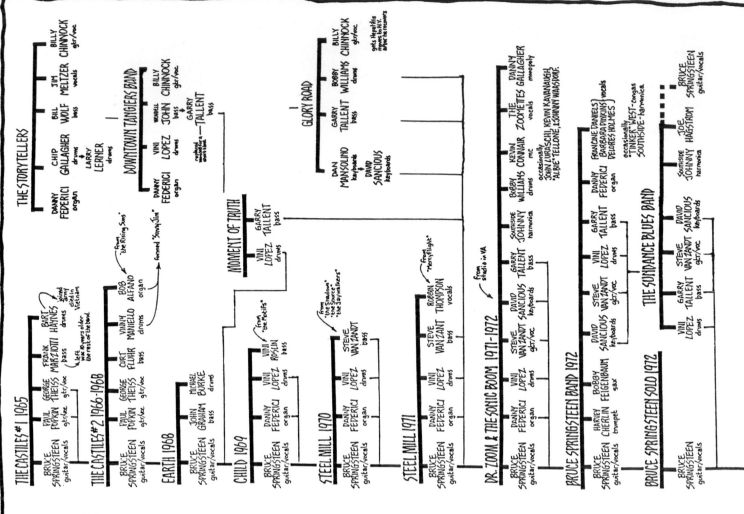

THE CASTILES were formed in 1965 in Freehold, NJ and they were managed by Gordon "Tex" Vinyard. The members at the time were George Theiss (vocals and guitar), Bart Haynes (drums), Frank Marziotti (bass), and Paul Popkin (tambourine, guitar, vocals). They soon added a young guitar player named Bruce Springsteen who also sang occasional vocals. The first change in the band came in 1966 when Bart Haynes went off to Vietnam (he later was killed in action). Next Frank Marziotti left the band — he was ten years older than the rest of the guys and couldn't afford to be in a band that was still struggling. Frank was replaced by Curt Fluhr and Haynes was replaced by Vinny "Skibotts" Maniello. It was this line-up that recorded the single "Baby I" on May 16, 1966 in the Bricktown Studio. Later Bob Alfano (from the Rising Suns) was added on organ. The band broke up by 1968. Theiss went off to form a band called the Rusty Chain while Alfano and Maniello formed a band called Sunny Jim.

Bruce met John Graham and Michael Burke while enrolled at Ocean County College in 1968. Together they formed **EARTH** (Bruce played guitar and sang vocals, Burke played drums and Graham played bass). They were a power trio and were managed by Fran Duffy and Rick "Spanky" Spachter, who called themselves "Ooze and Oz Productions." They played on the Shore throughout 1968.

That summer Bruce began to frequent the Upstage, a new club on Cookman Avenue in Asbury Park. From the instant he arrived he gained a reputation for being a fast guitarist. Vini Lopez was also hanging around the Upstage at the time and was looking to start a new band. Lopez had previously played with Moment of Truth (along with Garry Tallent) and with the Downtown Tangiers Band (with Dan Federici and Billy Chinnock). Lopez approached the new guitar whiz and together they formed **CHILD**. The line-up featured Bruce on guitar and vocals, Lopez on drums, Federici on organ and Vini Roslin (formerly of the Motifs) on bass. Child played regularly throughout 1969 calling Pandemonium (an Ocean Township club) their home. Advertisements for some of their shows read "Pandemonium gives birth to Child," and "It's a Birthquake with Child." Their shows included a gig opening for blues great James Cotton.

After hearing of another band from Long Island named Child also, they changed their name to **STEEL MILL**. The name came about one day when Bruce, their manager Carl "Tinker" West and a friend named Chuck Dillon were sitting in a bar called the Inkwell in Monmouth County thinking up new names for the band. Dillon suggested the name Steel Mill, Bruce liked the name and it stuck. Not long after switching to the new name, Roslin left to be replaced by Steve Van Zandt (formerly of the Shadows and the Source from Middletown, and the Jaywalkers from Asbury Park).

Steel Mill played the Shore during 1970 and were the top local band of the time. They also found a second home in Richmond, Virginia and even considered relocating there at one point. Tinker booked them on a tour of California and they went out to San Francisco where their Matrix show received rave reviews and interested Bill Graham. Graham recorded three of their songs in his studio and made them an offer (he now cites it as the biggest mistake of his career not to sign them at any cost). Manager West turned it down and the band returned to New Jersey. Back in New Jersey the band continued as a popular Shore band sometimes playing to crowds over 10,000. They added Robbin Thompson as a second vocalist (he'd come from the band Mercy Flight in Richmond) and their draw continued strong. The band eventually broke up in January of 1971 after playing a series of "final" shows at the Upstage. They never released a record.

Springsteen decided to go off in a more R&B direction and abandoned the heavy metal sound of Steel Mill. He formed a big band and called it **DR. ZOOM AND THE SONIC BOOM**. The Zoom Band consisted of a rotating line-up including Vini Lopez and "Big Bad" Bobby Williams on drums, Garry Tallent on bass and tuba, Bruce and Steve Van Zandt sharing guitar and vocals, Southside Johnny on harmonica, David Sancious on keyboards, and a female vocalist section known as the "Zoomettes." Kevin "Bird" Connair served as the MC and other local musicians such as "Big" Danny Gallagher, John Luraschi, Kevin Kavanaugh (eventually of the Jukes), "Albie" Tellone and Johnny "Hot Keys" Waasdorp joined the band occasionally playing everything from vibraphones to monopoly on stage.

The Zoom band was too large to ever make any money or to play regularly (most members had other band projects on the outside). Bruce formed a slimmed-down version of the band and called it **THE BRUCE SPRINGSTEEN BAND**. Shows, however, were done under such names as The Bruce Springsteen Blues Band and Bruce Springsteen and the Friendly Enemies. This band featured Lopez on drums, Tallent on bass, Van Zandt on guitar, Sancious on keyboards, Harvey Cherlin on trumpet, and Francine Daniels, Barbara Dinkins and Delores Holmes on vocals. Manager West even occasionally played congas and Southside Johnny played harp whenever he was available.

THE E STREET BAND FAMILY TREE

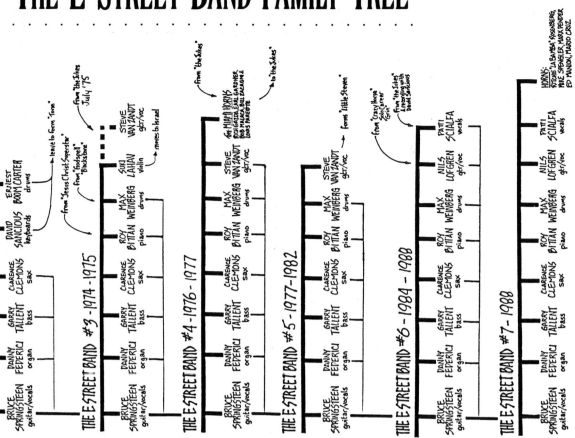

THE E STREET BAND #1 - 1972-1974
BRUCE SPRINGSTEEN guitar/vocals — GARRY TALLENT bass — DAVID SANCIOUS keyboards — CLARENCE CLEMONS sax — VINI LOPEZ drums — DANNY FEDERICI organ *(from "Joyful Noyze" Vibratones)* *(to bar runner)*
Joins tour June '73

THE E STREET BAND #2 - 1974
BRUCE SPRINGSTEEN guitar/vocals — DANNY FEDERICI organ — GARRY TALLENT bass — CLARENCE CLEMONS sax — DAVID SANCIOUS keyboards — ERNEST BOOM CARTER drums *(leave to form "Tone")*

THE E STREET BAND #3 - 1974-1975
BRUCE SPRINGSTEEN guitar/vocals — DANNY FEDERICI organ — GARRY TALLENT bass — CLARENCE CLEMONS sax — ROY BITTAN piano — MAX WEINBERG drums — SUKI LAHAV violin — STEVE VAN ZANDT gtr/voc *(from "Jesus Christ Superstar")* *(from "Godspell" "Blackbone")* *(from "the Jukes")* *(moves to Israel)* *(July '75)*

THE E STREET BAND #4 - 1976-1977
BRUCE SPRINGSTEEN guitar/vocals — DANNY FEDERICI organ — GARRY TALLENT bass — CLARENCE CLEMONS sax — ROY BITTAN piano — MAX WEINBERG drums — STEVE VAN ZANDT gtr/voc *(to "the Jukes")*

THE E STREET BAND #5 - 1977-1982
BRUCE SPRINGSTEEN guitar/vocals — DANNY FEDERICI organ — GARRY TALLENT bass — CLARENCE CLEMONS sax — ROY BITTAN piano — MAX WEINBERG drums — STEVE VAN ZANDT gtr/voc *(form "Little Steven")*

THE E STREET BAND #6 - 1984-1988
BRUCE SPRINGSTEEN guitar/vocals — DANNY FEDERICI organ — GARRY TALLENT bass — CLARENCE CLEMONS sax — ROY BITTAN piano — MAX WEINBERG drums — NILS LOFGREN gtr/voc — PATTI SCIALFA vocals *(from "Crazy Horse" Solo Career, Grin)* *(from "the Jukes" [recording with David Sancious])*

THE E STREET BAND #7 - 1988
BRUCE SPRINGSTEEN guitar/vocals — DANNY FEDERICI organ — GARRY TALLENT bass — CLARENCE CLEMONS sax — ROY BITTAN piano — MAX WEINBERG drums — NILS LOFGREN gtr/voc — PATTI SCIALFA vocals

the MIAMI HORNS: *are* RICH GAZDA, EARL GARDNER, BOB MALACH, BILL ZACAGNI & LOUIS PARENTE

HORNS: RITCHIE "LA BAMBA" ROSENBERG, MIKE SPENGLER, MARK PENDER, ED MANION, MARIO CRUZ

At the same time across town, Southside, Lopez, Van Zandt, Tallent and Joe Hagstrom were in a group called the **SUNDANCE BLUES BAND**. It was the first band where Southside really made a name for himself. Springsteen was an occasional member of this outfit, joining in on vocals.

Even the scaled down Bruce Springsteen Band had trouble finding work and making money so **BRUCE SPRINGSTEEN** went off **SOLO** and played throughout 1972 by himself. Tinker West introduced Bruce to Mike Appel who signed on as Bruce's manager. Appel managed to get Springsteen an audition with John Hammond of CBS Records. Hammond liked what he heard and signed Springsteen to CBS with plans for an album. Both Hammond and Appel saw Springsteen at the time as a solo artist, very much in line with the folk scene that was happening at the time. Bruce, however, insisted that he be allowed to form a band. Hammond said he couldn't imagine how Springsteen would be able to pull off such songs as "Growin' Up" and "Saint in the City" with a full band but he finally allowed Springsteen the chance. Bruce called together his old Asbury Park cohorts including Lopez, Van Zandt, Sancious, Tallent, Federici, and former Joyfull of Noyze sax player Clarence Clemons. They rehearsed in Point Pleasant, NJ before going into the studio to record **Greetings from Asbury Park, NJ.** Van Zandt soon left the band however to work construction and to tour with the Dovells on the oldies circuit (the band was hardly making any money at the time). The band was called the E Street Band, named after a street in the area near their rehearsal space.

That core formed the **E STREET BAND** from 1973 through 1974. In February of 1974 Vini Lopez became the first E Streeter to leave. Now called "Mad Dog" and with a reputation for outlandishness, his personal style clashed with the rest of the band and his drumming style was not the precise machine fueled drums that Springsteen's new material called for. He was sacked in February of 1974. Before Lopez was fired the band had already booked a couple of dates and one of them — at the Starlight in Cooktown, NJ — couldn't be cancelled. So the band needed a drummer and fast. Ernest "Boom" Carter, a friend of Davey Sancious, was recruited and with less than two days of rehearsals played his first date with the band on Feb. 23 at the Starlight Lounge. Carter stayed with the band until August of that year when he and Sancious played their last gigs as E Streeters. They left to form Tone, a fusion jazz group (a group that Patti Scialfa would incidentally sing with). Sancious' departure was expected — he had long wanted to go off on his own — but it left the group without a musical core.

The next group of E Streeters were to come from an unusual source — an ad in the Village Voice. Many different players were auditioned though eventually Max Weinberg and Roy Bittan were added to the band. Both had done work on Broadway shows and done stints in rock bands and both were masters at their instruments. Roy, in particular, was a machine on the keyboards able to play "absolutely anything" as Mike Appel says. When the band started touring again that September they added Suki Lahav on violin. Lahav stayed through March of 1975 and many still call this the seminal period in E Street history. Bob Dylan's "I Want You" was the highlight of the set and many shows started off with "Incident on 57th Street" — experimentation was the matter of the day.

After Lahav left, Springsteen decided a guitar attack was in order and added Miami Steve Van Zandt to the band again. Van Zandt took on a Keith Richards-styled rhythm role and had the job of musical arranger whenever something unusual was called for. Steve also directed the Miami Horns who joined the band during their 1976 tour and played over 50 shows with the band. The horn section included Rich Gazda, Earl Gardner, Bob Malach, Bill Zacagni and Louis Parente. Apart from the addition of the horns, the core of the E Street Band remained the same for the longest period of its history — until Steve left in 1982.

In 1984 the E Street Band thought of auditioning guitar players but one special player already stood out — Nils Lofgren. Lofgren had extensive experience as a solo artist, with Neil Young's band Crazy Horse and with his own band, Grin. He took on the Van Zandt slot in 1984. Patti Scialfa also joined the band in 1984 — she had previously toured with the Jukes and had sung with David Sancious. She became only the second female to join the E Street clan. That line-up finished up the lengthy **Born in the USA** tour but for the **Tunnel of Love** tour Bruce again added a horn section — this time around made up of Ritchie "La Bamba" Rosenberg, Ed Manion, Mark Pender, Mike Spengler and Mario Cruz. The E Street Band has remained relatively stable when compared to many other bands that have been around for 15 years, but one would expect further changes are down the road as Bruce adds ideas or concepts to his ever changing body of work.

GEORGE THEISS
. . . .

Interview by Robert Santelli, June 1985

Serious fans of Bruce Springsteen know that the very first band he was a member of — and the only one in which he was not the undisputed leader — was the Castiles. This mid-sixties outfit wore matching shirts and vests onstage and played mostly covers by such groups as the Rolling Stones, the Who, and the Doors. It was based in Freehold, Springsteen's hometown.

Managed by the late Tex Vinyard, the Castiles quickly became one of the premier bands on the Jersey Shore in 1965 and 1966. The Castiles played teen dances, band contests, area Hullabaloo clubs, and nonalcoholic coffeehouses like the Left Foot. But unlike other young Shore bands, the Castiles, with Vinyard's guidance, eventually made it up to New York City and on a number of occasions they performed at the Cafe Wha? in Greenwich Village.

The Castiles even made a record — albeit a very amateur one — at a recording booth in Brick Town, New Jersey. It was, however, the very first time Springsteen's voice and guitar were captured on vinyl. Unfortunately, only a couple of copies of the record exist today.

Recently, *Backstreets* had the opportunity to speak with George Theiss, a member of the Castiles back then, and today a respected Shore musician who's in the process of re-forming the acclaimed George Theiss Band. As the lead singer and rhythm guitarist, Theiss's role in the Castiles was an important one. One winter night in Freehold, where he still resides, Theiss recalled the days when the Castiles were, as he put it, "one of the best bands on the Jersey Shore, maybe the best."

. . . . .

BACKSTREETS: *If I recall correctly, didn't the Castiles sort of evolve out of the Sierras, the band which included you and Vini Roslin, who later played bass in Child and Steel Mill?*

GEORGE THEISS: Yeah, indirectly the Castiles grew out of the Sierras. Both were Freehold bands.
Was Bruce an original member of the group?
No. He came in after the group was formed. At the time I was going out with Bruce's sister, Ginny, so it was very convenient for me to have Bruce in the band. (Laughs.)
Looking back, it seems that much of the credit for the success that the Castiles achieved should go to Tex Vinyard, the group's manager. Would you agree with that?
Oh yes, definitely. The Sierras used to rehearse right next door to Tex's. The drummer lived there. So, naturally, Tex heard us playing. One day he came over, and I guess he felt sorry for us, because from then on, we started rehearsing in his dining room. He and his wife, Marion, did a whole lot for us. They got rid of all their dining room furniture and replaced it with amps and drums. They adopted us. We ate there, hung out there, watched TV there. For a good three years, we were there steady. And it wasn't just the band, it was friends of the band, girlfriends, the whole bit. It must have amounted to about 12 to 15 people on pretty much a regular basis.
How important was Tex's guidance and advice? He certainly did more than simply let you rehearse in his house.
Oh yeah. We definitely wouldn't have gone as far as we did without him, that's for sure. All we wanted to do was play and have a good time. Tex took care of everything else. He was a great manager. He even bought us equipment. Tex also was a big ego builder. He would sit there and tell you how the girls were going crazy over you. At 16 or 17, that's just what you wanted to hear. He made sure we were confident.
What year was the band formed?
I think it was 1965. And it went to about 1968.
What caused the band to break up?
Tex claimed he fired us. But I think it just got to the point where we weren't getting along too well. A couple of the guys were going to go to college. I

The Castiles, 1965: (L to R): Frank Marziotti, Bruce Springsteen, George Theiss, Paul Popkin, Vinny Manneillo.

didn't know what I was going to do. Bruce was already working on his next thing. He was already jamming with the guys he would form Earth with. So, as soon as the Castiles broke up, he just took over what booking we had and went on.

Musically, what was so special about the Castiles?

We went out and played with confidence. We played without being afraid of blowing it. It was the feeling of thinking we were good which was the thing that made us good. We certainly weren't the best musicians around, but often we sounded like we were — because of our confidence.

Where did the name come from?

Shampoo. At the time, that's the kind of shampoo everyone was using. The name also had a nice ring to it, if you know what I mean.

What was the purpose of making a record? Did you actually plan to distribute it? Was it considered a stepping stone to a recording contract with a record company?

Tex just said, "Let's make a record," so we did. We didn't have any idea of distribution or getting signed to a label. We didn't think that collectively, that much I know. Bruce was probably thinking

along those lines, and I know I did at times. But I don't think the other members of the band did. We were too much involved in the present to really think about what could happen in the future.

Onstage, the band certainly had a sharp, polished look, with those vests, white shirts, and black pants.

Yeah. Tex thought it was important to look good, to have that uniform look. In fact, he called them uniforms. It looked real professional to him to have us all look alike up there on the stage. We didn't care. Later on, we got into the Sgt. Pepper look, with boots and jackets. There was a poster we had made. We were all dressed up in long military jackets. We looked great.

Looking back, did it ever occur to you...

That Bruce would become as big as he has become? *Well, yeah.*

Sometimes its hard to believe how big he really is. But there was always something different about Bruce. He always seemed to know something we didn't. It was as if he always had a plan and that he knew exactly where he was heading.

—Robert Santelli

REMEMBERING THE UPSTAGE

Where the Band Was Just Boppin' the Blues

The Upstage: Is there any longtime, serious Springsteen fan who doesn't know about the legendary Asbury Park club where, in the late sixties, the Boss, future E Street Band members, and the Jukes cut their musical teeth?

Much has been written about the Upstage — the all-night jams, the formation of groups such as Springsteen's Steel Mill that resulted from them, and the intense interplay, both onstage and off, of the Shore's best young musicians back then — but those who have told tales of the Upstage are those who have told them time and time again. The same voices, the same stories. The truth is, the Upstage supported a large and varied cast of characters. Some of them, like Springsteen, Steve Van Zandt, Southside Johnny, Garry Tallent, Danny Federici, David Sancious, Kevin Kavanaugh, and Billy Chinnock were fortunate enough to go on to bigger and better things. But there were others, many others, who were indeed integral players in the Upstage experience, but who have not had the chance to look back in print. Here for the first time three of them recall the club and what went down. In their own words, they remember the Upstage.

. . . . .

BIG DANNY GALLAGHER

Big Danny Gallagher is a mountain of a man with a long red beard and eyes like lasers. Friends of his say he was always to be found at the Upstage when the best music was flying. "Danny had a real good sense about that," said one friend. "And if it wasn't happening, he'd be the kind of guy to make it happen."

A pedal steel guitar player and a vocalist with one of the best blues voices this side of the boardwalk, Big Danny these days fronts Big Danny and the Boppers. He's also had a hand in the High Tide Cafe, an Asbury Park club which could well become a modern day Upstage. "The Shore needs another Upstage type club so the younger musicians can

have the same opportunities to jam and learn and experiment as we did. I'm just trying to do my part to make sure that happens."

. . . .

The Upstage started with some of the real old local musicians, guys like Harry the Hat and a lot of Margaret Potter's friends. The word then started to leak out about this place that she and her husband opened. People started coming from all over. The Upstage was the cheapest motel room in town. Two bucks to get in and you could hang out until dawn when you could go to the beach and sleep there all day — legally. Everybody lived for the weekend when the Upstage was open. Things were good. But when Brucie arrived on the scene, they got great. Everybody knew as soon as they heard him play.

Now there were a lot of real good guitar players at the Upstage — there was Billy Ryan, Ricky DeSarno, Stevie Van Zandt. But no one had it together like Brucie did. Brucie used the Upstage as a perch; he hung out there; he formed his bands there; he used it as a rehearsal hall.

At the time of the Upstage, there were only like eight or nine places for bands to play. By the time Brucie signed his recording contract, there were like forty or fifty places to play up and down the Shore.

Some Sufi guy once said that there are three kinds of music: there's the kind that will move you, the kind that will touch your soul, and the kind that will touch your heart. It seemed like Brucie had all three. And you could hear how he developed all three if you were at the Upstage back in those days. He'd play with Vini Lopez, and afterwards I'd ask Vini, I'd say, "Hey man, are you sure you and him didn't rehearse that stuff you just played?" And he'd laugh. He'd say no, and he wasn't lying. It was all spontaneous. That's what made the club special.

There was a lot of blues played. And old rock 'n' roll. Rockabilly, too. Once we had a fifties party at

The Sundance Blues Band, Upstage Club, Asbury Park, N.J., 1970 (L to R): Steven Van Zandt, Joe Hagstrom, Vini Lopez, Southside Johnny Lyon, Garry Tallent.

the club. Margaret made a garbage can full of spaghetti, everybody rolled up their sleeves and greased up and went on stage and played what today you'd call classic rock 'n' roll. That's how the Zoom band started, at one of those parties. Brucie said, "Hey, why don't we just take everybody we know and party on the stage while we're playing." And next up was Dr. Zoom and the Sonic Boom. I was in the band. I played Monopoly and drank wine. That was my part in the band. We tried to get a guy to fix an engine onstage. But he said it was too much of a hassle to do it for just a few songs. We had baton twirlers, an emcee. People were in tuxedos.

There used to be lines at three in the morning to get in the Upstage. People were three and four across, and the line would wrap around the corner. This was in the middle of the night. Fortunately, the police were cool. They knew they had a good thing. Hell, they knew where every kid in the area was every Friday, Saturday, and Sunday night.

Southside, Big Bobby Williams, Van Zandt,

these guys were there all the time, so they kind of ran the stage at the club. You wanted to play, well, you had to see one of them. I had no considerations about playing prime time in those days. I wasn't no great musician. But I took part when I was able to. I enjoyed myself. I contributed. I have good memories of those days that nobody can take away from me.

· · · ·

MARGARET POTTER

It was Margaret Potter and her husband, Tom, who opened the Upstage back in 1968. At the time, she was fronting her own band, Margaret and the Distractions. They became the Upstage house band. Both she and Tom were hairdressers, and they lived and worked two doors down from the Upstage.

After the Upstage closed in 1971, Margaret and Tom separated. Tom moved to Florida. Margaret stayed in Asbury Park and continued to work as a hairdresser. She dropped out of the Asbury Park music circle, however. "I needed to earn a living and try to make my life work," she said. "I loved music just as much as I ever did, but I had to

First show as Dr. Zoom and the Sonic Boom, Sunshine Inn, Asbury Park, N.J., May 14, 1971.

put bread on the table." Little was heard of Margaret Potter until recently, when she joined a band, the Final Cut, which includes original Upstage drummer Big Bobby Williams. "We don't play on a regular basis," said Margaret. "But when we do play, we enjoy it. It kind of reminds me of the old days."

. . . . .

I'm so happy that people want to know about the Upstage almost twenty years after it opened. Those were great days. Lots of people ask me if the club had anything to do with Bruce's success. I don't know. If anyone deserved to make it, Bruce did. He worked so hard. His desire and his straight, right-down-the-line approach to music is what did it, I think. I give the credit to him, not to the club.

Still, the Upstage was special because it was a place for the local musicians — young kids — to find themselves. You can have a bunch of young players playing in their basements, but they can't all meet there. They could at the Upstage.

You know, with the amount of kids we had at the Upstage week in and week out, we never had any real problems. Sure, there were a couple of incidents. Like the time Big Bobby, who was a bouncer at the club when he wasn't playing drums, had a gun put to his head. Thank God nothing

more happened. And there was another time we had a local motorcycle gang show up. Fortunately there were no ugly confrontations. They came, they enjoyed themselves, and then they left, although one of them wanted to take me with him. Other than that, we had no big problems.

We had two sessions at the Upstage. We opened at 9:00 P.M. for minors, kids under 18. That's when my band, Margaret and the Distractions, would usually play, although there were times when we had other bands perform, too, and we had our share of jamming. But at midnight the Upstage closed for an hour. All the minors left and we cleaned up the place. An hour later, at one in the morning, we opened up again. This time you had to be 18 to be let in, although if you had a driver's license, I let you in. I was usually at the door collecting money. The difference between 17 and 18 wasn't so much. We weren't serving alcohol or anything. And this is when the jams were best. You'd get some musicians to come down and jam for the early session, but most came later, and they usually stayed until dawn. Then everybody would go home or to the beach.

One thing unique about the Upstage — and I haven't seen it since — was that you could come all by yourself, whether you were a member of a band or not, and play. You didn't have to bring your instrument. We had house instruments, house equipment. This has become lost here in Asbury Park. It's inhibited the young kids. Some kids today don't even know about the blues. But back then, it was loose, if you know what I mean.

There was a spirit that the musicians had. They respected each other. They knew who was good and who needed to get better. But they worked it out, they really did. It just sort of worked out naturally who got to go onstage this time and who didn't. There was competition, sure, but it was a healthy competition. And it made them all better players.

There's not much else to say other than it's gone now, a part of history. Everybody's grown up. God, when I see some of those kids, well, they're not kids anymore, are they? But we were all like one big happy family. I miss those days, I really do.

. . . .

JOHNNY LURASCHI

Johnny Luraschi was one of the youngest of the Upstage regulars (along with David Sancious). "My father and mother died when I was young, so I lived with my older brother," recalls Luraschi. "That meant I was pretty much able to do whatever I wanted at 15 years old." What he did was hang out at the Upstage and learn all he could about rock 'n' roll and the bass. Luraschi played in a number of popular Shore bands over the years, including Cahoots; Cold, Blast and Steel; and Hot Romance.

. . . .

This guy Tom Potter, he was a hairdresser. He had this idea to open up a place where musicians could come and hang out and jam, have some coffee and a good time. I first heard about the Upstage from some of the older musicians. I remember they used to rave about this club in Asbury. I was younger than most everybody else, but I knew I had to go to this place they called the Upstage. Everybody was buzzin' about Bruce. Everybody would say, "There's this kid who plays guitar and comes to the Upstage, and he's incredible. You got to check him out." I was living with my older brother, so I got to do what I wanted, you know.

I used to go with my brother Eddie to the Upstage. He used to play a little keyboards, but he was a big guy, so he wound up being a bouncer. But I played all I could. You had to get in on the roster, though. They had these 40-minute jams set up. You'd try to get together with some guys who you knew were going to get the chance to play. You had to work your way in.

Every once in a while you'd get some New York hippies who came down to play. Leslie West and the Vagrants came down one night, I remember. Members of the Rock 'n' Roll Ensemble would come down. But most of the players were local. If you were too cool to go to the CYO dances and stuff, you came to the Upstage.

Me and Davey Sancious used to walk to the Upstage from Belmar, where we both lived. Later, when I was old enough to drive, I rode my motorcycle there. The whole thing about the Upstage and Asbury Park was timing. Asbury Park was — and still is — in a sort of Bermuda Triangle. You didn't play there for money or anything. You played because it was the thing to do. All of your musician friends were trying to get onstage, so you did the same. Most of the guys came every week. Bruce, Steve, they'd be there all the time. Even back then Bruce had that take-charge ability when he walked onstage. And whenever he played, there was magic at the Upstage. You could feel it, you could touch it. It was all around you. And you could definitely hear it.

It was a wild place to look at, too. I mean, the whole place was painted in psychedelic colors and Day-Glo. There were black lights that made the place cool. It was real easy to have all this happen because all you had to do was bring your instrument. The amps and sound equipment were there. All you had to do was plug in. One complete wall of the place was speakers. So you'd walk up on the stage and plug in.

It's hard to say why the Upstage finally closed. It was around when everybody was going through a real creative period, I guess, and when people moved on to the bars and formed bands, there weren't enough younger players to carry the torch. You couldn't make any money at the Upstage; it wasn't that kind of place. So the musicians, if they wanted to stay musicians, had to look for work. And when they were old enough — when they turned 21 — they moved on to the bars and the Jersey Shore. It was a matter of survival. And even then, a lot of musicians didn't make it. They stopped playing and moved on to other things. After the Upstage, the scene sort of moved to the Student Prince, a bar in Asbury, as well as a club called Pandemonium. But it just wasn't the same afterwards. It couldn't be. ***—Robert Santelli***

SOUTHSIDE JOHNNY
. . . .

Interview by Charles R. Cross, December 1984

W hen God was dishing out talent to the Asbury Park set, he gave Bruce Springsteen songwriting, Miami Steve producing, and for Southside Johnny Lyon, he saved something very special: *The Voice.* Southside may very well have one of the purest rhythm-and-blues voices this side of Otis Redding. Watching him perform in a small, smoke-filled club with his band, the Jukes, one of the best bar bands in America, is something akin to the second coming of rhythm and blues.

Southside grew up in Ocean Grove, right next to Asbury Park, and he was a seminal figure in that early scene, jamming in countless bands with Bruce, Steve, and a host of other local legends. From his very start in the business, everyone knew he had *The Voice,* so Southside was always the choice when a Shore band needed a singer. He knew the lyrics to over a thousand songs, and his understanding of and appreciation for early R&B is rivaled by few.

Based on the massive popularity of his club shows and the tremendous talent of his band (which included Steve Van Zandt before he joined Bruce's band), Southside was signed to a record deal in the mid-seventies and put out several classic albums — most notably 1978's *Hearts of Stone.* Southside was great at singing, performing, and putting out records. He was admittedly less than great at the business aspects of music, and almost from its very inception, his career has been marked by a nightmarish battle with record companies.

This interview was conducted in early December 1984 over the course of several hours (and several beers), first in a bar, then in a dressing room, and finally on the Jukes' bus.

. . . . .

BACKSTREETS: *Let's start with your roots. It must*

◀ *Southside Johnny, Parker's Ballroom, December 1984.*

have been something growing up near Asbury with the local music scene what it was in those days.
SOUTHSIDE JOHNNY: Yeah, even before I started playing I would go to the clubs. I had this friend, Buzzy Labinski. Buzzy started collecting records and he'd run dances. I worked for him — I would guard his records and help him set up. He'd take me to see all these different bands when I was 14 years old. These were the great local legends. He took me to see James Brown at the Convention Hall, which turned my head around quite nicely.
Speaking of record collecting, I understand you've got quite a collection of James Brown and other early R&B.
Yeah, I don't do it so much anymore. The competition on the East Coast is fierce.
I'm sure collectors of your records wonder if there is much unreleased Jukes material.
Not really. Unlike Bruce, we don't go in and record a whole bunch of songs. Bruce is searching for the pith, I guess, of what he feels like at the time. I just try to pick the ten best songs. We've got a lot of demos we've done on 16-track — we must have 20, 30 songs from the last few years. The only album where we have a real backlog of stuff is the *Hearts of Stone* record. We recorded eight songs and decided we didn't like the direction we were going, so we threw away seven of them. There are some Bruce tunes, a couple of my songs, but they weren't coming out the way we wanted them. One of the reasons *Hearts of Stone* never got the promotion it should have was because we alienated the record company by going over budget and over time.
That's a real shame, since I think that's your best record and should have been a monster hit.
Yeah, it's a shame. When it first came out it was picked up by 125 stations. but I saw a record-company memo that had both Cheap Trick's marketing plan (posters, radio ads, tie-ins, giveaways) and our marketing plan. Our plan said "release album, see what happens." That was the entire promotion for the record.

Your career seems to have been one continuing nightmare of problems with record companies.

Well, we're a difficult proposition for a record company. They want to be on top of the next big thing so they can sell millions of records. And from our very first record we were considered established artists, so they figured if our record didn't immediately sell 300,000 copies it was dead. Instead of treating us like a group that could be promoted, they figured we'd already been promoted. There are a lot of people in the music business who don't know what they're doing.

There were a lot of mistakes that were made, but we made as many as they did by letting them do the things they did to us. There's too much money in the music business now. Now it's the music business, the video business, and *then* music.

But in many ways we've been our own worst enemies. I'm not ambitious to be a rock 'n' roll star. Consequently, I'm not willing to do all the things people do to promote themselves. Those outrageous images are just alien to me. I wouldn't look good as Boy George, Prince, or Dee Snider. It's hurt the sales of the albums, the success of the band but it's the only way I know how to stay sane in this ridiculous nightmare of the music business.

A lot of your longtime fans were really disappointed in Trash It Up. *What's the story behind that record?*

Yeah, I wasn't happy with it either. The story behind that was that after doing the live album and having Mercury completely ignore it, I got pissed off and left. At that point I was so frustrated I never wanted to make another record. It took me a year to get over that feeling. Then Billy [Rush] and I spent a year putting together new material and trying to get another record company that we wanted to work with.

Finally there came a point where if I didn't make another record, my career as a recording artist was going to be in serious jeopardy. And Billy had written a bunch of songs and he'd been listening to the dance charts and he had an idea for a new kind of R&B sound for us. I said yeah, but I didn't want to produce it. Jerry Greenburg played it for Nile Rogers, and Nile said he wanted to produce it. It sounded like a great idea but I think Nile stretched himself a little too thin. He was working on three other projects at the time and doing a new Chic record. And I also get the feeling that Nile doesn't like to work with musicians so much. We like to be in the studio and he likes to do his own thing,

which in its own way is brilliant. So at that point I said he could have complete control — I didn't want anything to do with it. Billy took over my position and I started drinking and a lot of things happened that were unprofessional. Consequently, a lot of things on that album came out less than they could have been.

You seem surprisingly aware of your own limitations.

Well, I learned a lot during those years I took off between the live album and *Trash It Up*. You have to remember too that I started singing almost by accident. I drifted into it. I used to sing on the street with friends, Italian guys. One day Sonny Kenn asked me to join his band and sing and I also played harmonica 'cause I knew a little of that. I just always took things for granted. The things I took for granted most people never get. I've learned that you may have a natural talent, a gift, but sometimes those things aren't enough. Sometimes you have to get in there and start punching.

I think the whole nature of the music business has changed too. There was an optimism back in the seventies in Asbury Park when you were first signed.

They had so much money then. We signed for $35,000, the price of the first album — Steven and I got the money and we used it to pay for the recording of the first record.

In the late seventies the money dried up and a lot of bands like ours, who didn't sell millions of records, weren't taken seriously. And we had the problem of who we were. We don't look like a unified theme. We look like an American band that plays American music and really wants the audience to have a good time. That's not a very marketable idea for a corporate thinker.

I'll always remember something Miami Steve told me. I was in the studio singing "The Fever" when a bunch of executives walked in and Steve told me to stop singing. I don't like to stop singing, so I asked him why. He said, "These guys don't want to see what you do. It just makes them nervous. All they want is the album, the album cover, and the publicity pictures. They never want to meet us. All they want is the product to sell." He's right.

Getting back to your roots, your father was a musician, wasn't he?

My father was a musician and my mother loves music. I was very lucky to have parents that really loved music. There was no Muzak in our house. When they turned it on, they turned it up. I could have been in a lot of trouble if I stayed on the

Southside Johnny, Parker's Ballroom, Seattle, Wash., December 1984.

streets 'cause I was very wild in those days. Without some kind of direction that takes you out of that, you don't escape. You end up working in some shitty job in Asbury Park, getting in trouble on weekends, and before you know it you're 60 years old.

It was almost as if the fates destined me for a musical career, because of my parents and Sonny. I met Bruce and Steven. Other than meeting them, I'd still be in Asbury Park with a very popular band, making a lot of money. They were ambitious and I wasn't.

I've never read an article about you that didn't mention Bruce Springsteen, and I'm falling victim here myself. Do you ever get sick of hearing that connection?

There was a period between the second and third albums when I felt, "Hey, what about me?" I don't care about the analogies as long as you get a chance to see me and the band play. It's an easy linchpin — like last night's review, "Bruce's Friend Puts on a Great Show." It can be bothersome, but it could be a lot worse. If it has to be anybody, I can't think anyone better than Bruce. He's one of the most honest, straightforward guys with the most integ-

rity and he's given me some great songs and some good advice. He's been decent to me all these years, and I'm sure it pisses him off more than it pisses me off.

There was talk that Steven's leaving the Jukes to join Bruce's band left some bad feelings.

That only happened later. Him leaving the band wasn't a problem — we all knew he was. Steven and I talked about it long before it happened. He came and asked me and I said definitely go with Bruce; he had a hit record and we were still trying to get our foot in the door. Plus, Bruce and Steven had been friends for a long time. And Bruce needs friends like that. Bruce doesn't get that close to people, and when he does get close to someone like Steven, it helps him function.

When Steve was leaving the Jukes, unfortunately other businessmen got involved and created some problems which Steven and I have patched up now. In the early days Steven and I even lived together for a number of years in a number of places. We were very close.

Before forming the Jukes, you were in a number of bands with various names and styles. Were any particularly

Southside Johnny, Cleveland, Ohio, 1978.

memorable? And who were your major influences then?
There were a million bands. In Asbury Park, we'd
have like "band of the week." Someone would con
a bar owner into hiring them for a couple of weeks
and we'd run out and get together a band. We'd
get Garry on bass, Vini on drums, and me to sing.
We'd take three days and learn 25 R&B songs.

We formed hundreds of bands for particular
things we'd get interested in. Steven would want to
do an Allman Brothers thing, so he'd put together
a band. I'd want to do something like Otis Redding
or Muddy Waters, so I'd put together a band.
Bruce would want to do Van Morrison or Dylan,
so we'd try to find musicians who would play that
stuff and an outlet to play it in. If we couldn't, we'd
do it at the Upstage.

The Upstage is a place of legend in the Asbury Park lore.
Many great stories came out of that place, but the
best thing was the musical interaction. It was a situation where you'd be playing with someone you
didn't know, so you have to react to them, to this
unknown quality. And it gave me an insight into
what can happen onstage: great things or terrible
things. It made all of us more loose. We learned
early in our careers that you could do some oddball
stuff and it wouldn't ruin your career.

*I'm a big fan of the early Steel Mill stuff — particularly
the Allman Brothers sound.*
Yeah, that stuff was great. And the Allman
Brothers were a big influence then. When Steve
and I had the Sundance Blues Band, Bruce came
back from California and he wanted to put together
a horn band, but he also wanted to get some cash
and have some fun, so we made Dr. Zoom and the
Sonic Boom. There were 13 musicians plus a
chorus, Monopoly game, baton twirlers, announcer.

*Back to your present-day career — despite all your frustra-
tions, you still seem to really love performing.*
You go on faith in music. You're willing to swallow
a lot of garbage to get to do the thing you love the
most. For a musician in the business, you've got to
put up with a lot of stupid people who don't know
what they're doing.

On the one hand, if you don't have success you're
frustrated. But on the other hand, if you have success, like Michael Jackson, you've got problems of
your own. He's going to have a hell of a time doing
anything again. It's become a media circus.

*Sometimes I worry that by selling 5 million records Bruce
has entered the circus arena whether he likes it or not.*
Bruce has the strength to get through anything. He
chooses to live in New Jersey — he can't go walk
down the streets sometimes. I'm sure he didn't
choose that, but he wants to be what he is. And I
think that's more important to him than being able
to go to the pizzeria. In his case I think you can say
that his stance, his lyrics, his music, are all more
important to him than his own personal privacy.
Anyways, if you're onstage it's okay for 20,000
people to go crazy over you.

*Speaking of going crazy — you're crazy about Otis Red-
ding. I know he's one of your favorite performers and one of
your great inspirations.*
Yeah, "Try a Little Tenderness." I remember the
first time I heard that song I was with my friend
Chucky Anderson. We were delivering a TV for
his father, who owned a TV repair shop. We were
riding into Asbury Park and this song came on and
we almost drove right into the lake. It was such a
dynamite, unbelievably tension-filled performance
— it killed us. You can't believe how intense that
song is.

That song would scare the shit out of anybody
today. If you brought that song in to some record
company executive or a radio programmer, he'd
throw it out the window he'd be so frightened.

—*Charles R. Cross*

Tour Guide for Asbury Park, New Jersey

Cruising Down Kingsley

Here on the Jersey Shore, especially in Asbury Park, we see it each summer: Springsteen fans from all over pull into town, wide-eyed and excited and eager to embrace the rich musical tradition of the area. For many, the trip to Asbury Park is the culmination of a rock 'n' roll pilgrimage — it reaffirms their commitment to the message and spirit of Springsteen's songs, and qualifies them as fans of the highest order.

They come to experience first hand the culture and musical climate that continues to inspire much of Springsteen's lyrical imagery. They come, too, with the hope of spotting Springsteen in a local club or, better yet, of catching an impromptu performance by the Boss with one of the area's many local bar bands.

They also come because Asbury Park is not only the mythical home of Springsteen and the E Street Band, but also of Southside Johnny and the Jukes, John Eddie, Little Steven, and a certain kind of

Madam Marie, Asbury Park, N.J.

rock 'n' roll that is as honest and time-tested and as grassroots and distinctively American as the rock 'n' roll you'll find in other regional musical meccas like Macon, Georgia, and Austin, Texas.

If you're a serious Springsteen fan and have thought about visiting Asbury Park, now is the time to do it. The reason? The city is about to undergo a massive renewal that will permanently alter its look, its soul, and, most important, its rock 'n' roll tradition. Soon the Stone Pony, the Shore's flagship club, will be but a memory.

For those who do come to Asbury Park soon, here is a guide to the must-see spots that bear importance to the Springsteen legacy and that have served to make this seaside resort a truly classic rock 'n' roll town.

· · · · ·

THE STONE PONY
913 Ocean Avenue

One of the most famous of all American rock 'n' roll clubs, the Stone Pony could be called "the house that Bruce built." Springsteen, however, did not begin his career here, as many think. It opened in 1974. At that time, Springsteen was on tour promoting his second album, *The Wild, the Innocent and the E Street Shuffle.*

But Springsteen has performed at the Pony on countless occasions over the years. During one winter stretch in the early eighties he played practically every Sunday night with the group Cats on a Smooth Surface. Springsteen even launched his now legendary *Born in the USA* tour from the Pony stage in June 1984. He's played more in this club than any other hall.

Southside Johnny and the Asbury Jukes were the Pony's first house band. In 1976 a live broadcast from the club introduced the Jukes and their debut album, *I Don't Want to Go Home,* to rock fans across America. Since then, hundreds of great rockers have played the Pony, including Elvis Costello, Little Steven, and Bon Jovi.

ASBURY PARK ROCK 'N' ROLL MUSEUM
Check phonebook for location

No visit to Asbury Park would be complete without visiting the Asbury Park Rock 'n' Roll Museum. Unfortunately, the museum's location is presently up in the air due to the redevelopment of Asbury Park. Springsteen fans can easily spend a couple of hours looking at the many photos and bits of memorabilia that pack the walls and cases of the museum's collection. So can fans of the Jersey Shore's other favorite rock sons, such as Southside Johnny, Little Steven, Jon Bon Jovi, and an entire cast of lesser-known musicians. The posters alone are worth the price of admission.

Curators Billy Smith and Steve Bumball are experts in Springsteen and Jersey Shore rock history. They almost always take the time to elaborate on the museum's many treasures, and they'll certainly answer your questions. Featured in the museum are rare photos of Steel Mill, Springsteen's most important pre-E Street Band outfit; the psychedelic sign from the Upstage; promo posters; instruments; and relics from a number of area musicians. Among the most prized items on display is one of the only copies known to exist of the Castiles' record, "That's What You Get"/"Baby I." The single was recorded in 1966; only a couple of copies of it are still known to exist.

Check a local phonebook for the museum's current location, or write to P.O. Box 296, Allenhurst, N.J., 07711.

PALACE AMUSEMENTS ARCADE
Cookman and Second avenues

This classic amusement center was partly responsible for the inspiration behind the title track of *Tunnel of Love.* In fact, one of the *Tunnel of Love Express* tour T-shirts for sale at Springsteen concerts had the familiar "Palace face" emblazoned on the front of it. The Palace was well-documented in Springsteen songs and many promo pictures of Springsteen were taken here.

The building is now threatened by redevelopment and its future is in doubt.

CASINO ARENA
Asbury Park boardwalk

Located across from the Palace Amusements Arcade at the southern end of the Asbury Park boardwalk is the Casino Arena. During the early seventies New Jersey rock promoter John Scher regularly featured major concerts here from June through September. More recently, Springsteen filmed his "Tunnel of Love" video in the Casino Arena. Unfortunately, the venue is in desperate need of repair. Whether it will be spared the wrecking ball remains to be seen.

At one time there were rumors that a renovated, remodeled Casino Arena would house a "new" Stone Pony, an expanded Asbury Park Rock 'n' Roll Museum, a Hard Rock Cafe, and perhaps even a state-of-the-art recording studio. Time will tell what the future holds for the Casino Arena.

THE WONDER BAR
1213 Ocean Avenue

Speaking of Springsteen videos, it was at the Wonder Bar that Bruce filmed his "One Step Up" video. When it comes to classic Asbury Park beer joints, the Wonder Bar fits the description perfectly. Over the years a number of Asbury Park musicians have played the bar, including Springsteen, former E Street Band drummer Vini Lopez, former Dr. Zoom Monopoly player Big Danny Gallagher and many more. These days the Wonder Bar rarely features big-name local bands — what you'll hear instead are copy bands, if that. But you've got to grab a beer or two at the Wonder Bar just for the experience. Here's another club that probably won't be around once the renovation of Asbury Park's beachfront begins in earnest.

THE CIRCUIT
Ocean and Kingsley avenues

"The Circuit" comprises Ocean and Kingsley avenues; together they form a long loop around Asbury Park's beachfront area. During the summer, and on Saturday nights the rest of the year, Ocean Avenue, which parallels the boardwalk, is alive with fast cars and Harley-Davidsons. You'll find the Wonder Bar and the Stone Pony on Ocean Avenue, as well as Mrs. Jay's, known as a biker bar and a place where some of the best bar bands play. Kingsley is one block west of Ocean Avenue. You'll find rock clubs on this street, too, including Dimples and Club Xanadu, where Springsteen first performed "Dancing in the Dark" live. He played it with the local group Bystander. Springsteen mentioned the Circuit in his songs "Night"

The Stone Pony, Asbury Park, N.J.

and "Fourth of July, Asbury Park (Sandy)," to name but two. For years the Circuit was the place to be seen and to see others — especially if you had a hot set of wheels. You can't do it too fast — the traffic lights are tuned to stop speeding.

· · · · ·

ASBURY PARK BOARDWALK
One block over from Ocean Avenue

Any visitor to Asbury Park has to take at least one stroll on this famed boardwalk. The seedy shops, the sausage stands, the pizza parlors, and the amusement rides are all destined for destruction soon. In their place will rise — you guessed it — condos and walkways. There's a lot of Asbury Park musical history embedded in these boards. Numerous Springsteen and the E Street Band photo sessions took place here — you might recognize some of the settings. Southside Johnny and the Asbury Jukes used it, too, as did many other local bands. Boardwalk images and themes swirl about early Springsteen songs. Perhaps his best known

boardwalk tune is "Fourth of July, Asbury Park (Sandy)."

· · · · ·

MADAM MARIE'S
Boardwalk and Fourth Avenue

This small fortune-teller's stand is also mentioned in "Fourth of July, Asbury Park (Sandy)." It's not any more important than the other Asbury Park landmarks mentioned in Springsteen songs. It's just more obvious. It also makes an excellent backdrop for a photograph. Madam Marie still works the tourists, too.

· · · · ·

CONVENTION HALL
Boardwalk, between Fifth and Sunset avenues

This is the largest venue on the Jersey Shore, excluding the Garden State Arts Center in Holmdel Township. Back in the 1960s, impresario Moe Septee presented such bands as the Rolling Stones, the Who, the Jefferson Airplane, and the Doors at

St. Rose of Lima School, Freehold, N.J.

Convention Hall. Southside Johnny and the Jukes performed here a number of times over the years.

. . . .

PARAMOUNT THEATRE
Boardwalk and Fifth Avenue

Soundwise, the Paramount has always had it over Convention Hall by leaps and bounds. Many concerts were held here, too. There are plans to refurbish the theater in the near future. Springsteen and the E Street Band rehearsed here before setting out on their 1978 tour to promote *Darkness*.

. . . .

DIMPLES
911 Kingsley Avenue

Years ago, Dimples was called the Student Prince. A popular hangout for Monmouth College students during the late sixties and early seventies, the Student Prince regularly featured Springsteen and his various pre-E Street Bands. It was at the Student Prince, as legend has it, that Springsteen first met up with Clarence Clemons.

. . . .

PARKING LOT
Kingsley and 1st avenues

Here once stood the Hullabaloo, a mid-sixties teen club where many of the area's young musicians performed in groups like the Motifs, Sonny and the Starfires, and the Castiles, Springsteen's first group. Later on, the Hullabaloo became the Sunshine Inn. Springsteen performed in this sleazy yet popular venue on many occasions. Perhaps the most memorable show he did at the Sunshine Inn was with the short-lived group Dr. Zoom and the Sonic Boom. Like Convention Hall, the Sunshine Inn featured many up-and-coming bands that would later rise to superstardom, including Kiss and the Allman Brothers Band.

. . . .

UPSTAGE
702 Cookman Avenue

The Upstage ranks with the Stone Pony as the most popular and most important club, historically speaking, of all the Asbury Park and Jersey Shore clubs. It was located atop a Thom McAn's shoe store; today it's OK Shoes. From 1968 through 1970, the Upstage was where not only Springsteen but such members of the E Street Band as Garry Tallent and Danny Federici, plus former E Streeters Davey Sancious, Vini Lopez, and Miami Steve Van Zandt (Little Steven) jammed until dawn each weekend. Southside Johnny, members of the old Asbury Jukes, Billy Chinnock, and dozens of other talented but lesser-known area musicians also hung out and performed here. The Upstage gave local musicians valuable stage experience and sparked the formation of numerous bands, including Steel Mill, Springsteen's heavy-metal blues outfit.

. . . .

FAST LANE
206 Fourth Avenue

Like the Upstage, the Fast Lane is but a memory. In the late seventies and early eighties, when the Fast Lane was the most popular club in town, groups like Beaver Brown and the Rest, Jon Bon Jovi's early band, performed there regularly. Springsteen frequently hung out at the club and often jumped onstage to jam with visiting and local bands. Many of the best English New Wave bands of the era played the Fast Lane. Joe Jackson even began one of his American tours at the club.

—Robert Santelli

Stone Pony, Asbury Park, N.J., August 21, 1987. ▶

TOUR GUIDE FOR FREEHOLD, NEW JERSEY

My Hometown, U.S.A.

For years, Asbury Park has gotten most of the spotlight as the symbolic home and stomping grounds of Bruce Springsteen. A lot of fans actually think he was born there. Some fans who are really dancing in the dark believe he lives there now.

Even those fans with only cursory knowledge of Springsteen's past know it was Freehold and not Asbury Park where the Boss grew up and first discovered rock 'n' roll. He was actually born in Long Branch, at Monmouth Medical Center, about ten miles away. But until he graduated from high school in 1967, Bruce Springsteen lived in Freehold, an old town that, at one time, was better known for its Revolutionary War lore (Molly Pitcher and the Battle of Monmouth) and its racetrack (Freehold Raceway) than for its special place in rock 'n' roll history.

It was in Freehold, for instance, that Springsteen's first band, the Castiles, was based. All those tales Springsteen has told from the stage — touching vignettes about his relationship with his father, about his neighbors, about learning to play his guitar — have a Freehold setting. In 1985, when the 3M Company announced that it would lay off 360 workers, and when Springsteen came to their aid with money and moral support, the plant where the jobs were lost was in Freehold. And of course the main inspiration for one of Springsteen's most deeply felt songs, "My Hometown," is Freehold, too.

Without doubt, Freehold has played as much a role in Springsteen's life and music as has Asbury Park. Fans who come to the Jersey Shore to take in Asbury's rock 'n' roll sights should then drive to Freehold to complete their tour of Springsteen's Jersey Shore.

. . . .

Bruce Springsteen's childhood was spent in three Freehold homes, two of which are still standing.

When Adele and Douglas Springsteen brought their new son home from the hospital in September 1949, they brought him to 87 Randolph Street. It was here where, in 1957, Springsteen saw Elvis Presley on "The Ed Sullivan Show" and begged his mother to buy him a guitar.

The Springsteens resided on Randolph Street, with little Bruce's grandparents on his father's side, until he was eight or nine years old. Unfortunately, the house was torn down years ago. In its place is a driveway that leads to St. Rose of Lima Church.

The Springsteens then moved to 39½ Institute Street. The blue and white house with the cozy front porch was, back then, located in a typical middle-class neighborhood. The sycamore tree on the side of the house is the one against which Springsteen is leaning in the photo on the lyric sheet of *Born in the USA*.

A few years later, Springsteen's parents made their last Freehold move before leaving the town for good and starting a new life in northern California. (Bruce, of course, remained in New Jersey.) The house they moved into, at 68 South Street, still stands. From a historical perspective, it is the most important house of the three, since it was here that Springsteen learned to play his guitar by listening to songs on the radio, and became, as one longtime friend put it, "obsessed" with rock 'n' roll. (Today the houses that Springsteen grew up in are inhabited by new families. Please be courteous and respectful of their property and privacy when you visit Freehold.)

Springsteen attended grammar school at St. Rose of Lima, located at the corner of South and Lincoln streets, just a short distance from Springsteen's South Street house. The Catholic school experience was not a pleasant one for him. In fact, scattered through a number of his early songs are lyrics that bitterly depict the difficulty he had with Catholic education and unbending nuns.

After graduating from St. Rose, Springsteen

The house Bruce Springsteen grew up in, corner of Institute and South streets, Freehold, N.J.

attended Freehold High School, on Broadway and Robertville Road, from 1963 to 1967. During his sophomore year he joined the Castiles and spent most of the time he wasn't in school hanging out at Tex Vinyard's house on Center Street, which has since been demolished. Vinyard was the Castiles' manager and practically a second father to Springsteen. Under Vinyard's guidance, the Castiles went on to become one of the most popular Freehold bands in the mid-sixties.

The Castiles played in front of an audience for the very first time in 1965. The place was the Woodhaven Swim Club, on East Freehold Road in the neighboring town of Freehold Township. The Swim Club is no longer around, either. Today its buildings are occupied by the local YMCA chapter.

In an interview with Springsteen's biographer, Dave Marsh, Vinyard recalled more than a decade ago that the band received $35 for its first gig. "It was a suck-ass job to get," Vinyard said. "George [Theiss, the Castiles' lead singer and rhythm guitarist] knew somebody who knew somebody who knew the principal. We got the last open gig of the season."

The Castiles went on to play a number of other venues in and around the Freehold area. Teen

clubs were popular at the Jersey Shore in the mid-sixties, and the Castiles played them. But the band also played school and CYO (Catholic Youth Organization) dances, battle-of-the-band contests, YMCA functions, and private parties.

In the late sixties, three things occurred that prompted Springsteen to leave Freehold: he graduated from high school, his family moved to California, and the Castiles broke up. Since Springsteen had tried unsuccessfully to pursue a college education — he briefly attended Ocean County College, on Hooper Avenue in Toms River — he had turned to what he loved and knew best: music.

By this time he had made friends with a number of other Shore musicians, many of whom lived east of Freehold and closer to the beach, in towns like Neptune, Long Branch, and, of course, Asbury Park. So that was where he drifted and where his next two bands, Child and Earth, mostly played.

Once he was on his own, Springsteen was rarely in a house or apartment long enough to call it home. When he was broke, he'd return to the Vinyards' house in Freehold. But mostly he roomed with friends in cheap, seedy apartments in Asbury and Long Branch, or close to Monmouth College in West Long Branch.

It made sense for Springsteen to live in this section of the Jersey Shore rather than in Freehold. Most of the clubs and coffee houses that featured live music were located there, including the Upstage, and a real music scene was actually beginning to develop there. To complete your Springsteen tour of the Jersey Shore, there are a few other landmarks worth visiting, not located in either Asbury Park or Freehold.

· · · ·

BIG MAN'S WEST
129 Monmouth Street, Red Bank

Today you'll find the World Gym in the building that once was home to Big Man's West, the club opened by E Street Band member Clarence Clemons in 1981. "I want the club to feature the best local and national talent and become a hangout for Shore musicians," said the Big Man himself after he, Springsteen, and the rest of the E Street Band opened the club on a steamy summer night

◄ *The Wonder Bar, Asbury Park, N.J., February 15, 1988. For the video of "One Step Up" Springsteen was made up to look like an old man, though in the final version of the video this footage was not used.*

Institute and South streets, Freehold, N.J.

eight years ago. It became just what Clemons hoped it would become. The club also helped the Shore music scene rebound from a particularly low period in the late seventies. During the two-and-a-half-year existence of Big Man's West, Springsteen jammed there a number of times. John Eddie got his start at the club.

· · · ·

CHALLENGER EAST SURFBOARD FACTORY
3505 Sunset Avenue, Ocean Township

During the days of Steel Mill, Springsteen's most successful pre–E Street band, he and Mill members Danny Federici and Vini Lopez lived here. The band also rehearsed in the building. Tinker West, a local surfboard manufacturer, was also Steel Mill's manager.

· · · ·

ROUTES 9, 88, AND 33

These main Jersey Shore roads figure in the Springsteen legacy. Route 88, which runs through the Ocean County towns of Point Pleasant, Brick Township, and Lakewood, is represented in the song "Spirit in the Night." Route (or Highway) 9, a main Monmouth County artery that goes through Freehold, appears in "Born to Run." And Route 33 links Freehold to Asbury Park and other beach towns. Springsteen undoubtedly logged many hours on it. —*Robert Santelli*

TALK TO ME

Interviews with the Man and the Band

Walk like the Heroes: The E Street Band, 1975 (L to R): Clarence Clemons, Max Weinberg, Roy Bittan, Bruce Springsteen, Garry Tallent, Miami Steve Van Zandt and Danny Federici.

LOST IN THE FLOOD

. . . .

Bruce Springsteen Interviewed by Paul Williams, October 1974

---

aul Williams is credited with starting the very first rock magazine, *Crawdaddy*, back in January 1966. Under his leadership it predated *Rolling Stone* and literally helped mold the form of rock journalism — it was the first of its kind and, some argue, the best. One thing is certain: *Crawdaddy*'s persistent coverage of an unknown singer-songwriter from New Jersey played an essential role in establishing Bruce Springsteen's credentials; there are those who suggest that without promotion from *Crawdaddy* and other rock magazines of the sort, CBS might have dumped the Boss before *Born to Run* ever came out. Williams, and the editor who followed him, Peter Knobler, used *Crawdaddy* to spread the word on Bruce. *Crawdaddy* also was the one rock magazine Springsteen said, at the time, that he always read.

In 1973 and 1974, Williams followed the Springsteen tour for weeks, working on a story for *New Times* magazine. Researching the piece, he conducted an interview with Springsteen on October 13, 1974, less than a month after Max Weinberg and Roy Bittan joined the E Street Band. The interview was conducted the day after a show at Princeton University and a week before Bruce would heat up the Passaic Capitol Theater with the first of his many legendary shows there. Williams interviewed Bruce one evening at Bruce's apartment in Long Branch; Max Weinberg was also there in the background and can be heard pounding his drumsticks on a chair throughout the entire interview.

At the time of the interview, Springsteen was still writing most of the songs that would eventually appear on *Born to Run*. He was still working on the lyrics to "Jungleland," and Williams remembers writing down the lyrics for Dave Marsh, who at the time had just gotten into Bruce and was await-

ing the new album, due for release in 1975.

Williams's interview, however, was never used by *New Times*; they first put it off because they "weren't sure anybody would be interested in Bruce," Williams says. Soon afterwards, *New Times* folded. Williams did write a piece on Bruce for *Gallery*, a skin magazine, which CBS liked enough that they sent out photocopies with the script cover album. He also penned a story in the *Soho Weekly News* titled "You Don't Know Him, But You Will...."

. . . . .

PAUL WILLIAMS: *What Dylan influenced you musically?*

BRUCE SPRINGSTEEN: In 1968 I was into *John Wesley Harding*. I never listened to anything after *John Wesley Harding*. I listened to *Bringing It All Back Home, Highway 61, Blonde on Blonde*. That's it. I never had his early albums and to this day I don't have them, and I never had his later albums. I might have heard them once, though. There was only a short period of time when I related, there was only that period when he was important to me, you know, where he was giving me what I needed. That was it. *That was really true for a lot of people.*

Yeah, it was the big three. I never was really into him until I heard "Like a Rolling Stone" on the radio, because it was a hit. FM radio at the time was just beginning, but even if there was no FM at the time, I never had an FM radio. In 1965 I was like 15 and there were no kids 15 who were into folk music. There had been a folk boom, but it was generally a college thing. There was really no way of knowing because AM radio was really an incredible must in those days. The one thing I dug about those albums was — I was never really into the folk or acoustic music thing — I dug the sound. Before I listened to what was happening in the song, you had the chorus and you had the band and it had incredible sound and that was what got me. *What about the Stones?*

◄ *Paramount Theater, Seattle, Wash., October 26, 1975. The simultaneous* Newsweek *and* Time *covers would hit stands and be dated the following day.*

Yeah, I was into the Stones. I dug the first few Stones albums, the first three or four maybe. After that I haven't heard any of it lately except the singles, "Tumbling Dice" and stuff like that — it was great. There was *December's Children* and *Aftermath...*

And Between the Buttons *and...*

Between the Buttons was when I started to lose contact with the Stones. It was right around there.

What came after Between the Buttons*?*

First Their Satanic Majesties, *then* Let it Bleed...

See, I never had a record player for years and years. It was a space from when my parents moved out west and I started to live by myself, from when I was 17 until I was 24, and I never had a record player. So it was like I never heard any albums that came out after, like, '67. (Laughs.) And I was never a social person who went over to other people's houses and got loaded and listened to records — I never did that. And I didn't have an FM radio, so I never heard anything. From that time on, from around '67, until just recently when I got a record player. I lived with Diane [Rosito] and she had an old beat-up one that only old records sounded good on. So that's all I played. Those old Fats Domino records, they sounded great on it. If they were trashed, they sounded terrific. A lot of those acts lost what was important after they could really be heard — it just didn't hold. They didn't seem to be able to go further and further. They made their statement. They'd make the same statement every record, basically, without elaborating that much on it.

How about the Yardbirds? Did you listen to them?

Oh yeah. I listened to the Yardbirds' first two albums. And the Zombies, all those groups. And Them.

That's funny for the people who talk about your Van Morrison influence, that it really came from the Them *records.*

Yeah, that was the stuff I liked. There's some great stuff on those records. When he was doing stuff like "Out-A-Sight James Brown."

But mostly your contact has been through jukeboxes and AM radio?

I guess, yeah. I stopped listening to AM radio, too, because it got really trashy and I didn't have a car. I got a classic example right here *(reaches down and picks up a record.)* You've got your Andy Kim records.

And you've got stuff like "The Night Chicago Died." Those are the same guys who wrote "Billy, Don't Be a Hero."

Oh God. If somebody shot those guys, there's not a jury in the land, there's not a jury in the land that would find them guilty. (Laughs.)

But it was like that in the sixties prior to the Beach Boys.

Yeah, a wasteland.

Union, N.J., September 22, 1974.

Yeah, "Poetry in Motion." But maybe there's hope. It's all cyclical. I sometimes wonder, though, if what the record business is like these days could stop things from happening. I mean at least on the radio.

Only to a certain degree. I don't want to get into specifics because I know some things that have been done to me. I don't want to sound like — I don't want to whine — but at least to a degree they can't stop you from going out there and playing every night. They can't stop you from being good if you've got it. They *can* keep it off the radio. They *can* make sure it gets little airplay, or no airplay, which, really, it hurts you.

Like look at us: we've been going for two years and the second record is at 70,000. That's nothing.

Trenton, N.J., November 30, 1974. ►

That really is nothing. That's zero. It depends on who they're dealing with, who they're messing with. It depends on the person. It's like anything — some people can be stopped and other people can't be stopped. It's just like me — I can't stop, they can't make me stop ever, because I can't stop. It's like once you stop, that's it — I don't know what I'd do. But it's like that, though — if you're dealing with people who say, "Ah hell, I gotta go back to hanging wallpaper," or who say, "Ah, I'm gonna go back to college and forget this stuff" — that's what people always say — "I don't know if I want to play or if I want to get married." If you have to decide, then the answer is don't do it. If you have a choice, then the answer is no. I like to use the term "the record company" because they always get painted as the bad guys. But the pressures of the business are powerless in the face of what is real.

It's like what happens when they push you to make a hit single. Then you get a hit and they push you to go on the road because now you can make $10,000 a night and you might only be able to make $10 a night five years from now. It happens to a lot of people, most people. Then you get out on the road and you can't write anymore and then you can't figure out what the hell else is happening besides.

What happens is there are certain realities that force you into things right now. We got a band; we got a blue bus; we got a sound man; we got an office in New York. Those are the sort of things that influence my decisions. We have to play, because if we don't, everything falls apart. We don't make any money off records. We have to go out and play every week, as much as we can. If not, nobody gets paid. In order to maintain and raise the quality of what we're doing, we gotta play all the time.

At this point you're on salary?

Yeah.

And is that it? Does everything else go back into it?

Everything else pays for the blue bus and everything else.

And you got debts, I bet?

Oh, we owe like a mint.

Some people don't realize that the economic remuneration at this point is like working in an office.

At best. Diane came in and said "Oh, this is terrific. I just got a raise working at my newspaper job in Boston." She said, "Now I'll be getting this

◀ *Philadelphia, Pa., December 30, 1975.*

much." And I realized that was how much I was making. There's no money saved at all. You can't sell 80,000 records and have any money saved. Unless you're totally by yourself and you're your own manager. Then you can make a thousand dollars and stick it all in your own pocket and go home and put some in the bank. But when you're trying to do what we're trying to do, there's no way.

The thing that bothers me, that you seem to have gotten around, is that there seems to be nowhere to play except big arenas, new acts or old acts.

What you gotta do is, like...I did the Chicago tour. I did that tour because I had never played big places. And I said, "I ain't gonna say no because I don't know what they're like." So we went and played it, about 14 nights in a row. I went crazy — I went insane during that tour. It was the worst state of mind I've ever been in, I think, and just because of the playing conditions for our band. The best part of the tour was the guys in Chicago — they are great guys. They are really, really real. But I couldn't play those big places. It had nothing to do with anything, but I couldn't do it. It had nothing to do with anything that had anything to do with me, those big arenas. So I won't go to those places again. That was it. Usually we won't play anyplace over 3,000 — that's the highest we want to do. We don't want to get any bigger. And that's even too big.

The challenge comes when you get more popular, which is inevitable.

But there's no way. I'm always disappointed in acts that go out and play those places. I don't know how the band can go out and play like that. I don't know how Joni Mitchell can do it. You can't. You can't effectively do it.

But then there's the Who. They announce they're playing Madison Square Garden and it sells out in an hour. So I'd guess they'd have to book a week, a whole week.

You gotta do that. And if you get that big, you gotta realize that some people who want to see you ain't gonna see you. I'm not in that position and I don't know if I'll ever be in that position. All I know is that those big coliseums ain't where it's supposed to be. There's always something else going on all over the room. You go to the back row, you can't see the stage, talk about what's on it. You see a blot of light. You better bring your binocs.

I guess people go for the event.

What happens is you go to those places and it turns into something else that it ain't. It becomes an

New York, N.Y., 1975. An outtake from the "Born to Run" album cover sessions.

event. It's hard to play. That's where everybody is playing, though. I don't know how they do it. I don't know what people expect you to do in a place like that. Especially our band — it would be impossible to reach out there the way we try to do. Forget it!

Listen, I got the word from somebody in New York that you're a real sex star now.

Who?

Well, a girl who works at the newspaper. She's 26. I guess 26-year-old women haven't found anything for years that they could get off on.

That's interesting.

And like, pow, they went to your show at the Bottom Line and Schaffer and it's natural because it's all part of the thing. It was a big thrill for them.

Well, we do some pretty heavy things onstage sometimes. There's lots of different currents, lots of different types of energy going on in each song, and that current is very strong. But that's interesting.

I tried to get her to describe why. I made notes as she was talking over the phone. She said it's like "he knows that you know that he knows what he's doing." She said certain

circles are really aware of what a joke it is because it's done really totally seriously. But she also says she'll sit there and laugh her ass off.

There's so many different conflicts and tensions going on in each tune. It can affect people in totally different ways. That's what a lot of the act is based on — it's setting up certain conflicts and tensions. We're going for the moment and then, there'll be no . . . release.

And you'll say, "We'll be back next time."

Really. And that's the way this life is. Next, next, next, next. No matter how heavy one thing hits you, no matter how intense any experience is, there's always, like, next. And that's the way some things we do are structured, for there never to be any resolve, for there never to be a way out, or an answer, or a way in, anything! It's like a constant motion in a circle.

And the two-hour sets are a manifestation of that, needing room to build?

That's a lot. Right now that's the utmost amount we could ever do. It could work better than it's been. It's just a question of finding the right spot

TALK TO ME

6 3

for everything, where things make more sense than other things, what's just the right place. When we were playing the Bottom Line we'd do an hour and a half. And those were long. We'd do an oldie, we'd do "Saint in the City." we'd do "Jungleland," we'd do "Kitty's Back," we'd do "New York City," we'd do "Rosalita" sometimes. We'd do like ten things. Now we're doing like . . . one . . . two . . . we're doing "Lost in the Flood," we haven't been doing that . . . we're doing that new song "She's the One" and a few other things. We're going about two hours. I think the longest we did was Avery Fisher, which was about two-twenty.

Most acts will do that with an intermission.

An intermission might be a smart idea just because it will set up a reference point where people can collect their thoughts. At clubs I never expect people to order alcohol because they're too tired. I know I'm pooped, I figure they're dead. There's outlets for a lot of different things in our shows, a lot of different emotions. It runs the gamut, from violence to anything. It runs through a lot of different outlets. We try to make people as close to it as they want to get.

There are a couple of songs on the first album, "Growin' Up," and "For You," that are more personal.

Well, we were doing "For You" for a while with the new band a few weeks ago, but there's just no time. You gotta realize there's just no time.

Also, I feel the new songs have been more towards archetypes and away from . . .

Yeah, to a degree. I think what happened is I'm using a slightly different language to express the same thing. The songs haven't gotten any less personal — probably just more and more.

They're not as first-personal. On those songs on the first record, you identified with the singer.

I find that if it gets too personal, people get too high. So you've got to use this second person. I tend to be more direct. I'm just getting down there, you know. I think it gets harder to do if you want to continue reaching out there, if you don't want to fall back and play it safe.

I like "Jungleland" a lot.

That's been coming along. There's a verse that's not really finished. It goes . . . there's a chorus that goes . . . "The street's alive with tough kid jets in nova light machines."

Tough kids in nova light machines?

"Boys flash guitars like bayonets, and rip holes in their jeans. The hungry and the hunted explode into rock 'n' roll bands that face off against each other in the street, down in jungleland."

Then the band plays. And what goes next . . . uh . . . I think the next part is the slow part. It goes "beneath the city, two hearts beat, soul engines warm and tender, in a bedroom locked, silent whispers soft refusal and then surrender. In the tunnel machine, the rat chases his dreams on a forever lasting night. Till the barefoot girl brings him to bed, shakes her head and with a sigh turns out the light."

Tunnel machines?

Yeah. (Sings/talks.) "Outside the street's on fire in a real death waltz, between what's flesh and what's fantasy. The poets down here don't write nothing at all, they just sit back and let it be. In the quick of the night, they reach for their moment and try to make an honest stand. But they wind up wounded and not even dead. Tonight in jungleland." Those are some of the words. There's a new verse and some that's not done, but that's the slow part.

"In the quick of the night, they reach for their moment."

Yeah. That's it.

Jungleland. That makes a nice title. It's a nice word.

Yeah, it resolves.

You could call the whole album that because it fits all your songs.

I thought of that. I'm thinking of titles for the next album, that was my initial thought. That's one of them.

It fits. It makes sense.

Yeah, but I usually change them. I work a lot on the lyrics before we record a song. I get self-conscious about them. So I change them. It's the same with a lot of the old songs. I notice them so even on some of the old songs I add new bits. There's a bit on "E Street" and that one on "New York City." It's done differently.

And I like the violin.

Yeah, it's great.

Well, I better call a taxi.

Yeah, what time is it?

Bruce Has the Fever

. . . .

Bruce Springsteen Interviewed by Ed Sciaky, August 1978

Ed Sciaky is one of the original Boss Jocks — along with Kid Leo in Cleveland, his early support of Bruce Springsteen was essential to the band's survival during the lean years when most radio stations wouldn't even consider playing a Bruce Springsteen record. Sciaky not only played Bruce, but helped to develop the loyal Philadelphia audience that to this day is the most fervent of all Springsteen crowds. He also introduced many of the early shows and did several on-air interviews with Bruce. During his years at WMMR and later WIOQ, he also always made it clear that he was a "fan," and his radio support has always had an enthusiastic flavor not found in other jocks.

The following interview was conducted in the early-morning hours of August 19, 1978, after Springsteen's show at the Philadelphia Spectrum. An edited version of the interview was broadcast later in the day on station WIOQ. The full, unedited version of the interview follows.

. . . . .

ED SCIAKY: *I'm beat, I have nothing to say.*
BRUCE SPRINGSTEEN: Well, Eddie, you did a hell of a show — that's why. No wonder you're tired.
Well, I was a little far back tonight. I was about seventh row, and I like to be a little closer.
Must have been murder.
Tonight was the most high-energy show I can ever remember at the Spectrum. I rate them, you know, and I'd put this in the top five. Do you rate them like that?
Sometimes. There's ones that you can say, "Wow, this one's really up there; that one was, like, way up there; this one was really something." But this one tonight was pretty wild. It just felt right — it felt good.

◀ *With Ed Sciaky, Philadelphia, Pa., 1978.*

I was just blown away. There were certain highlights and certain changes from the last time you were here, like "Because the Night" which you didn't do last time.
Last time we were here, it was the third show on the tour, and we weren't doing "Darkness on the Edge of Town," we didn't do "Factory," we didn't do "Because the Night," we didn't do "The Fever."
Wait a minute — you didn't do "Fever" for about five years. Now why is "Fever" back?
It was just a surprise, you know. We'd done it two or three times and the tape had gotten out through someone's help whose name I won't mention. So we did it a few times and we had to do it here. I used to have kids run up on stage and yell in my ear, "BRUCE! 'FEVER'!" That was always a request.
You used to say you didn't like the song, and a lot of people think it's one of your best.
I don't know. It was just something that I wrote so long ago. It was just an older song and never a real favorite of mine. I liked it, I always liked it. But just for myself. I liked Johnny's version — I liked what he did with it a lot. But we wanted to have something extra, so we pulled it out.
I saw you down in Washington the other night, and I thought you'd do something for Elvis, like "Wear My Ring," for his anniversary.
I had a song we were gonna do, but in the end we didn't learn it in time. I wanted to do — what's the song from *Blue Hawaii*? It was his theme song. One which everyone relates to his Las Vegas period: "I Can't Help Falling in Love with You." Which I think is a great song. But everyone relates to it as being Las Vegas-y, but I don't think it is. I wanted to do that one. But we just didn't get a chance to run it down before the show. It was something because when we went down to Memphis, Bruce Jackson, the fellow that does our sound, did sound for Elvis for a long, long time, and I went up to Graceland there.
This was recently?

Yeah, it was a couple of weeks ago.

Is it true what you said in Rolling Stone *about the time you tried to sneak in there?*

Oh, that time, yeah, that was two years before then. It was just real late at night and we were looking for something to do. And we got in the cab with this guy and we said — it was me and Miami Steve — and we said, "Listen, we wanna get something to eat." And this guys says, "I know, I'll take you to Fridays." And we said, "We don't want, like a hangout — we want a place where we can go and eat." So he says, "There's a place out by Elvis's house." We said [snaps his fingers], "You mean there's a place out by Elvis's house?" And he said, "Yeah," and I said, "Take me to Elvis's right now." He says, "You guys celebrities?" We say, "Yeah, yeah, we're celebrities." So he says, "Oh." We tell him who we were and he says, "Can I tell my dispatcher that I got some celebrities in the cab?" We said, "Sure, sure." So he gets on the thing and says, "Joe, Joe, I got some celebrities in my cab." And Joe says, "Yeah, who ya got there?" And into it he says, "I got, I got..." Then he shoves the mike right in my face because he doesn't know who we are, and I say, "Bruce Springsteen and the E Street Band, we're from New Jersey, blah, blah, blah." And the cabdriver says, "Yeah, I got them and we're going out to Elvis's." The dispatcher says, "Damn." He thinks we're, like, going out to have coffee with Elvis or something.

So we get out there and I'm standing up and looking at those gates — he's got a big, long driveway and I saw a light on. And I say, "I gotta find out if he's home, Steve." And I said, "I can't stand here — I gotta find out if he's home." So I jumped over the wall, a stone wall. And the cabdriver is going, "Man, there's dogs in there. You're gonna get it. You're gonna be in trouble." But I gotta find out, so I ran up the driveway and there was nobody. And I ran up to the front door. And I got to the front door and I knocked. And I knocked... And then, from out of the woods, I see somebody watching me. And I figure I'm just going to go over and I'm going to say hello and tell this guy I just came to see Elvis or whatever. So I walk over towards the woods and out comes this security guy. And he says, "What are you doing?" I said "Well, I came to see Elvis. I'm in a band. I play the guitar." "Well," he says, "Elvis ain't home. Elvis is in Lake Tahoe." And I say, "Are you sure?" And he said,

"Yeah, yeah." I said, "Well, if he comes back, tell him Bruce Springsteen..." And he didn't know me from nobody, you know from Joe Schmo. I said, "Listen, I was on *Time*, I was on *Newsweek*." He said, "Ah, sure, buddy. Well, listen, you gotta go outside now." So he took me on down to the gate and just dumped me out, back onto the street.

What if he had been home, would you have gone in?

I tried, that's why I went up there.

You saw him at the Spectrum once, remember, and you didn't try to meet him.

It was different then. It was a funny kind of thing. I never liked, you know, going backstage and stuff. I just feel uncomfortable when that happens — I don't know why. But if I could have snuck in and saw him, it would have been different — it woulda just been different.

So you can dig people that want to break into your house and all?

(Laughs.) They want to break into my house?

You know, people that follow you around and all, and people who want to relate to you the way you relate to Elvis.

It's hard for me to put it together like that. Sometimes kids come up and say "Hi" or something. It's hard for me to relate to it the same way. It's different — it just seems different to me on some level, though I guess maybe it isn't. I could just never put it together. I still feel like more the fan than the other thing — the performer. It's like I can't relate. I relate easier from that viewpoint than the other.

I think I've lately seen a change in how you relate to people. You're dealing a little more with the press and the realities of the record business and all that kind of stuff, sort of getting to be the "rock star." I mean dealing with all the different aspects rather than just going out and having the fun of playing.

The *Born to Run* thing — I just got blown away by that particular side of it. I was just too raw and green about it or stupid. And this time I was a little more prepared for people writing stories about [me] and things like that. Plus I was really interested in, and I believed in, the record a lot. I was interested in it getting out there. I thought it was a more difficult record to get into than *Born to Run* was. It was something that I spent 11 months doing and I was just glad I did it. I liked it. I loved playing all the songs from it — it's the most fun of the night. So I said to myself, "Hey, I'm going to get on out there and hustle it." Ya got to get it out to people for people to hear it. I used to think that being on *Time* and *Newsweek* was bad — that's bad

New York, N.Y., 1975. Outtake from the "Born to Run" album cover sessions.

for *me*. It made me feel funny. I just felt funny about it. Then later I looked back on it and thought it was good because maybe somebody read a story and bought the record and it meant something to them and that was good. What was bad was the way I let it get to me on certain levels. And that was my own fault.

It was an unusual situation. Nobody usually goes through that.

Yeah, it was unusual. So this time out I was interested. I said, "Hey, I wanna get it out to as many as I can."

You've had some criticism about the record — some of it mixed — that it was intense, with no "Rosalita"-type songs on it. You said that doing the new LP is the most fun part of the night for you, more fun than the oldies and "Rosalita," the fun songs?

It's a different kind of fun. It's more fulfilling. I don't mean they're fuller. There's this stretch where we go from "Darkness" to "Thunder Road," a stretch of songs that we do basically in the same order every night because there's this continuity thing that happens. It makes connections and it

gives the rest of the show resonance. So then we can blow it out on "Rosalita." Or we got this new song we're doing, called "Sherry Darling."

You've always been praised as a performer first. That's the main thing people say about you — that you're an incredible performer, which you are. But it seems to me now that you're talking about you the songwriter. You're more serious about the songwriting on this album. It seems to me you're very proud of the songs and of the concept of the album.

I'm not more serious about it. It's just different things at different times. Like "Rosalita"...well ...they just mirror the particular perspectives I have at that moment. The next album will be different again.

Was the intensity of this album, as most people are assuming, the result of your being down about the legal hassles?

I don't know. I wasn't really down about it. It was a funny sort of thing — there were only a few days where I got down about the legal thing. This is stuff that matters but it doesn't matter. It's like as much as all this stuff is in the world, like all this stuff — all of it — they can take this away, they can take that, they can take the rights to this, or

money, or whatever, but the one thing that is truly mine, the one thing I value the most, is the ability to create a moment where everything is alive, or it happened. There's no papers or stuff that can take that kind of stuff from ya. You do it one place or you do it another, whether you do it in a club or a concert. But there were a lot of different sides to it. At the bottom, I always felt that way. That was always real consoling. And on the other side, I said I wrote "Born to Run," and the money from that song, maybe that belongs to somebody else, maybe somebody else is responsible for the money that that song made. Maybe that's true. But that song, that song belongs to *me*. Because that's just mine. So that was sorta my attitude about it. I was interested in those things during the lawsuit, but I knew that no matter how many times they sue you or you sue them, or it goes to court or you're doing a record and you get held up doing that, or they try to attach the box office, or this or that . . . no matter how much of that went down, there was always the reason that I felt I could so something that can't get touched by that stuff in a certain kind of way.

So you're glad it's all over.

Yeah, it's all by the boards, it's finished, it's done, and it worked out for the best, in my mind. The whole thing with Mike, who was my old manager, like everybody painted him as the monster, this is the "good guy" and this is the "bad guy," it was like a big misunderstanding. He worked real hard for me for a long time — he did, he really believed in what me and the guys, what everybody was doing. So he got painted as being a little too much of a monster, I think sometimes, which he never was to me. I had a lot of great times with him. You get to a point with two grown men where they disagree or there's a misunderstanding that can't be resolved. And you have those things. It's like growing up.

You used to say you were writing about characters, not really you, not even people you knew, but people you thought existed or you made up. And now there's a little more personal you, a song for your father, more of the personal part of you, rather than fictional characters. Is that right?

A little bit. You're always writing about you. You're talking to yourself — that's essentially what you're doing when you write — and to other people at the same time. There's a little more of it — I don't know what you call it, the first person or second

◄ *Kutztown, Pa., July 26, 1975.*

person — and a little more directness. On this album I didn't write about the city as much because I grew up, basically, in a smaller town. I guess in a way this album was a little more real for me than some of the other ones.

Would you call it your favorite album?

I don't know. I have favorite songs and stuff.

How about "Because the Night." Tell us a little bit about how it happened that Patti Smith did it?

We were in the same studio and Jimmy — Jimmy Iovine — was producing her and he was engineering for us. And we were in a couple of nights at the same time and we had a different engineer or something. I had a tape of one song that I gave to her and he gave her the "Because the Night" tape. A long time ago he asked me if I was going to put it on the album and all. And she said she liked it. I said I don't have all the words done or anything and she said, "Oh," and she wrote the words. And that's pretty much how it went down.

Were you happy with it?

Yeah, yeah.

You're doing it now and it's unbelievable.

We didn't do it for a while and we just started doing it.

And of course you're not doing "Fire" anymore, which is the Robert Gordon thing.

We did that at first.

That reminds me: another major change over the last couple of years is that you're playing guitar so much now it's incredible. You had sort of gotten away from that. I remember the old days at the Main Point when you used to play a lot of guitar. That was before you got Steve in the band, I guess.

I used to play a lot. There was a period when the main thing that was important to me was the arrangement and the song; for a long time that was what mattered to me the most. For a long time I don't think I played any guitar, I mean lead guitar. And this tour there was just a couple of songs where I said, "Oh, I can take some solos here and there." And the guitar fit a little better into the tone of *Darkness* than the saxophone did this time. So there was a little more on the album, and in the show there was a little more than in the album.

That goes back to the old days, when you used to play a lot more lead guitar with your other bands, didn't you?

I used to be just a guitar player. I was never a singer.

What possessed you to say, "I'm not just going to be a guitar player, I'm going to write and I'm going to perform and do something else"?

There were so many guitar players. There were a

Springsteen and Karen Darbin, his girlfriend in 1975. From "Born to Run" cover sessions.

lot. I felt there were the Jeff Becks and the Eric Claptons, there were guys with personal styles, Jimi Hendrix. Guys who were great. I guess on the guitar I never felt I had enough personal style to pursue being just a guitarist. And when I started to write songs I seemed to have something; it was just something where I was communicating a little better. It wasn't a real choice, it just sort of fell that way.

At one time you wrote your first song?

Well, I did that since I started playing the guitar.

What was the first one? Do you remember?

I don't remember. It was some old song.

You've been listening to a lot of Buddy Holly lately?

I did when I was in California more. I go through lots of people. What I've been listening to now, which is funny, is a lot of Hank Williams.

I notice that there's a little hint of country on the record, like on "Factory."

But that was before I started listening to him. He was fantastic. God, he's just incredible. It's hard to describe.

You've always liked Sam and Dave and Chuck Berry, and I guess Elvis. Those were some of your influences.

The rockabilly guys. I listened to a lot of rockabilly this tour. We opened with "Summertime Blues" tonight. I listen to a lot of other stuff.

Is there a performer that you've seen live that does to you what people tell you you do to them? That magic experience live. I've always felt sorry that you couldn't see yourself live sometimes, because you'd love "you." You do something to people and I'm not sure if you know what that is, and I don't know if you've seen that in another performer.

I haven't seen that many shows.

Well, we know it wasn't Led Zeppelin. We know at least that much.

I've seen a lot of good bands. I'm trying to think who I've seen live.

Elvis didn't impress you? That was sort of the end for him? What did you think of the show?

That wasn't a good night. I saw him at Madison Square Garden and he was really great. I saw him the first time he went to New York, and he was really good — he was great. And then on the '68 special, he was just the greatest. It's a shame — he was so good on that 1968 TV special. He was only

Philadelphia, Pa., October 25, 1976 ▶

about 32 at the time, and man, he was good.

It was also a very honest show.

I just loved that show.

You ever thinking about doing TV or movies now?

No, I haven't thought about that much. We were gonna do a TV commercial because there's places, like down South and in the Midwest, where we're not very well known. It's getting better, though. This time we're not super well known, but...We were gonna do us playing or something for 30 seconds. That's about as close to TV as I guess I'm gonna get. And another thing is because of the lawsuit, I'm a little behind. I got records I gotta make. I got a lot of songs I want to get out, and big allegiance to music. That's what I do — that's my job. The other stuff — if it was something that was really good and I had the time. But I've always got a lot of stuff to do and I have a lot of catching up to do.

Well, do you have a final word to all the people who remember you from the moldy oldie days?

I just want to say the crowd was fantastic tonight — it was great. I was thinking that because this was summertime and all, it was going to be a letdown. And tomorrow night, if those girls would not jump up and kiss me when I'm singing. It sounds funny and all, but it's sorta true because you can't sing when somebody jumps up and kisses ya and does all that stuff. So if you can sorta just stay down, off the stage, it would be appreciated. I don't like to have security in front of there and stuff, so I just depend on the fans to be okay. So less kissing would be appreciated.

We're going to set you up in a little booth in the lobby, and you're gonna kiss all the girls, okay?

I don't know about that.

Does it freak you out when they get up and do that?

It's funny, you know. It's fun. But what happens is, when a whole mess do it, you can't play. You gotta stop singing. And these security guys, I guess they think this 15-year-old girl is gonna knock me out or something.

Does it happen everywhere, or just in Philadelphia?

No, it was much more tonight than ever before. There was never that many.

Do you remember that guy who called me up on the air?

Oh, that was funny.

Remember, he was the guy who called me up and said he screamed "Bruce" during a quiet part of a song. And I asked him why he did that and he said, "During the quiet part is the only time when I can establish one-to-one communication with Bruce."

He had a good reason. He had a good answer.

And that's what running onstage is about, isn't it? That's one-to-one.

That's about as one-to-one as you're gonna get. But it does make it hard to play and stuff, and I'm always worried. It makes it difficult. And I don't like people getting hustled off and stuff.

Do you have any fond memories of the old days at the Main Point? Was that typical for you, too? You've played lots of small clubs around the country, but to me that was special because I saw that and I didn't see those other places.

We played a lot of great nights there. I'll always remember Travis Shook.

Yeah, you opened for them in 1973.

They were nice people.

I remember you also opened in 1973 for Chicago, and that was a bad experience.

That was one of the worst shows we ever did.

And then you said you'd never play the big places, but now you're doing it and you're doing it well.

What happened on the Chicago tour was that at the time we were not known, and it was difficult to come out and go on. We went on at eight-thirty and we'd be off by nine every night. The guys in Chicago were great — they were some of the nicest people that I ever met. I had fun on the tour like that, but it sort of put me off bigger places. And this [the Spectrum] was the first big place we played after that because there were so many people who wanted to come. And after that it just felt so good. It's been good experiences.

We thank you, Bruce, and we'll see you again Saturday night at the Spectrum.

I'll be there, Eddie.

I hope so. And the Shockmobile did make it tonight. Got 94,000 miles on it.

It did? What was that, a Rambler? A Rambler. The Shockmobile. Well, good luck with that thing, Eddie.

◄ *Philadelphia, Pa., October 27, 1976.*

OUT IN THE STREETS
· · · · · · · · · · · · · ·

Bruce Springsteen Interviewed by Robert Hilburn, October 1980

Though Dave Marsh is the journalist most usually associated with Bruce Springsteen, *Los Angeles Times* critic Robert Hilburn has probably interviewed Springsteen more than any other journalist. *LA Times* readers know that Springsteen has been a popular subject with Hilburn through the years and Hilburn put together material from his many interviews with lavish photos for his 1985 book *Springsteen.*

At the start of *The River* tour back in 1980, after seeing a concert in Cleveland, Ohio, Hilburn wrote one of the best pieces on Springsteen from that period. He described Springsteen at the time as "a blending of Presley's dynamics and Dylan's inspiring vision."

Hilburn interviewed Springsteen in Bruce's hotel that night. Springsteen spoke in detail about *The River* album, which had just been released, about his rock idealism and the public image of rock's destructive life style. The text of the interview follows.

· · · ·

ROBERT HILBURN: *What about the destructiveness? All the deaths, including now Led Zeppelin's John Bonham, must make you worry at times about the demands on you.*
BRUCE SPRINGSTEEN: Rock has never been a destructive thing for me. In fact, it was the first thing that gave me self-respect and strength. But I totally understand how it can be destructive to people. There was a point when I felt very low after *Born to Run.* I felt bad for two, three, maybe four months. Before that, it had been me and the band and we'd go out and play. We'd sleep where we could and drive to the next show. All of a sudden I became a person who could make money for other people, and that brings new forces and distractions into your life.

◄ *New York, N.Y., September 22, 1979.*

What does that do to you?
Two things happen. Either you are seduced by the distractions of success and fame and money or you're not. Look at all the examples of people in rock and what happened to them — people who once played great but don't play great anymore, people who once wrote great songs but don't write great songs anymore. It's like they got distracted by *things.* You can get hooked on things as much as you can on drugs.
What led to your confusion?
I felt like I had lost a certain control of myself. There was all the publicity and all the backlash. I felt the thing I wanted most in my life — my music — being swept away and I didn't know if I could do anything about it. I remember during that period that someone wrote, "If Bruce Springsteen didn't exist, rock critics would invent him." That bothered me a lot, being perceived as an invention, a ship passing by. I'd been playing for ten years. I knew where I came from, every inch of the way. I knew what I believed and what I wanted.
What was the low point?
One night in Detroit, I didn't want to go onstage. That was the only time in my life — that period — that happened. At that moment I could see how people get into drinking or into drugs, because the one thing you want at a time like that is to be distracted — in a big way. I was lucky. I had my band, which was people I had grown up with. No matter where we went, they were always there for support.
Don't the pressures continue when you get more successful? Do they ever stop?
Yes, it keeps coming, more so. But I'm a different person now. When you're young and vulnerable, you listen to people whose ideas and direction may not be what you want. But you don't know that. You just stepped off the street and walked into the studio. On the first album there's almost no electric guitar. If anyone ever told me I was going to make a record without guitars, I would have flipped out.

Seattle, Wash., December 20, 1978, third encore.

I would not have believed him. But I did make an album like that.

Why do you still work so hard on the stage? Don't most performers tend to ease up as time goes by?

I don't know how people do that — if that's what they do. To me, you do that when you're dead. You don't live anymore. You don't exist. That's what "Point Blank" on the new album is a little about.

There's a lot of idealism and inspiration in your work. What were the things that inspired you?

When you listen to those early rock records or any great rock 'n' roll, or see a great movie, there are human values that are presented. They're important things. I got inspired mainly, I guess, by the records, a certain purity in them.

I just know that when I started to play, it was like a gift. I started to feel alive. It was like some guy

◄ *Austin, Tex., November 9, 1980.*

stumbling down a street and finding a key. Rock 'n' roll was the only thing I ever liked about myself.

On the new album I wrote this song called "Out on the Street." I wasn't gonna put it on the album because it's all idealism. It's about people being together and sharing a certain feeling of joy. I know it's real, but it's hard to see sometimes. You go out in the street and there's a chance you get hit over the head or mugged. The song's not realistic in a way, but there's something very real at the heart of it.

But there's also a lot of struggle in your music.

Life is a struggle. That's basically what the songs are about. It's the fight everyone goes through every day. Some people have more success with it than others. I'm a romantic. To me, the idea of a romantic is someone who sees the reality, lives the reality every day, but knows about the possibilities too. You can't lose sight of the dreams.

That's what great rock is about to me, it makes

the dream seem possible. It's like I felt more dead than alive before I started music. I said that before, but it's true. I go to places and see people all the time, and what they're doing ain't at all livin'. They're dyin'. They're just taking a real long time about it.

I found something in rock that says it doesn't have to be that way. We try to say that to people in the songs, and they say it back to you with their reaction. The greatest part of the show is that they will sing the words back.

I came out the first night of the tour in Ann Arbor to do "Born to Run" and I forgot the words. I knew it was gonna happen. I listened to the song ten times just before the show, but when I walked up to the microphone my mind was blank. I went back to the drums and all of a sudden I heard the words faintly in the back of my mind and I realized the audience was singing. That was a real thrill. It was like a special bond. They weren't just sitting out there; they were really involved.

I started sensing that bond during the last tour. It's more than just that you're successful or a big rock star. There's something else happening. I meet kids in the street and there's something we have in common — something they know and I know, even if we don't talk about it.

On the new album, there's more of a balance between the idealism and the realism than before.

Rock 'n' roll has always been this joy, this certain happiness that is, in its way, the most beautiful thing in life. But rock also is about hardness and coldness and being alone. With *Darkness* it was hard for me to make those things coexist. How could a happy song like "Sherry Darling" coexist with "Point Blank" or "Darkness on the Edge of Town"? I could not face that.

I wasn't ready for some reason within myself to feel those things. It was too confusing, too paradoxical. But I finally got to the place where I realized life had paradoxes, a lot of them, and you've got to live with them.

You talk a lot on the album about dreams, losing them and regaining them.

That's one of the things that happens in life. The great possibilities you have in your early twenties. When you're in your thirties or late thirties, the world is different. At least it looks different. You may not have the same expectations. You're not as open to options. You may have a wife and a kid and a job. It's all you can do to keep those things

straight. You let the possibilities go. What happens to most people is when their first dreams get killed off nothing ever takes its place. The important thing is to keep holding out for possibilities, even if no one really ever makes it. There was a Norman Mailer article that said the one freedom that people want most is the one they can't have: the freedom from dread. That idea is somewhere at the heart of the new album. I know it is.

A lot of the songs on the album talk about marriage, but many are yearning for it and others are racing away from it.

One of the ideas this time was to touch on the feelings that everyone has. People want to be part of a group, yet they also want to disassociate themselves. People go through these conflicts every day in little ways. Do you wanna go to the movies tonight with your friends, or stay home? I wanted to get part of that on the record — the need for community, which is what "Out on the Street" is about. Songs like "Ties That Bind" and "Two Hearts" deal with that too. But there's also the other side, the need to be alone.

You used to say that it was harder to write songs because they got more personal.

That's what writing and growth are all about, I guess. I had an album of 13 songs finished a year ago September, but I didn't put the record out because it wasn't personal enough. This album seems much more personal to me.

In many of your songs you deal with the same images: streets and cars. One of the critical complaints about you is that they become almost cliches.

The songs are always different to me. I became fascinated with John Ford movies in the fact that they were all Westerns. I watched the early ones and the late ones. It was fascinating to me how he'd film the same scene — a dance scene or a confrontation — and make it different in every picture. There was a lot of continuity in his work. I liked that.

Why?

You go back to the previous movie and have a clearer understanding of where he was coming from. What he was saying in this film was changing the shape of what he said in another one.

Why cars and streets?

I always liked those images. That's American, in some ways. If you're outside of the big cities, there's people and there's cars — there's transition. That's why people are moving so much in my songs. They're always going from one place to another, and it seemed the natural place for them. Besides, I

New York, N.Y., September 15, 1978. (L to R): Danny Federici, Garry Tallent, Max Weinberg, Miami Steve Van Zandt, and Roy Bittan.

love the road. I like to get on the bus after the show and ride all night.

Do you like to leave a town after the show?

Yes, I'd rather go on the bus to another city than stay in a hotel. I don't like *staying*. It's funny. It makes me feel uncomfortable.

Why so much night imagery?

I don't know. I think there seem to be more possibilities at night. You look up ahead and you can't see nothin'. You don't know what's there until you get there. And I've been playing in bars since I was 15. I live by night. I was never up during the day. People are alive at night.

Looking ahead, what do you see for yourself over the next five years?

I don't do that. Now is now. Tonight you can do something. I don't count on my tomorrows. I don't like to let myself think about the next night. If you

do that, you begin to plan too much and begin rationing yourself.

What do you mean by "rationing"?

There may be no tomorrow, there may be no next record. If you start rationing, you're living life bit by bit when you can live it all at once. I like the latter. That's what I get the most satisfaction out of: to know that tonight when I go to bed I did my best. It's corny, I guess, but isn't that what living is all about? If you go to the show, the kid has a ticket for tonight. He's got no ticket for the show in L.A. or New York. He doesn't have a ticket for Detroit. He only has a ticket for Cleveland. You can't live on what you did yesterday or plan on what's gonna happen tomorrow. So if you fall into that trap, you don't belong onstage. That's what rock 'n' roll is: a promise, an oath. It's about being as true as you can be at any particular moment.

MAX WEINBERG

. . . .

Interview by Charles R. Cross, July 1984

Bruce Springsteen has been called the hardest-working man in show business, and if there's any truth to that, then Max Weinberg, as the E Street Band's drummer, can top that claim. Long ago, Bruce dubbed him Mighty Max, and there is perhaps no other nickname in the band that's as appropriate.

Born in 1951, Weinberg grew up in north Jersey, around Newark and Maplewood. By his early teens he was already playing with several local bands, backing up lounge acts and even working as a drummer for Broadway shows.

In 1974 he saw a classified ad in the *Village Voice* that changed his life — "Drummer (No Jr. Ginger Bakers)," it said, and gave a Columbia Records contact number. Max auditioned (the first song he played was "Let the Four Winds Blow"), and both Weinberg and Springsteen describe it as just short of love at first sight.

Apart from his body of work with the E Street Band, Weinberg has been active during off seasons doing seminal work with Southside Johnny and playing a host of other session dates. In 1984 he turned his talents elsewhere and authored *The Big Beat,* a book of conversations with rock's finest drummers. It is an admirably well-written book, and despite its central focus on drummers, it is of great interest to any fan of rock 'n' roll. Weinberg's theory is that although the drummer is infrequently in the spotlight, he is still an integral part of rock history. And for some reason they always have great stories to tell.

We decided to apply this concept to the E Street Band, and found Max one of the easiest band members to talk to, and truly a nice guy. This interview took place over the course of a couple of

◄ *Max Weinberg, Brooklyn, N.Y., February 1984.*

days in July 1984 in Cleveland, Ohio, first in a hotel room and then backstage after the show, while Weinberg soaked his hands.

BACKSTREETS: *First I wonder if you could clear up some of the rumors I've heard about the recording of* Born in the USA *and* Nebraska. *What kind of stuff didn't make it on the record?*

MAX WEINBERG: Well, we recorded about 80 songs for *Born in the USA*. Some of them are great. "This Hard Land," which didn't make it on the record, is just fantastic. That's probably my favorite song we've done.

I know there are rockabilly versions of most everything on The River, *but is there really an electric* Nebraska?

Yeah, we did a lot of those songs with the band.

One of my personal obsessions is with the River *outtakes, which I happen to think are better than the actual commercial album — songs like "Cindy" and "Roulette." What's the story behind "Roulette"?*

Yeah, that's a great song. That was the very first song we recorded when we went into the studio to do *The River*. I don't know, but for some reason it just never made it on the record.

Tell me about your problems with your hands. I understand there was a chance you might never drum again.

I developed incredibly bad tendonitis in my hands. I had these hand operations. It was very painful, that's why I'm soaking my hands in ice now.

I noticed in your book you thank your doctor.

Yeah, Richard Eaton. He's acknowledged as the greatest hand surgeon in the world. I sat down at the table, my hands spread out like this with a drape. I'm a drummer and I'm giving him my hands and he fixed me up.

Are these shows hard for you? I know your hands are rumored to bleed after most shows.

I've been working out for this — woodshedding for about four months. I got done with *The Big Beat* in March, so from March until when we left, I didn't do much but drum. I've got sort of a studio in my basement and I'd just go down there every

TALK TO ME

8 3

day and play until I'm tired. I work out real heavy — I run a lot, I do weights.

Why did you decide to write The Big Beat?

The book came about because I've always been interested in talking to drummers and musicians. *The Big Beat* is a result of my special fascination with the drummers that are in the book and the era in which they played. Ringo and Charlie Watts, Dave Clark of the Dave Clark Five, these are the guys I listened to when I was becoming a drummer, when I was a kid. These are still my favorite drummers. That's not to say that they're the only drummers I listen to. I like Stewart Copeland, Simon Phillips is great, the guy from Talking Heads is great. Strictly speaking in rock, these are my all-time favorites, my heroes more or less.

One thing that surprised me was that you didn't write of any jazz drummers.

Well, I love jazz drummers. Buddy Rich is probably my all-time favorite jazz drummer and all-around drummer but in the book I strictly deal with rock 'n' roll 'cause that's what I play and that's what I know best. It's not a technical book, it's a book that the fan of rock 'n' roll can really gain a lot of information from. It's a tribute, my way of putting the spotlight on these guys and also giving them a chance to tell some of their stories. These guys were eyewitnesses to some of the greatest history in rock 'n' roll. Ringo, Levon Helm, Dino Dannelli with the Young Rascals, D.J. Fontana, who was Elvis Presley's drummer — they all have fascinating stories.

One of the best things about The Big Beat, *I think, is that it really does, as you say, put the spotlight for once on this usually unknown member of the band.*

The drummer's always in the back. And if you're doing your job as a drummer, you're solid but you don't stick out. You're not singing the song, you're not writing the words. The foundation of the band begins with the drummer. You can't build a building without architecture, and the drummer is the main architect if he's doing his job. He can cause it to crumble if he's not doing his job. There's a picture of Ringo in the book that's never been used before. I love this picture because the spotlight's on Ringo, and John, Paul, and George are in silhouette. I thought it was particularly fitting because when I looked at the Beatles I saw Ringo.

It was watching Elvis Presley, wasn't it, that you first became interested in music?

I had two older sisters and a younger sister. They were teenagers at the time, and naturally into Elvis.

I was about five or six and I remember vividly sitting down and dressing up as Elvis with a cardboard guitar and this hair and sideburns, it was very cute. And when he played "Hound Dog," the roll of D. J.'s was what really blew my mind. It got my attention immediately. I guess I was just always keyed into rhythm and percussion, because that made me want to develop my rhythmic sense. About a year or two later I got a little drum. I was really only about six or seven when I got my first drum. I was banging on that thing and I had a little promise. I got my first set, my parents bought me this little Japanese drum set — I think they went into hock, it was this little Japanese drum set that cost $125 — when I was in the end of sixth grade. I first heard of the Beatles in November of '63. By the time they were on Ed Sullivan I already had a drum set and a little band, and then when I saw Ringo, that just changed my life. That just made me want to be Ringo. I just wanted to be in a great rock 'n' roll band, playing for screaming people.

It must just have been a hell of a kick for you to be able to meet these drummers and talk about your craft.

Yeah, it was a total gas. Naturally I was nervous — I've never gotten over my nervousness talking to Ringo. It was great because I got to ask all the millions of questions I had when I was a kid, and these guys were so nice, warm, and engaging, it was a real pleasure. It's great when you have heroes and you come away after meeting them and they're bigger heroes. These guys are still big, big heroes to me. Every time I listen to Russ Kunkel I learn something, and that's what it's all about and I'm proud to be part of the tradition.

Bruce has been called the hardest-working man in show business and that makes you perhaps even harder-working, being the drummer. Playing a song like, let's take "Backstreets" from tonight, that must put some great physical demands on you.

It's emotionally hard. You try to conserve your physical energy as much as possible while at the same time giving a thousand percent. That's what economy of emotion and finesse technique are all about. But the emotional thing, I try to reach a certain emotion when I play, especially a song like "Backstreets," it's so emotional. And I've played that song, shit, I've played that song 500 times and every time I listen to it or play it, I just get choked up. I love that song. That song describes totally a period of my life for three years during the mid-seventies.

"Dancing in the Dark" has a different drum sound. Did you do anything special on that song?

It was just the straight beat. No fills. Bruce played that song in the studio, it was the last song we cut off *Born in the USA*. I've been listening, like everybody else, to a lot of Stewart Copeland and the Police. I was really into the Police and I had just seen the Police two days before we cut that track. They played "Every Breath You Take," and it's just groove and momentum. It's the exact opposite of "Born in the USA," which has its own groove and momentum, but "Born in the USA" is very busy drumming — I love that song. "Dancing in the Dark" — you play what the song dictates, and that's what the song dictates.

How do you consider yourself as a drummer? What do you think of your talents?

I have my moments, but I don't put myself in the same league as any of the guys in the book I wrote. I have my moments — it's about moments, trying to get as many of them as you can. But I don't put myself on the level of a Ringo — not that I'm putting myself down, but I never listen to myself like that. Only on a few things do I sound as good as I want to sound — "Born in the USA," that's how I want to play. I like "Dancing in the Dark," I like "Candy's Room." I play good on "Ramrod" — "Ramrod" is probably one of my favorite pieces of drumming I've done. "Born in the USA," that's really me drumming, you've got the true Max Weinberg, Mighty Max, on "Born in the USA." I hit something out there on that one — it's real pleasing to me.

You've done a weird potpourri of session work. What kind of stuff remains that you want to do?

I'd like to do a lot more session work. I've been doing some movie stuff — I did some stuff for *Streets of Fire*, that song "Nowhere Fast," and I'm on *Sixteen Candles*.

Do you get lots of phone calls and requests to play on records?

No. When you're in a big group, people don't think you do stuff. They never ask who the drummer is unless they want my sound. And that's how I get work — I average a few things a month, but I could be busier. I'm going to be a lot busier. It's a little hard to think about what I'm going to do after this tour; this tour just started and we're going to be out here for a year and a half.

Chicago, Ill., July 17, 1984.

Looking into the future, what do you want to do after the E Street Band?

I don't even think about that. I do play every show like it was the last, though — that's the only way I can get through these shows. I don't think about anything but what's going down right now. Especially for drummers, when you start thinking about that shit, you lose your perspective. My job is to keep it happening like right now. I will always desire to play with Bruce Springsteen. He's the most inspirational, most dedicated, most committed, and most focused artist I've ever seen. I like to be around people like that, and there aren't many people like that. I only think about what I did tonight.

Thinking back to when you first saw D.J. Fontana kick in that great opening of "Hound Dog," did you ever imagine you'd become the drummer in a band like the E Street Band? Did you ever dream you'd be where you are now?

This is a dream come true.

—*Charles R. Cross*

LITTLE STEVEN VAN ZANDT

. . . .

Interviews by Charles R. Cross, December 1982,
by Marcello Villella, March 1987

L ittle Steven Van Zandt has been one of the most seminal figures of the E Street Sound. With his own work with the E Street Band, with South-side Johnny and the Jukes, and with his own solo career, Van Zandt has established himself as a true original — an artist of the highest personal integrity.

Backstreets has interviewed Van Zandt on four occasions. What follows are excerpts from the 1982 interview in which he first discussed his plans to leave the E Street Band, along with excerpts from a 1987 interview conducted by Marcello Villella, following the release of *Freedom, No Compromise.*

. . . . .

1982

BACKSTREETS: *My description of your music would be "soul with modern touches," at least the music on* Men Without Women. *I'd call it an amalgamation of some great old things and some great new things. I'd say part of your problem with radio is that what you're doing is not what one would call the popular music of the day.*

STEVE VAN ZANDT: The real problem is that whenever you do something that combines elements and just transcends categorization, you're in trouble until people get used to it. I'm not overly concerned — I think by the next record, or the one after that, radio will just get used to me. They'll realize I'm not going to fit into one of those categories. I'm always going to be combining different cultural elements because that's what I do. It's always going to be a combination of things because that's who I am. I hope, sooner or later, I'm going to hit some common ground.

You might feel like you're carrying a torch for soul music.

Well, I don't want to be thought of as carrying the torch for sixties soul music. The only common thread I'm very conscious of keeping is the passion

◄ *Stone Pony, Asbury Park, N.J., August 21, 1987.*

and the emotional side of that music. It basically started in the church and in the sixties was brought into a romantic setting; now I'm bringing it to the next evolution, which is carrying that emotional commitment to one's work, to one's life. I'm really not into being nostalgic or anachronistic about it. I am trying to redefine it. It's going to take a little time.

On completely another track, I was listening to a Steel Mill demo tape the other day, and despite the fact that it was years old, the songs seemed timeless. I think Steel Mill would be very popular today with the heavy metal generation.

Yeah, it was a heavy metal band. It was one of the first before heavy metal really happened, so it had the very, very early elements of it. We had a bit more melody and a bit more to the lyrical side of it than a lot of the hardcore stuff today.

Both through your own work and your work with the E Street Band, you've collected a band of followers who are fanatical, to say the least. They're just nuts.

I think we're different. I know, speaking for myself, the fans understand we're artists concerned with communicating. We're not there to entertain and we're not there to take advantage of anybody or retire next week. We've been there a long time and we're going to be here a lot longer. We're going to be playing forever. We have a certain integrity that comes through. We're not temporary. We're not trying to hustle up some bread and buy a house and fade away. We're gonna be here tomorrow, so we have a relationship with people that's permanent.

Your whole career seems to me to have been one best described as "outlaw." You've broken the rules of rock 'n' roll, the first one being that kids from New Jersey wouldn't get a record contract and wouldn't go on to be important in any way. In 1970, the story of your success and that of the other Jersey musicians would have been a shocker.

That's very true, and it's still true. We're still rebels in the way we do things. That's particularly true with me and my band. The rebellion has also taken a new turn. It's a more focused rebellion. I know what I want to accomplish. You're not going to accomplish anything by screaming real loud and banging your head against the wall. I think in the next 20 years you're going to see rock 'n' roll get more involved in politics, and I think the rebellion of it is going to take on a very interesting focus. The communication that can exist between people of different countries is going to happen through rock 'n' roll.

From what I know of your early history, growing up around Asbury Park, you guys would hang out together, play Monopoly, and jam together all night long. Comparing the material you wrote back then, which has a sense of you struggling on the street, to the material you're writing today, has there been any sense of a loss of innocence?

The innocence is certainly gone, as it is from America — there's no question about it. On the other hand, I've never stopped being on the street or being the underdog. Nothing's changed. Through fate, or whatever, I haven't changed that much. You get more mature and you get better, but basically I'm still talking about the same things. I think if you look at the lyrics on *Men Without Women*, you get both sides. I still have the same anger. "Lyin' in a Bed of Fire" is as angry as I've ever felt.

Considering the creative freedom you've had, at this point in your career do you feel lucky?

I do feel lucky. I'm glad that I'm able to make a living doing what I want to do. That's the great thing about rock 'n' roll: That you can create your own world. If you're good enough, you can play what you want. I'm not doing this in the short run. The audience knows that — you're not going to compromise if you're doing something long-term. This is the only thing I can do. Rock 'n' roll will always be my life. I've always been a gypsy.

Have you ever considered that the music you've created, and the music Springsteen has created, has changed the entire world for kids growing up in New Jersey? It used to be that New Jersey was a joke — you both have worked to make that no longer so.

That's good. What we accomplished could have been accomplished in any little town in America. I think it's really great that Bruce and I did it for New Jersey. It gave hope to all the Des Moineses of the world.

Steve, the thing most people want to know at the moment is whether or not you'll continue with the E Street Band. To this point you haven't told anyone. Only you and your hairdresser know.

It's not my central focus. Miami has retired really. It's just Little Steven now. When I can I still want to, you know, whatever, help out Bruce or play on a record or do a couple of shows but it's really not my central focus. My central focus and my first priority is my own work now.

Are you saying you've rested the Miami Steve title for good?

Yeah, he's gone pretty much, retired to a condo in Tampa. It's a new band, it's a new day, I want it all to be new and that even includes the people who are going to enjoy it. I don't want them to think it has anything to do with the past because it really doesn't.

If you're saying goodbye to the E Street Band aren't you going to miss occasionally playing all those great songs?

I've played them enough. Really. Once you start playing your own music it becomes a big part of you. It's all encompassing and your focus is changed. And this is not something new for me: It's been coming for a while. —*Charles R. Cross*

. . . .

1987

BACKSTREETS: *Last time we spoke, you had just released* Sun City *and you expressed a lot of hope for its message, if not its sales. And I think the impact of that message has been very strong. Paul Simon recently credited you with interesting him in the issue. Were you happy with the response to that record?*

LITTLE STEVEN: I'm very, very happy with the record, the video, the full length documentary, and the book. I'm happy with the way it reached people. We accomplished everything we set out to accomplish. Our main goal was to reach our own people — those in the entertainment world. And as far as I know, no major star has played Sun City since the record came out.

We wanted also to increase awareness about the issue and we wanted to give the whole movement a little push. Which finally resulted in what I'll call the "symbolic sanctions" of our government. But as symbolic as they were, they were very significant, because Reagan had said "never." It was important at least to break that wall down.

The other thing that was important was to send a message to the South African people that we care — that even we in America and England care, the two biggest supporters of South Africa.

Your message, it seems, was that not all Americans believe in the official government policy on South Africa.

Washington, D.C., August 1985. ▶

Philadelphia, Pa., 1975. The only picture ever published of Steve Van Zandt after he joined the E Street Band without a hat on.

Exactly. So that was very good. The problem now is that a lot of people think that because these sanctions have gone through, that's the end. Which is, of course, wrong. These symbolic sanctions are only the beginning. Now we have to find a way to keep the issue alive.

What concerns me is that some people may have the perception that things have changed there and consequently the issue is not such an important one for them.

True, but nothing's changed there — it's just as bad as ever. Right now, nobody knows, but right now somewhere between ten and twenty thousand people are detained. About a third of them are children. Things are very, very bad, and very little of this gets out because they have censored the media.

On to your new record: it seems to me that you are continuing the strong messages that you started with Voice of America. *I saw that album presenting an alternative party, and that party is freedom. And with this record, I see you presenting the platform of that party — freedom around the world.*

I think you have perceived it very well — it is meant to be an extension of *Voice of America,* part of

an evolution. There are some similar themes: one being Latin America. The political party thing I've taken to a more literal place on this record, with "No More Parties." This is an evolution of what I've talked about before: people have more loyalty to their party than to the truth. When we elect politicians, we should elect them because they are the most educated, not because they belong to the same club your father was in. In America, because of the way people are elected, with the economics of politics, we are left with virtually no democracy, just a veneer of democracy. We're not that different from the Soviet Union. We have a little more freedom and we dress it up better, but it's the same thing. We elect people by television commercials — who has the money to pay for that?

Despite the power of your message, many people say — with their own reasons — that they don't want any politics in their music.

I had a record that we're going to release as a B-side — it's called "Vote." It was written for the 1984 election, and the message was we must vote — we must use this democracy we theoretically have in place. If we don't use it, then we're going to continue to be manipulated. The problem now is the right wing, the more conservative element — you can use the word *fascist* if you'd like. They are more organized, just like the left wing was more organized in the sixties.

Bruce, of course, joins you on "Native Americans." I think that perhaps finally with "Sun City" you were able to leave the Springsteen references aside. That probably was liberating for you.

Actually, it was the *Voice of America* record that did that for me. I think "Sun City" was also a help. But *Voice of America* was accepted, I think, as something that was uniquely me, that was not like any other record, really.

Do you remain among the believers?

I think it's an important role for an artist to present ideas. We need to wonder what is the ideal. With each record I try to present one song that shows us some ideals. Some people may call that naive, but I feel we need to show the possibilities. The difficult part is fighting the cynicism within ourselves. It's important to fight that as, in the end, that's all that matters. The day we stop fighting, it's over.

— *Marcello Villella*

Philadelphia, Pa., December 8, 1980. ▶

CLARENCE CLEMONS
. . . .

Interview by Marcello Villella, February 1986

They call him the Big Man. For years, Clarence Clemons held that nickname just because of his size; he had a physique so imposing that in the E Street Band's early days it was an insurance policy that the band would get paid. But now a much slimmer Clarence (from a strict diet and exercise program) has another reason for the name: his solo career. His second album, *Hero,* was one of the biggest success stories of 1985. Buoyed by a hit video, two singles, and a successful tour of the world, it was a hot record for more than a year.

We caught up with Clarence in Italy at the end of his *Hero* tour in 1986.

. . . .

BACKSTREETS: *Let's start back at the beginning, Clarence, with your hometown. You were born in Norfolk, Virginia. And from there you went on to play football.*
CLARENCE CLEMONS: I left there when I was about 18 years old to go off to college. My father had bought me a saxophone when I was nine.
I remember the story of how you'd asked for a train and instead had gotten a sax....
Yeah. I'd asked for the train and he bought the sax and I've never gotten over it. Anyway, I went off to college and I majored in football, but I always had the sax in my car, looking for what I really wanted to do. I knew that what I was doing wasn't it. College wasn't what I wanted to do, and what they were preparing me for I wasn't really ready to do. I wanted to play music. So I was searching for the missing link in my life. And that came when I met Bruce.
Before you met Bruce, what was the style of music that interested you?
I grew up in a very religious house. We didn't listen to a lot of the radio, so I grew up listening to

◄ *Seattle, Wash., October 24, 1980.*

a church choir. It was music that made you feel good. It was old gospel music, which really was where rock 'n' roll and the blues came from. So when I finally got into rock 'n' roll, it was an easy transition. I grew up listening to the Coasters when I got exposed to music, the stuff with King Curtis on sax, and this is really where my roots are.
That's really the sound that I think one hears on your first album, Rescue. *Sort of like Otis Redding.*
Yeah, that's it man, exactly it. Otis.
In contrast to that, I was very surprised when I first heard Hero; *it's a very different sort of sound and approach. It has a much more modern sound, and more of a commercial orientation.*
I look at it as growth. You move from the unknown to the known. When you start something for the first time, you do what you know best. So that's what I did: I started with my roots. This time I wanted to do my own thing. And the music grew from that and it became more modern. I look at it as "the Big Man moves into the eighties." It's called growin' up.
What happened to the Red Bank Rockers?
The Red Bank Rockers died when my drummer, Wells Kelly, died two years ago. He was the heart and soul of the band. So when I first started thinking about this album I had planned to use him a lot more than just as a drummer — he had a great, great voice and I wanted to use him a lot more vocally. I was starting to write songs around him. With the loss of him, the idea was also lost, so that's when I decided to do it myself.
"You're a Friend of Mine" obviously was written about Springsteen. How was it that Jackson Browne ended up doing the duet with you?
The song was written with Bruce in mind. But he had just gotten married and he was in the middle of the biggest tour in the history of rock 'n' roll, so I had to go find someone else to do it with. So I called Jackson. He was a friend of mine for many years, and he liked it and we decided to do it.

Tacoma, Wash., May 5, 1988.

It's safe to say now — you've got a big hit on your hands with your album and the single. This record also seems to me to be promoted now as a Clarence Clemons record, in contrast to your last album, which seemed to me to always be billed as "Clarence Clemons, from Bruce Springsteen's E Street Band." Did that sort of promo bother you?

I was annoyed last time. This time it's a lot different. But I cannot deny that connection, and I don't really get upset when it's referred to a lot, because these are my roots and this is my background. And you can never get away from that. I'm just happy that this time I'm being considered on my own and my career is solidifying itself. I'm a solid solo artist now.

What's the story behind the addition of Mokshagun to your name? Obviously there's religious significance.

It's a name that was given to me by my guru. It means "liberation fire." He says my whole purpose in life is to bring light into the world, to destroy ignorance, to become a liberated fire, a liberated flame for the people. I've really found myself through meditation. I meditate every day.

Going back to the beginning again — would you recount, just one last time, the great story of how you first met Bruce?

It's just like he tells. He was playing in a bar down the street from where I was playing. And it was a dark and rainy night — it was cold. I walked out on the street and saw him and asked if I could sit in with him. He said "Sure," and the magic started.

Let me pose one last question to you. In the great story that introduces "Growin' Up," Bruce speaks of the gypsy lady who granted any wish you'd ask her. If you were in front of her today, and she had the power to grant any wish you asked, what would you wish for?

I would wish that God's will be done. That's the greatest wish that anyone could have.

—*Marcello Villella*

Landover, Md., August 24, 1984. ►

NILS LOFGREN

· · · · · · · · · ·

Interview by Ruth Atherly, August 1985

Nils Lofgren became the first new member of the E Street Band in ten years when he replaced Steve Van Zandt on guitar in 1984. Lofgren was a crowd favorite throughout the *Born in the USA* tour, wooing audiences with his backflip during "Rosalita," with his Keith Richards tribute on "Street Fighting Man," and with his solid guitar work and background vocals. His vocals have added a dimension to the E Street sound.

In addition to his work with the E Street Band, Lofgren is a noted and distinguished musician in his own right. His solo career spans the last decade and a half, and he's received almost as many critical accolades as Springsteen. His work with his early band Grin is legendary, while his contributions to Neil Young's band (particularly on the *Tonight's the Night* album) are considerable. Lofgren also has a solo career of note, and several classic LPs.

We caught up with Nils in 1985, when the band was in Toronto for its stadium gig.

· · · · ·

BACKSTREETS: *Let's start with the big question: Are you going to stay in the E Street Band, or is this just a contract basis for this tour?*
NILS LOFGREN: Oh, no, no, no contract; Bruce asked me to join his band and I said yes. I'm definitely in the band. And I'll just . . . uh . . . when Bruce needs me, I'm there. And when he's not working, I'll continue to do my own shows and records.
Does being with a band of such magnitude, with the tour going a year and a half, interfere with your solo career?
No, it's given me a lot of confidence. Physically it's kind of tough. It's kind of like two jobs. But for me, anyway, emotionally it's been a real help. It's given me a lot of confidence to work with Bruce and the

◄ *Tacoma, Wash., October 19, 1984.*

band. When there's time off to do my own stuff, I'm in a whole other world. Then, when it's time to go back with the band, it makes it even fresher for me. So it's an exciting thing trying to walk in and out of these two worlds.
It must be tiring. . . .
That it is. As long as my health holds out, it's something I really enjoy doing.
How did you come to join the E Street Band?
Well, I'd been up to visit Bruce when he finished *Born in the USA* but before it was released, just to listen to the mixes and visit him for a couple of days. At the time nobody knew, including Bruce or Steve, what was gonna really happen. Just in passing, I mentioned that if he needed a guitar player I wanted an audition. A couple months later, just before the album came out, he called me and asked me to come up and jam, and I went up and jammed with the band for a couple of days. He asked me to join.
You write your own songs, you're a world-renowned performer. Do you have any freedom when it comes to the songs on this tour?
Well, it's more a question of the musical freedom we all have within the context of what's right for the song. But that's why we're all there — because it's natural to us, because we understand Bruce's music and all feel it and love it. So whenever we're doing something new or working on an arrangement, we all throw our two cents in. But of course it's Bruce's song, and any bandleader should be the one to decide what the best ideas are. A lot of times he'll have specific ideas for songs, and other times everyone just plays what they feel.

Ultimately, of course, Bruce decides what's best for each song or the instrumentation or this or that, but we all throw out our ideas in the studio and onstage within a format of the emotional content of each song. We are all free to do what we want; we have to keep the shows fresh for us to make it a genuine thing for the audience. We make a point of that so it's kind of a natural thing. It's a very subtle change, but none of us ever played the exact same part in any song, night to night, except for maybe one particular line that you double with somebody. You kind of just naturally take the freedom to improvise a little bit within the emotional structure of the tune.

Is it hard for you — being the leader of your own band — to have to deal with bowing to someone else's authority?

No, it doesn't feel like that. It's a welcome break from always being the bandleader — always being the guy who hires and fires everybody and sings all the songs. I love being just a guitar player. At least with this band — they are very easy to work with — it's a very positive thing. I don't have that much experience with other bands, though. It's very rare when I know in my heart I can give myself completely to somebody else.

The only other opportunity I've had to do that was with Neil Young, and on a small scale, for a couple of weeks, I played with the Pretenders on the road. I love them dearly, they're a great band. It's got to be a natural thing; otherwise, there is no way you could really spend this much time on the road and still enjoy it.

What does it feel like when you play to 50,000 or 70,000 people? Is that a big thrill?

Yeah, it is a big thrill. When you get house lights on in a 70,000-seat stadium and everyone is just dancing or swaying or singing, it does hit you a little more. But when it's magic and it's special, it can be the same feeling in front of 500 people, and that's really what you want in any environment. There's a big difference in the numbers, and all but those differences actually get much smaller when we start to play the music. The main thing is to get across emotionally to the audience, whether it's five people or 50,000.

Is there a big difference in how the audience reacts from if you were playing a small venue of, say, 15,000 to what you're playing now?

No, the only real difference is the numbers. There are a lot of people who are farther away and we've got big video screens so they can see. That's about the only difference. We still do the same — perform the music and approach it the same way. Of course, we have some ramps to get out closer to the audience because we have to have a higher stage and be a bit farther away so people can see. But once we start playing, we do the same things that we do in a little club. You want to relate to the

Sydney, Australia, March 23, 1985.

people, so you run out on ramps and you get closer to them just to remind them that you're there. Of course, from that distance we all look like ants from the back of the stadium, but the music stays.

We've done 135 shows now; the band is better than it's ever been, and so is Bruce. It's always been a positive thing, but it's at the point now where it's just the best time of day for me. The phone stops ringing, people don't knock at my door and no one can bother me. I get to play with the band, so it's my favorite time of the day.

While you've been on tour, have you been writing songs? The songs on your new album, were they written while you were on tour?

Most of them had been written. I was just about to start rehearsing the album when I joined Bruce's band. I do get a lot of ideas on the road, and I'll jot them down in a notebook and put some musical riffs on a cassette, but usually it won't be until I get home and have a block of time to sit down and really put the two columns together and turn it into a song. I do tend to get more ideas on the road, but as far as really putting it into a song, I do that usually more at home.

Have you been influenced on this tour? Has your music changed at all?

The biggest thing that I've gotten out of this whole tour is confidence. The experience has given me a lot of confidence that I know I wouldn't have had, had it not been for Bruce and the band. I'd still be making records and getting better at it, which I still am, and probably expect to do the rest of my life. But after 135 shows with Bruce and the band, to walk right in the studio and do my own record, having practiced playing guitar, it was just a level of confidence which was the big difference.

In your videos, do you come up with the concept?

Basically I work with the director and bounce ideas off the record company and my manager. We just basically bounce ideas around until you come up with a concept that everyone likes and agrees on, and then you go for things, they change minute to minute, that's the nature of video.

I've done a lot of gymnastics in my videos, and those are my favorite parts of it. The acting thing, which I just started doing, is a little uncomfortable, but it's fun.

Is it hard to take direction from a director?

It depends on how you set it up. The only directors I've worked with are people I've chosen and had an understanding with. It's just like making a record. Someone says, "Hey, that was a good solo but you can do it better, you're a little tired today, let's pick it up tomorrow." Sometimes you're so anxious to get it done, you need somebody to tell you that. That you respect.

It's such an intense project and it happens so fast. The things that have been exciting or different for me are the gymnastic bits. The most bizarre thing was working on the horizontal bar in "Secrets in the Street." I had a chance to work out with a great coach from the University of Maryland and then I picked it up in London, where I went to film it, with the British National champion. That was very exciting. Just being in a gymnasium and working out with a gymnastic team was just a whole different world from rock 'n' roll. And that has been the most fun I've had in making videos. When I was a kid I was a gymnast, and it was nice to get back in that environment.

The "Secrets in the Street" video has the flavor of a young fellow that the father doesn't like because he's a street fellow. Does that fall in with a Springsteen influence on you?

No, not really. I wrote that song before the tour started. Let's put it this way: I've known Bruce, we're the same age, we grew up with the same music, I've always loved his music and, you know, saw his shows whenever I could, and it's just — it's osmosis.

If you love rock and roll and love that feeling or emotion, you can't look at somebody like Jimi Hendrix or Little Richard and be unaffected by it. I think Prince is great, and it's obvious that he loves Jimi Hendrix and Little Richard. Everyone has said that in a good way. How can you not like those people if you can feel the music? Just like Bruce got his main influence from Elvis initially. I started a little bit later, with the Beatles and the Stones. In general, it's just anybody good rubs off on you a little bit. So, sure, Bruce has rubbed off on me.

Do you think you've rubbed off on him?

Well, you'd have to ask him that; I don't want to speculate. I'm just really glad to be in the band.

With such wild momentum on this tour, where does it stop?

I hope it never stops. The magic of this tour is a very special thing. I'm just trying to get better at what I do, sing and play, make my own records and tour when Bruce isn't working. When Bruce is working, I'll be there as the guitar player, if he needs me. He made *Nebraska* without any band at all. And I love Bruce — he should do whatever he wants to do. If he wants to make a record, however he wants to do it, whenever he needs me I'll be there and when he's not working I'll just continue to do my own albums and tour. And, health permitting, I would like to stay as busy as possible indefinitely.

What do you do between shows to relax?

I used to try to play basketball or work out at a gym. But for this whole year, ever since I made my own album, I've kind of had two jobs. On my days off I just do interviews and things involving my own album, and on show days with Bruce, I don't do anything except get myself mentally and physically ready to do the best show that I can.

Are your shows going to be as long as usual, as long as the Springsteen shows?

I'd like to do three hours without a break with an acoustic section, where I just play alone acoustically. But what that actually turns into on the road depends. I like to play a long time, and I enjoy long shows.

Can you go out without being recognized?

Bruce is the only one at this point really that has a bit of a problem with that. Maybe Clarence too. But we all pretty much go where we want without any hassles. Maybe once in a while someone will ask you for an autograph, but it's not like Bruce, who is very recognizable now.   *—Ruth Atherley*

VINI LOPEZ

. . . .

Interview by Robert Santelli, September 1985

Vini Lopez is the Pete Best of the E Street Band. An original member of not only the E Street Band, but also of such early Springsteen-led outfits as Child, Steel Mill, Dr. Zoom and the Sonic Boom, and the Bruce Springsteen Band, Lopez was the one who supplied the backbeat from 1968 to the end of 1973.

Lopez, however, was fired from the band after the recording of *The Wild, the Innocent, and the E Street Shuffle.* A lot has been written purporting to explain why he was fired. In this exclusive interview, Lopez tells his side of the story.

An explosive drummer, one very much influenced by the style of Ginger Baker, and, in his words, "one who experimented all the time," Lopez's fiery drum style was packed with power and emotion. "I played every song with as much energy as I could," he recalls. "I worked the drums as hard as I could."

After his dismissal from the E Street Band, Lopez played for a number of Asbury Park-based bands. The more prominent ones included Cold, Blast and Steel; the Shakes; and Lord Gunner. Today, Lopez, now married and working as a carpenter, resides in upstate New York.

. . . .

BACKSTREETS: *Let's get right to the heart of the matter. You were fired from the band in 1973. Why?*
VINI LOPEZ: I'm a fighter. I was back then and I am now. Back then I felt we [Bruce and the E Street Band] were getting a raw deal from our manager, Mike Appel. I didn't hide my resentment. I let him [Appel] and everyone else know it.
Be more specific. Was there a particular incident which prompted the firing?
Well, I just got fed up. I mean Clarence [Clemons] had been arrested because our manager didn't pay Clarence's alimony like he was supposed to. There were money problems. I didn't care about having

ten less dollars or whatever. But it was the point. We were being cheated. Well, Mike Appel's brother and I had a few words. I pushed him and he went down. After that, I was told I was to leave the band.
Did you resent being kicked out of the band? You and Bruce went back a long way.
I resented it, but there was nothing I could do except ask for a second chance. Which I did. But I didn't get it. There were times when guys in the band today got a second chance because of something that happened. But I didn't. That hurt.
What are your comments concerning the things that have been written about your drum playing? Some people obviously feel the reason you were fired was that your drum playing simply wasn't good enough.
I'm not denying I ever made any mistakes as a drummer. I never said I was a perfect drummer. But I could play. There's a mistake on the second album, on the song "Rosalita." After cutting the song all night, we went back to the studio the next day and I heard the mistake. So I said, "Hey, let me do that part again." Mike Appel said no. And we didn't. So what can I say? If anyone doesn't believe I can play the drums, let them come and check me out. I can keep a backbeat.
Go back for a moment to the early days. How did you and Bruce team up?
I was in a band called the Moment of Truth. When the band broke up, I wanted to get a new band together that played original music. I had heard about Bruce, so me and a friend went to this place called the I.A.M.A., an Italian-American club where Bruce was playing with his band Earth. I introduced myself, told him I was thinking of putting together an original band, and invited him down to the Upstage club to jam. Months later we finally hooked up at the Upstage and played together for the first time. It was me and Bruce and Little Vini [Roslin]. After we were through playing, Bruce and I went downstairs to the Green Mermaid Room [bottom floor of Upstage] and talked. I said,

Vini Lopez, Asbury Park, N.J., July 18, 1970.

"Let's put something together, something with original music." And he told me he'd been writing some songs. So I said, "Let's do it," and we did. I knew Danny Federici and brought him into the group. Little Vini was the bass player.

And that group eventually became Steel Mill.

Yeah, but first we were Child.

In the old days, everyone in the band lived together.

Yup. I lived in a bathroom at Tinker's surfboard factory. Danny lived in another bathroom. Bruce and Tinker lived around front, in the office.

Back then, and even today, you're known affectionately in some circles, and not so affectionately in other circles, as "Mad Dog."

At first they called me "Loper." That was my nickname. During the Dr. Zoom period I was "Mad Man." It wasn't until the second album that I became "Mad Dog."

During those days when everyone was given nicknames, what was Bruce called?

Not the Boss. That came much, much later. He was known as the Doctor.

As in Dr. Zoom.

That's right. And Johnny Lyon became Southside Johnny. Garry Tallent was the Funky Chicken. He still is. Steve [Van Zandt] became Miami Steve. I wanted to call him Vegas Van Zandt. He was a *heavy* card player back then.

Did you live up to your Mad Dog and Mad Man nicknames?

I was the only drummer I knew with 360-degree hair. And I was a homicidal, schizophrenic, paranoid Roman Catholic. That says it all.

Let's jump, for a minute, to the E Street Band and the recording of the first two albums. There are a number of tapes floating around with songs recorded by the band that never made it onto either record. What are your recollections of those songs?

Well, I loved "The Fever," the tune Bruce eventually gave Southside. Back when we did it, we were in the studio and someone rolled the tape and recorded it. That's how "Sandy" came about, too. There were a lot of songs Bruce wrote and we played in the studio that never appeared on record and were never played live. We kept a pretty basic song list for a long time.

Looking back to those days, the days when you were in the band, what goes through your mind?

Lots of things. But I try not to dwell on them. Those were great days for me. I wish they never had to end. I guess I would do things differently. But what happened, happened. *—Robert Santelli*

BOOM CARTER

. . . .

Interview by Robert Santelli, April 1986

Drummer Ernest Carter, better known at the Jersey Shore as "Boom," joined the E Street Band after the departure of Vini Lopez. Born and raised in Asbury Park, Carter was a close friend of David Sancious and part of the original Upstage crowd.

Carter's drum style was markedly different from Lopez's. Able to play all forms of rock as well as rhythm and blues, soul, and jazz, and formally trained, Carter blended a variety of these influences into his drumming, the same way David Sancious did on keyboards.

Whereas Lopez often attacked his drums in a rhythmic frenzy, Carter approached playing the drums with deliberate delicacy. He was, and still is, a finesse drummer. "One of the things Bruce liked about me as a drummer," Carter recalls, "was the way I pushed the band. Bruce pushed me, and I pushed the band."

Carter was a member of the E Street Band for nine months, after which he left to join David Sancious's new band, Tone. Carter played drums on all six Tone albums. Currently, Carter plays with a Jersey Shore blues band, the Fairlanes. I caught up with him just prior to a gig at the Cafe Bar on the boardwalk in Long Branch, just up the road from Asbury Park.

. . . . .

BACKSTREETS: *When you joined the E Street Band in 1974, almost at once you were playing live with Bruce and the band. What kinds of songs made up the set back then?*
BOOM CARTER: We were playing tunes like "Jungleland," which, back then, before Bruce recorded it, sounded totally different. But David Sancious's keyboards made a big difference in the way it sounded. And we played other tunes that would eventually be heard on the *Born to Run* album, plus things from the first two albums.
Is it true that Sancious was responsible for bringing you

into the E Street fold? You joined the band with him?
Yeah, that's right. David told Bruce about me, because Bruce was looking for a new drummer after Vini [Lopez] had left. I auditioned for the job at Garry Tallent's parents' house. Bruce liked what I played, and so I got the gig.
What were you doing at the time? Were you in another band?
I was on the road, mostly down South, with a band called Little Royal and the Swing Masters. Little Royal was like Soul Brother Number Two. He looked like James Brown and sang like James Brown; his songs were James Brown takeoffs. At the time, I was living in Atlanta, Georgia. Davey called me up from New Jersey and asked me if I might be interested in joining the E Street Band. I told him yeah, sure. So Davey told me that the band would be playing in Atlanta and that I should stop by backstage after the show and speak to Bruce.
Was that the first time you met Bruce?
No, I knew him from the Student Prince and also the Upstage.
You and David were childhood friends, yet from what I remember, you two never played in the same band until the E Street Band. Is that correct?
Yes and no. We never played in a New Jersey band together, although we jammed a lot. But when we lived in Virginia, we had a couple of bands together. That was in 1971, I guess. But when Bruce began recording *Greetings From Asbury Park, N.J.*, David went north to work with him.
Richmond, Virginia, was home away from home for a number of Asbury Park musicians in the early seventies. You and David Sancious, Southside Johnny, and Garry Tallent all lived there at one time or another. What was the attraction?
David knew some people who were going to open a recording studio there. When they did, he went down and became the studio's keyboards player. He got me a gig doing sessions there, too. We'd record in the day and play out with our band at

night. We were called Cinnamon, and it was me on drums and David on piano, and that was it.

You were an E Street Band member when the Born to Run *sessions began. What were they like?*

Recording was like trial and error. Bruce had so many different ideas about how the songs should sound. I think we tried them all and then some. We'd be on the road, come back home, and then go into the studio. We did a song at a time.

What made you leave the band right in the middle of the sessions?

I was closer with David than with Bruce. He was someone I grew up with. And when he decided to leave the band, I felt I should go too. Plus, we had this music that we always wanted to do, and we had the chance to do it. David had a record contract and I wanted to be part of whatever music he was going to put on his album. I loved playing with Bruce, but I couldn't play with Bruce and David at the same time. So I had to quit. I don't regret the decision, looking back. It was what I really wanted to do.

Was Bruce surprised at your decision?

It was always there that David wanted to leave and that I'd probably go with him. It was only a matter of time.

You, of course, played on the song "Born to Run." Were there any other songs you recorded with Bruce and the band?

No. It was just that one track.

Was the legendary roll that begins the song your idea or Bruce's?

It was Bruce's idea. He told me what he wanted and I played it.

You played with David's band, Tone, until it dissolved. What did you do then?

David and I did sessions. I toured Europe with Paul Butterfield. Eventually I joined the Jukes and played percussion, drums, and even guitar.

Are there any plans to one day reunite with David and start perhaps a contemporary version of Tone?

We think about it a lot. We keep in touch. I'd certainly like to do something with him again. I think he feels the same.   —*Robert Santelli*

Bryn Mawr, Pa., February 25, 1974. ▶

SUKI LAHAV

. . . .

Interview by Steven Allan, December 1985

eeing the E Street Band today, playing to stadium-sized crowds, it's hard to imagine their sound as anything but the raucous, guitar-dominated playing that's best exhibited by songs like "Glory Days" and "Born in the USA." But long-time fans of the band know it hasn't always been like that — in the early seventies the band had a dramatically different sound. Until *Born to Run,* the band was very much keyboard-dominated, due in part to David Sancious's jazz background. Springsteen's songs themselves tended more toward the theatrical and there was still strong evidence of Bruce's early fascination with Bob Dylan; in fact, the band was as likely to pull out a Dylan number for an encore as they were to break into "Twist and Shout."

Part of the reason for that unique sound was the presence of Suki Lahav, the first female member of the E Street Band. Suki was the resident E Street violinist from September 1974 to March 1975. Though she recorded many songs in the studio, on record she can only be found as a vocalist on "Sandy" and "Incident on 57th Street," while her violin playing shines only on "Jungleland."

But onstage, for her brief tenure with the band, Suki made quite a lasting impact. Her violin playing gave a romantic and intellectual feel to Springsteen's shows and added another haunting element to many of the early songs. In particular, her playing on the E Street version of Dylan's "I Want You" was wonderful. Many of the shows at that time would open with Bruce alone at the microphone, with Suki in the rear of the stage, spotlights on both; it was powerful visually as well as musically.

Suki's original introduction into the band had been through her husband Louis Lahav, the engineer for the second album. Her career with the E

Street Band ended when she and Louis decided to return to Israel. She now lives with her second husband and two children in Jerusalem, where *Backstreets* caught up with her.

. . . . .

BACKSTREETS: *How did you meet Bruce Springsteen?*
SUKI LAHAV: Louis was working with Mike Appel in the 914 Sound Studios as an engineer. Mike arrived with Bruce and I remember as soon as he came into the studio it was obvious, even then, that he was a giant, that one day he'd just explode into stardom.

As soon as I heard those recordings, I became just as convinced. By the music, the lyrics, and, later on, after I got to know him, by Bruce as a person.
What year was that?
We arrived in the States in 1971 and everything seemed to happen with Bruce around 1973 and 1974.
Whose idea was it to use the violin in the band?
Bruce was the first to suggest it. At first everyone laughed. "What, a violin in a rock 'n' roll band!" seemed to be everyone's attitude. But, as always, if Bruce said so, then everyone went straight along with it. And I think he proved that he was right.
So he offered you the chance?
Well, not exactly straightaway. He had some auditions but he couldn't find anyone to fit his demands. Even then he was the big perfectionist. I was only in the picture because I was Louis's wife. I remember once they invited a children's choir to record on the track "Sandy." They didn't turn up, so Bruce decided to record me over and over, track on track, and make it sound like a choir. That was hard work, trying to sound like a choir. That's the only official recording I appear on.
How do you feel about not being put on record?
I don't mind that at all. What was more important to me was the experience I gained from working together with such a great artist. I personally don't think I was good enough for him anyway.

Where did you first appear live with the band?
In Lincoln Center. After that — since the response was so good — we carried on with it. Bruce used the violin only for the romantic side of him. I played only on the slow songs.

How was it to work with him?
Bruce was in total control, the one and only "Boss." But still he worked always together with everyone as a team. He didn't have to impose himself — he was willing to accept suggestions, but always, he had the last say. Even then he used to record loads of songs and only use a few of them. In my opinion, some of those songs that have never been released are his best. Especially the lyrics — he wrote like a madman, a natural phenomenon.

What was the band like?
I became friendly with everyone. But especially with Max. We used to talk about Bruce a lot. He was amazed by him. And he was very loyal to him — he seemed to play just for him. I remember Max telling me how hard it was for him, being the drummer. He was always in the background onstage and couldn't hear Bruce sing all the time. He wanted to be able to hear all the words to be able to get more into the music. Clarence is just a heap of warmth and tenderness. It's a pity, but he's less apparent on the *Born in the USA* album.

What do you think of Born in the USA?
I'm not all that much of a rock 'n' roller these days. So altogether I'm less interested in that type of music. I feel it was done very professionally and I can understand why people like it. But that type of music has less affect on me than, say, *Nebraska*, which was, for me, his best album yet.

There's a problem as one becomes a star, especially in the States. The American culture and entertainment industry have such big demands that one can easily be turned into a music factory. Even Bruce — though I'm sure much less than others — has become part of the great media controlled music, where other people decide what to do and what not to do. But I'm not worried about Bruce. As always, I'm sure he's under control of everything — and still the same, down-to-earth, simple but great artist. Even when he sings "We Are the World," he stands out more than anyone, with the feeling and power he puts into those simple words. He's more representative of America than the president. He's a true American figure and not a result

Suki Lahav, Tel Aviv, Israel, December 1985.

of public relations. He doesn't act — he really is himself.

How did your involvement with the E Street Band end?
I wanted to come back home. I believe my place is here in Israel. Louis and I decided to come back to Israel before the split with Mike.

Have you been in touch with Bruce since?
About six years back, a film producer friend of mine wanted to use three of Bruce's songs for an Israeli film of his. He had trouble getting the okay from CBS. So I called Bruce up on the phone. It took me a few days to find him at home, but in the end he answered. He was really pleased to hear from me and right away said that there's no problem in using those songs ["Jungleland," "Hungry Heart," and "Point Blank"]. He was really nice about it. CBS made a promotional disc of that film with those three songs on it. I heard it's become quite a collector's item, being that they only had thirty printed.

What do you do now?
Most of my time I'm at home with my children — far away from the lights and excitement of those early days with Bruce.   —*Steven Allan*

East Rutherford, N.J., August 1986. ▶

TALK TO ME

THE TIES THAT BIND

Fans Behind the Scenes

Angel on My Chest: Los Angeles, Calif., July 1978.

COVER ME

· · · · · · · ·

Behind the Design of Born in the USA

Making an album that's as successful as *Born in the USA* entails more than just writing and recording the songs. It also involves marketing and design. The packaging of the music and the classic design of the cover certainly contributed to the success of *Born in the USA*.

That design was the work of New York designer Andrea Klein. Her involvement with Springsteen stretches back to *Born to Run*, and she designed both the *Nebraska* and *Born in the USA* album covers. She also designed five of the seven singles sleeves of *Born in the USA*, most of the sheet music, the great songbooks to both *Nebraska* and *Born in the USA*, and the beautiful *Born in the USA* tour program. For several years she was the designer behind the look of Bruce Springsteen's printed work — an important job indeed. Much of the imagery the public associates with Bruce Springsteen's music comes from the work of Andrea Klein.

We sent *Backstreets* contributing editor Arlen Schumer, himself a New York graphic designer, to interview Klein on the making of an album cover. In this interview, she discusses the ideas and concepts behind *Darkness* and *Nebraska* and the making of the *Born in the USA* image.

· · · · ·

BACKSTREETS: *How did you begin at CBS Records?*
ANDREA KLEIN: I had taken a course in paste-ups and mechanicals and did very well in that class. The woman teaching the course was at one time the production manager at CBS Records, and when the class was finished, she sent three of us on an interview — she knew there was a job open — and I got the job!
What did you show the CBS people?
I must've shown them some work I had done in college — I graduated from Syracuse in 1971. I was a painter for about five or six years, and I had

a few paintings I had done that were used as jazz album covers. And then I showed them paste-ups and mechanicals, because that's what they wanted to see.
So paste-ups and mechanicals do pay off?
You don't get a job without them. Six months after I was in that department, I was promoted to junior designer.
Just from doing paste-ups?
I was doing some little bits of design work.
For John Berg?
And Paula Scher was very much a part of it. She was wonderful to work with. They used to throw work my way. I started out doing back covers of classical albums. They continued to give me more important work, and then I was promoted. They knew my intention was not to stay in paste-ups. Some people are there just to do that; that's all they want to do. Some of us who were doing paste-ups made it very clear that we did not want to remain in that area.
What did you think of Berg's previous work? Did you respect him?
Oh, completely. I think he's a genius.
The Born to Run *album cover was...*
Brilliant.
Well, Eric Meola's a great photographer...
But that's not why that album cover is great; I just don't believe that. An album cover is great because it's a great *graphic*; it's a package design. And an *art director* is the one who puts it together, who crops that picture, who picks the type, whose eye has made that look like what it does.
And yet the photographer seems to get the glory.
What I'm saying is that John Berg decided with Bruce what the photo was going to look like. He decided to make it black and white, decided to shoot him on a white, seamless backdrop, and chose to wrap the photo from front to back. It was John Berg's genius that created that cover.
One of the things I like about the Darkness *cover is the*

way the black and white inner sleeve pulls out from the color cover.

I designed the sleeve. It was on *my* typewriter. The type was originally typed out by me on an old manual typewriter.

Is the type a straight blow-up from crummy bond paper?

Exactly. I had been involved with the cover design and had met Bruce. He would come up to CBS — he had his fans by then, and he would come into my office with his sunglasses on. I was comping type, painting "Darkness on the Edge of Town" on clear acetate. He just sat there reading the paper — he obviously felt very comfortable. He just hung out.

There were many more typefaces to be done, and when it became obvious that this was going to take all day, Bruce said, "Look, I'll be at the studio. Come over when they're ready." And the next evening, with about fifty comps — they weren't all mine, everyone in the department was contributing — we went to the studio and spent quite a while there. John Berg had said, "Show 'em a million." We had them out against the wall on the floor so Bruce could see them all out in front of him. He'd go through them, "Okay, no...okay, yes..." It was fun. Bruce was very talkative and told some great stories. We picked the cover that night. And that's how *Darkness* happened.

I've heard Darkness *was the first album cover and promotion that Bruce took a real, personal involvement in, all the way to the final printing stages.*

He took a personal involvement mainly because he felt too commercialized from the *Born to Run* era. He wanted to make sure that the graphics that came out were not the least bit commercial and in no way was it going to be graphic and slick. He made sure he wasn't going to look too great. There was no retouching allowed, as always.

Who was making the decisions?

Bruce.

Bruce was acting as art director?

He makes all the decisions. You don't show him something you don't like.

So would you have retouched the cover shot?

Yes. I don't think *Darkness* is any great album cover, by *any* means. I don't think anybody does.

What about The River?

I had nothing to do with it. He was recording this out on the West Coast, and a friend of Bruce's...

Jimmy Wachtel "...for Dawn Patrol"?

I think he was friendly with Jackson Browne, and that's how they hooked up. That's all I know.

To me, the cover of The River *is redundant. It's another disheveled close-up of Bruce.*

Yes, and very intentional on Bruce's part.

They should've made the back cover the front cover; it's a nice editorial image.

Oh, I don't agree at all. The whole package design is poor. The back has nothing to do with the front. I don't really like the type.

It was the most logical step after Darkness's *typewriter type, this hand-lettered* River *logo.*

It's the same thing. He was very deliberate about making sure nothing was "professional-looking." Bruce is into this stuff.

Tell me the whole story of your involvement with Nebraska.

I was at CBS and decided to leave, to spend more time with my nine-month-old son. One of the last days I was there, I got a call from Jon Landau Management. They wanted me to do the next cover. They wanted to present CBS with a finished mechanical that I would do. I was thrilled. So I met with Jon Landau that day, and soon after started meeting Bruce at the studio. He played me all the stuff. The album wasn't completed, so he would play some of the songs that didn't even end up on the album. He played me the music and we talked about it. He would explain to me how he feels about the album.

How did he word these feelings?

He played me the music — that's how he worded it, I mean. It was in the music; I understood it.

But did he try to verbalize it?

Yes, a little bit. He was very private about it. He didn't want anybody knowing about it. He knew it was very different from his other albums. We talked about a feeling that he had about the album and how he felt possibly about the image on the cover. Right away we both agreed it should be black and white. He didn't have any other particular ideas. He said stuff like he didn't necessarily have to be on the cover.

Did he have the title at that point?

No. So what I did then was decide to show him some portfolios of photographers' work, people that I knew who did great black-and-white photography.

What type of portfolios were you calling up? Were you thinking of the Robert Frank, Diane Arbus types?

Yes. I was showing him more of, I'd say, an "artsier" type of black-and-white photography, as opposed to commercial, slicker stuff. It just seemed right for this. There was a book Bruce had always loved which he showed me — *The Americans*, by Robert Frank! He also showed me some pictures of himself that he liked. And it wasn't because of how he looked. It was because of the *feeling* that was evoked in the pictures. And that's how he explains these things to me. He doesn't have to use a lot of words. I understand what he means. So anyway, I showed him some stuff, and he really liked David Kennedy's work. And I did also.

What was his work like?

David wasn't a very well-known photographer; he was well-known among us up at CBS. He was a twenty-five-year-old guy that really did some nice stuff. David had a commercial side to his work, and then there's his personal side, still-life photos, portraits, stuff he would exhibit if he had an exhibit. This [the *Nebraska* album cover photo] happened to be one of those pictures, which Bruce really loved.

Bruce saw it and said, "Hold it — that's the cover!"?

No, he just really liked that photo. He said, "Okay, let's go ahead, let's give it a shot."

And you were the middle man, the mediator?

So we did a marathon photo session up in Brewster, New York, at David Kennedy's house, an old family home, which was a lot of fun.

The inner sleeve photo seems like a James Dean Giant *kind of tribute.*

Bruce liked it; I would've *loved* it for a front cover. Bruce felt it was a little cold.

I always thought he had a great rapport with the camera.

He's actually very much at ease in front of a camera. But everything to him is *contrived*. When he looks at pictures of himself that were taken by a photographer in a photo studio, he feels very much that they're contrived. Which they are. So he always likes "on location" pictures — which are *just* as contrived!

So when did you get a title to work with?

The title wasn't picked until the very last minute. There was another possibility — the other title was going to be *January 3, 1982.*

The day he recorded it?

Because it was that journalistic kind of title. I guess Jon Landau and Bruce thought it wasn't a good name for an album; it was too hard to say. Jon Landau and Bruce went through lyrics in the songs, looking for a title. They talked about *Open All Night* as a possibility. They thought *Nebraska*

was more wide open. Then Bruce showed me an old Chuck Berry album cover that he liked. It had the same sort of cover layout.

And the back cover?

I was doing some big type, and Bruce certainly was anxious to see it, and finish it that night. So he came over with Landau and sat down for a while, as I comped it out. I played him a Roxy Music album, *Avalon*, which I love. He told me later that he got turned on to it that night. The mechanical was done, and that was it. They handed the tape over with the mechanical to CBS. No one at CBS knew anything about it.

How did CBS feel about the design being outside their control?

They loved the cover, but probably would have preferred a picture of Bruce. Bruce felt very strong about it. It was a very personal thing. He was thrilled when it went number...three? I was thrilled that I had the opportunity to do it. Bruce said *Nebraska* was his favorite album cover. I never took it for granted whether I was going to be asked again or not, so I was surprised and thrilled when they called me to do the *Born in the USA* album. I guess we developed some sort of communication bond.

Tell me about your involvement with Born in the USA.

I met with Jon Landau in the spring or summer of '83, and he played me the title song.

What was your reaction?

It was more like *Born to Run;* it had that great, great music, and the great lyrical aura of the whole album. It was that thrilling. We talked about the album, that it was a very important album for Bruce, because it was coming after *Nebraska.*

Important in what way? To reestablish him commercially?

Yes. Bruce actually had a fear — he expressed that he didn't think he had any fans out there. He said that it was four years since his last full band album came out. And he didn't go on the road with *Nebraska;* he didn't make any new fans. His fans had grown up, had gone to college and graduated. That's how both he and Jon felt. So they were very much ready to establish him again commercially. I met with Bruce, and he played me all the music, about sixteen cuts. Again, the album wasn't finished. So we sat down and talked about the cover, and right away we both agreed it should be *color.* Coming from *Nebraska* — boom! Rock 'n' roll! Color! And he was ready to *look good*, as opposed to

The River *cover sessions, October 1979.* ▶

the *Darkness* cover, where he deliberately did not look his best. But, as always, he feels an album cover of his music should be *emotionally* accessible. He talks about the *feeling* that he wants it to have. We'd go to a bookstore, he'd pick out books, and I'd take them home — it was that kind of process.

What were some of the ideas you were picking up on?

Pretty much American, a lot of color. Bruce had an idea, a book he really liked. It was a book of photographs, and maybe even some poetry, by Joseph Szabo, called *Almost Grown.* They were beautiful pictures of adolescents. Bruce really liked the pictures. All he would say was "I don't know . . . all I know is I like these pictures." Period. He didn't go any further with it. I said, "Okay, let's get hold of these pictures, and maybe I'll do a photo collage." Which is what I did, but there was quite a long period in between, going through pictures with Bruce.

Did you meet Joseph Szabo?

Yes. We kept finding pictures, editing pictures. To make a long story short, he outgrew the idea. All the while I had presented him with some ideas that I had, which is part of my job as an art director/designer. My main idea was to have Bruce come into the studio, a real, live, controlled, professional studio, a let's-get-some-beautiful-pictures-here-of-Bruce session. I wanted to do a graphic flag — Bruce against stripes. I thought stripes were beautiful, graphically.

Was he agreeable to that idea?

He definitely considered it, although he didn't right away jump to the idea. And then, at some point, he was ready. He said finally, "Okay, look, I don't have any other ideas, sure, let's try it, why not?" We talked then about photographers. I felt it was very important for Bruce to get comfortable with the photographer.

So Bruce felt comfortable with Annie Leibovitz?

He mentioned that he liked her; she knew that he liked her. I thought she'd be right, and I called her.

Had you worked with her before?

No. My main fear about working with Annie was that she would not be willing to work with tight art direction. She was a journalistic photographer for magazines like *Rolling Stone*; she didn't go out on jobs with an art director. Journalists don't work that way. I also had a friend who'd worked with her shooting Cyndi Lauper, and Annie very much liked to take control of it. Which sometimes is great if you need somebody like that.

But with so tight an idea. . .

You don't always need that good a photographer. But yet you do. So I explained to her that it was going to be heavy art direction, and she really appreciated my honesty. She really wanted to do it, she would've done it for free. She *loves* Bruce. We sat down and talked about a bunch of ideas. She felt once we had him in the studio, we should do whatever we could. We rented the studio next door to her, where we had a series of stage sets Bruce could just walk into. He was very impressed by the whole thing. He walked in, and the first thing he saw was this big painted flag. I hired a scenic painter to do a Rauschenberg-looking flag; it was done on canvas, about fifteen feet wide. I stapled it to the wall and made it real weird. Then we went down the street to this garage we rented and did the fire shot, one of Annie's ideas.

That's real fire?

You could see it on Bruce's face — he was a little nervous about it. He looked a little like, "What *are* we doing here?"

The fire shot seemed to come out of left field, having nothing to do with the established Born in the USA *image campaign. It's a nice enough Bruce shot, but seems very. . . contrived.*

Right. Then there was the Keith Haring painted flag. We hired him to paint the wall of the garage. That was another one of Annie's ideas.

Interesting. . . Bruce goes East Village.

Well, he didn't know from Keith Haring.

I'll bet Keith Haring didn't know from Bruce Springsteen!

He did. He really did. But as far as I was concerned, Annie wanted to use him, I didn't. But I didn't think Keith Haring and Bruce Springsteen would exactly be the right match. So then we went back across the street into the other studio, where we had one big taut flag. Bruce really loved the idea.

Was that famous opening scene from Patton *in your head at all?*

No. It did come up later. We went through all the photos, blew them up, and did comps of the album cover. But Bruce felt he looked a little schlumpy. He didn't want to look ambiguous — he wanted a clear face. So we decided to go back into the studio and get the picture he liked. At that point I decided I wanted bigger stripes, a more graphic look. We bought a flag that was twenty-five feet wide by

Tacoma, Wash., October 19, 1984. ▶

London, England, July 6, 1985.

fifteen feet high. It couldn't even fit in Annie's studio! So we went to Silvertop Studios in Queens, where commercials are shot, and rigged it up. We did a whole bunch of sessions.

When I first saw the cover, I expected to see Bruce's face on the other side.

Bruce hoped to have his face on the cover, because he didn't have it on the cover of *Nebraska*. When all was said and done, he just didn't like any pictures of himself. He liked this image the best; he picked it. It came from the idea of a back cover. Bruce had his hat in his pocket. That's how he is — he sticks his hat in his pocket. Great back cover! Even though some of us talked about it being the front cover, Bruce kept saying, "Yeah, but I can't put my *butt* on the cover."

When did he cross that hurdle?

I don't know. He went home one weekend and called me. "Well, I think we gotta keep fishing." In other words, start from scratch — and the album was nearly finished!! I got off the phone, and I was very depressed. I think I burst out crying. "Keep fishing"! I thought I was gonna lose my mind!

What were you, as art director of the project, happy with at that point?

There were so many photo sessions — we did seven sessions in a year and a half — that there were a few things I loved. There were some portrait photos I liked, frontal versions, and some great type designs. Anyway, that Monday I got a call from Bruce, that that was *it*. He got nervous. Just when it was time to really make a decision, he totally withdrew.

Saner heads prevailed?

Right. He spent the weekend with Chuck Plotkin.

"Thanks to Chuck Plotkin for his assistance..."?

Yes. Thanks to Chuck Plotkin for your influence! The way Bruce has taken his career that's *different* from other huge personalities is that he just maintains complete control of his own image. And one way he does that is by making sure, from the graphics side of it, he sees and approves every single solitary thing that goes out. It gets down to the slash mark on the cover; he didn't think it should be there. That's how involved he gets.

Considering that it was 1984, an election year, did you fore-

see the immense coopting of the album's flag imagery as patriotic propaganda?

I think Bruce, at one point, did picture it. He was a little bit afraid to use the flag. We all knew the flag was a great marketable image. That was clear to all of us. But it was more coincidental, as far as I'm concerned. I could be wrong. But the title of the song is "Born in the USA," and that's where it came from. I don't think being an election year had anything to do with it.

The double-page spread of the flag in the field, from the first tour book, was another keynote image.

It was taken by Robert Lewis, a young, very unknown photographer who's great. He went out to shoot Bruce during rehearsal, and in his spare time he took the flag out to the fields. I wanted to make it a *poster*. Bruce loved the picture; I guess he didn't like the way I designed the poster — I used skywriting. He thought that was funny but too cute. "Nice try, Andy."

The "Dancing in the Dark" 45 sleeve threw me a little, because it appeared before the album, and its type style gave me the impression Bruce was moving in some slick, modern

direction. Then the album came out with a completely different look.

Type has to do with the graphic. To me, Bodoni Bold [*USA*'s typeface] is a more classic American type; it's been used on stamps.

What's been the fallout from this album design?

I would say that some of the work I've gotten has been a result of the album. Recently, I got a call from Chris Blackwell at Island Records — he loved the Run-DMC album cover I had finished for Profile Records, not knowing I had done Bruce's cover. He found out later I had done it. So they've hired me to do a bunch of work.

Has Annie Liebovitz received more of the credit, in your estimation, for the great cover?

In a way she did. I saw an article about Bruce, and next to the album cover was "Annie Liebovitz's classic photo," and to me that was a real misrepresentation. In other circles, people looking for art directors have come to me, not caring that Annie took that picture. So it's not something I regret. I'm thrilled the album was such a success.

—*Arlen Schumer*

THE NIGHT I MET BRUCE SPRINGSTEEN

I'd Drive All Night

The song leaped out of the radio and stopped my '66 Valiant dead. The sound was different from anything I had ever heard before in my life, yet was immediately recognizable; it seemed to contain a little bit of all my favorite songs...like a theme song for rock 'n' roll itself. It was thrilling, and instantly memorable. It was the summer of '75, and the song was "Born to Run."

I had become a Bruce Springsteen fan.

Everything you would expect followed: the records, the articles, the interviews, the concerts. But those things were not enough to satisfy my growing adulation. My most burning desire was to meet Bruce in person.

I got the chance three years later.

On the day *Darkness on the Edge of Town* was released, the record manager of Korvette's told me about *Thunder Road* magazine, and gave me the number of its editor and publisher, Ken Viola. I called him that night with the intention of contributing to the magazine. We met soon after and became good friends.

Ken also worked for John Scher, the concert promoter and owner of the Capitol Theater in Passaic, New Jersey. At the time, Scher was promoting Bruce's August date in Rochester, and through Ken's recommendation I illustrated the special shirts for the road crew (you can spot one in the roadie group shot in the *River* tour book). It was a good break.

But then came a real plum: to celebrate Bruce's "homecoming" after the triumphant summer of *Darkness*, Scher wanted a special marquee designed for the Capitol.

I worked on a design built around Bruce's guitar stance — to me, his leads were the key sound to

◄ *Passaic, N.J., September 19, 1978.*

both the album and the tour. After completing the artwork to Scher's satisfaction, I negotiated my fee; six sixth-row-center seats for opening night.

"Summer's hangin' on and the time is right for racin' in the street." On the first day of fall, five friends and I climbed into my car and drove to Passaic from Providence, where we were juniors at the Rhode Island School of Design. Two additions to the show promised to make it extra-special: it was going to be broadcast live throughout the East Coast, and Ken said there'd be a good chance we'd be able to meet Bruce afterwards.

Four hours later we were rounding the corner of Jefferson and Monroe streets, and we saw the marquee. Maybe it was the combination of the gritty Passaic environment, the crisp newness of the chill autumn night, and the sight of all those people milling around the Capitol entrance, but there was "Spirit in the Night": "They'll meet 'neath that giant Capitol sign that brings this fair city light."

As for the concert itself, anyone who heard the radio broadcast, live or on tape, knows what an incredible show it was. Of all the live tapes I've heard from the *Darkness* tour, that show contains what I feel are the definitive live versions of "Promised Land," "Prove It All Night," "Backstreets" (with the equally definitive "Drive All Night" interior monologue), "Because the Night," and the "Not Fade Away/She's the One" segue. (The bootlegged album, "Piece de Resistance," gets my vote for unofficial live album.) And seeing this music performed from the sixth row center — in a small (capacity 3,500) venue like the Capitol — was...unforgettable.

When the show ended, I met up with Ken and he advised me to hang out for an hour or so, because Bruce and the band would be coming out *front* stage.

And they did. First I saw Max, who was telling a friend that he was leaving to visit his mom. And

there was Bruce, entertaining a small group, telling old drinking stories. Then I spotted Jon Landau and approached him.

I introduced myself and told him I'd really like to meet the man who had changed my life. Landau smiled in agreement. "He changed my life, too." To my surprise, he went right up to Bruce and interrupted his anecdote, saying that there was someone special he wanted him to meet. All eyes shifted to me.

In one hand I held the original marquee art, the other had the Capitol program book opened to my marquee-inspired illustration (since bootlegged as a poster!), and I was wearing my own Rochester roadie shirt, to boot. Bruce looked over all the stuff, sort of nodded in approval, and signed the artwork for me.

Then I said something to him, something I had been wanting to tell him ever since I heard "Born to Run" that first time. I had read what rock 'n' roll meant to Bruce, how it entered his life and changed it forever. I wanted to try to communicate, with equal sincerity, what he meant in my life. Though I must've worn a smile from ear to ear, I didn't want to come across as just another gushing fan. The words came out very evenly: "Bruce, I just want to tell you that your music means more to me than anything else in the world."

We were both the same height, and I was looking straight into his eyes. There was that flash, when you can tell the other person knows exactly what you mean from the heart; it's a flash of connection. Bruce's sensitivity and generosity toward his fans after a show was already legend, but nothing prepared me for his reaction.

He hugged me like a brother.

And all I can recall is that the fans standing around us, including my friends, let out a spontaneous burst of exclamation, as if to say, "The Fan meets the Idol, and that's the way it *should* be."

Thanks to Murphy's Law, my friend David, who shot photos of the show, happened to run out of film. Only the memory remains.

True fans of any artist's work get to a point in their lives when the desire to meet the artist, to receive some form of personal acknowledgment, overwhelms even their adulation of the work itself. Some have yet to reach that point, while others move through it. I was fortunate enough to fulfill that desire.
— *Arlen Schumer*

The Marquee from the Capitol Theater designed by Arlen Schumer.

◄ *Rochester, N.Y., April 17, 1976.*

GLORY DAYS

. . . .

I Played Ball Against the Boss and Won (Sort Of)

---

ost fans of Bruce Springsteen already know that the Boss is a baseball fan. A bright red softball cap creeps out of the back pocket of his jeans on the cover of *Born in the USA*. "Glory Days," a whimsical song about a chance encounter with an old baseball buddy, was the fourth hit single off the album, and Bruce actually put on his softball clothes for the video.

Springsteen is well known for sprinkling his concerts with amusing tales that link the mythology of baseball to the bigger-than-life tradition of rock 'n' roll. But few of his fans have ever seen Springsteen play his favorite sport. Fewer still have had the privilege to play against him.

Ten years ago, I was a general-assignment reporter for an afternoon daily in New Orleans. Although I yearned to write features, I spent most of my days chasing fire trucks and talking to city planners. One small allowance my city editor gladly permitted me was a weekly rock column for the Saturday tab. No one else at the paper wanted it.

My first review for the tab was a ten-page, from-the-gut rave of Springsteen's New Orleans debut, a concert that kicked off his *Born to Run* tour in 1975, just weeks before he became a national phenom. *Time* and *Newsweek* writers were in town to catch the performance. When both magazines put Springsteen on their covers in October of that year, a legend was born.

After the show, I tracked Springsteen down at a small club in uptown New Orleans. He was shy and reclusive and told me he didn't give interviews. I put my notepad away, pried a couple of quotes from him, gushed like an unabashed fan of a big-league home-run king, and left in seventh heaven.

Eight months later, the show's promoter, Bill

◄ *East Rutherford N.J., September 1, 1985.*

Johnston, called me at the paper to tell me Springsteen was ending his tour in New Orleans. I was ecstatic: any time Springsteen comes to town is reason to celebrate. But the next words out of Johnston's mouth nearly knocked the wind out of me.

"Bruce and the band have been playing softball now that spring is here," he said. "He wants me to arrange a game with the local media. Would you like to be captain of the team?" Does the Pope have a vested interest in meeting St. Peter? If there's one thing in life I enjoy as much as seeing Bruce Springsteen, it's playing softball. For a rock 'n' roll softball junkie like me, playing softball with Bruce is as close to nirvana as I ever hope to achieve in this lifetime.

Springsteen's return concert was scheduled for Thursday. Mindful of the tiny pulls and jammed fingers that occasionally befall ballplayers, Springsteen wisely decided to hold the softball game after the concert, the next afternoon. When the local rock stations promoted the game, more than 500 of his fans showed up at the Audubon Park levee to watch. Many spread picnic lunches of Popeye's fried chicken or crawfish and Dixie beer, a local favorite.

Johnston, the promoter, wore a black and white striped shirt. He introduced me to my "team" — four or five hung-over DJs, several women who worked on his promotion staff, and a coterie of local rock critics, most of whom didn't like each other very much.

Springsteen and his band climbed out of their tour bus, parked on a lot at the edge of the field. They were dressed in their "uniforms," blue and white sleeveless basketball shirts that read "E Street Kings." Their gloves were still shiny, their rubber cleats new. Springsteen wore his trademark *Our Gang* hat. It flopped over his curly hair with exaggerated cockiness. His eyes were hidden by reflecting shades. He seemed vaguely uncomfortable.

At the pitcher's mound, Johnston introduced me

Philadelphia, Pa., September 19, 1988.

to my idol. Springsteen acknowledged we'd met once before, but didn't seem to care. Perhaps he was put off by my own sartorial choices. Like his fellows in the band, I wore a basketball tank top. But my hat was as nontraditional for a baseball diamond as Springsteen's — a wide-brimmed Panama plantation hat. Although it was perfect fare for the stifling pre-summer weather, it was inappropriate for the sport at hand.

Nevertheless, after the ground rules had been established, I turned to Springsteen and asked how his team had been playing. He said they'd won 19 out of 22 games on the tour so far — all promotional affairs with radio station disc jockeys and pop music critics. I asked him if he was confident

◀ *Houston, Tex., November 14, 1980.*

his team would win against my team. He smiled politely and declined to predict, but I knew in his cocky heart of hearts he was feeling confident.

"I'll bet my hat against yours that my team wins," I suggested. He looked at me suspiciously and at my hat with something close to disdain. Perhaps he was wondering what effect such a hat might have on his rock 'n' roll image. He shuffled his feet and begged off the proposal. "Hey, I just got this hat," he said. "Like, I'm attached to this hat, y' know? I wore it at the concert last night."

When I retreated to the sidelines, it was tough discerning my teammates from the onlookers, who pressed upon the scene right up to the basepaths. I jotted down my roster of 15 players; three were women. I promised them all I'd work them into the game at some point, and aligned my defense purely

University Park, Pa., February 19, 1974.

on instinct. "C'mon," I said as we took the field, "we can't lose a game to a bunch of musicians."

Lead guitarist Miami Steve Van Zandt led off the game with a home run. Next up was Springsteen, who singled, then scored along with organist Danny Federici on road manager Rick Seguso's base hit. But my hastily assembled batting lineup produced two big rallies, with five runs in the first and four runs in the second. After four innings we had a commanding 9-3 lead. Springsteen must have been relieved that he hadn't taken me up on my proposal.

In the top of the fifth, it was obvious to everyone that I had to make some obligatory lineup changes. The women on my team were anxious to play, and our lead looked safe. I replaced my three lightest hitters with three women. One turned in a stellar performance in right field. Unfortunately, the other two hadn't put on a glove since childhood and were purposely tested as often as possible by the E Street Band hitters. With Bruce and his buddies peppering ground balls and long flies to my unpracticed distaffers, our six-run lead wilted like a cotton plant in a drought.

We eked out an insurance run in the bottom of the sixth and took a 10-7 lead into the last inning. Danny Federici singled to start the seventh and Clarence Clemons, the band's "Big Man," put his weight behind a pitch and huffed and puffed his way around the bases for a home run to slice our lead to one precarious run.

On the sidelines, the crowd grew vociferous, cheering on the E Street rally. My teammates, miffed that Springsteen's team was hitting to our

worst fielders, demanded to come back into the game. The E Street Band, they noted, wasn't playing with women, why should we?

It was a legitimate point, but moot. I had already taken them out of the game. Springsteen knew the rules as well as I did. He wanted to win as much as I did. I probably would have done the same thing. I kept the women in the game.

We got Miami Steve Van Zandt to fly out to the left fielder before one of the roadies and Springsteen both singled. E Street's number-three hitter, Garry Tallent, came to the plate with the game on the line. On the first pitch, he hit a hard one-hopper back to me at shortstop. On instinct, I tagged the roadie going by me from second and pegged the ball to first to complete the double play and end the game.

Springsteen met me at the mound and pumped my hand. I asked him to sign the ball, and tucked it safely away in my glove. He was immediately surrounded by fans wielding pens and scraps of paper. With a huge grin plastered on his face, Springsteen gleefully signed autographs for ten minutes, honored to perform this mundane chore of Hall of Famers.

While Springsteen signed autographs for his fans, the rest of the band cleaned up the debris that had been left behind on the levee. Chicken bones, crawfish carcasses, and empty beer cans were strewn everywhere. In no time, the field was cleaner than it had been when the game started.

Only 15 or 20 people were left at the rim of the diamond when the "official scorekeeper," a Columbia Records representative, approached me with the scorebook. "Hey," she said, "you guys only scored four runs in the second inning, not five. The game is tied, 9-9."

I glanced around at the emptying field. I had three players left — enough to send to the plate for the last half of the seventh, but not enough to field a team in case we couldn't score a run. Springsteen and his band waited patiently for my next move, patting their gloves. In New Jersey, that's what's known as a squeeze play.

With a shake of my head, I stepped slowly out to the mound to confer with Johnston and Springsteen. I couldn't refute the evidence of the scorebook, but I didn't believe we had miscounted our total score, either.

"Look, Bruce, I have three guys here. We might be able to score a run and win this thing, but we

At the Main Point, 1976, visiting former E Streeters David Sancious (left) and Boom Carter (center). Photographer Phil Ceccola says this is the last known picture of Bruce with his beard — the next day he shaved it off and cut his hair.

might not. I can't field a team if we don't end the game, so why don't we just call it a tie and play a doubleheader the next time you come to town?'' I said.

Springsteen smiled and shook my hand. "Sounds good to me," he said. "Why don't we just trade hats?"

Sensing that my friends and future grandchildren would never believe my story, I asked a friend to take my picture with Springsteen while we enacted the swap. Johnston got into the middle of the picture, too, and we put our arms around each other.

When I arrived back home, I discovered there was no film in my camera. But Johnston called me about a month later and said there was a picture of him and Springsteen and me in *Rolling Stone* magazine and a capsule summary of the ball game. Naturally, I framed the story.

We've all gone on to bigger and better things. Springsteen fills stadiums now, and it wouldn't

surprise me if 50,000 fans showed up to watch him play softball. I'm writing features for a newspaper in Virginia, content to hang out at the local pub like a character in a Springsteen tune, boring folks with my softball glories, all my big baseball stories.

But Johnston has the greatest "what if" story of all. Springsteen was looking for new management during his trip to New Orleans and offered the position to Johnston, a savvy rock promoter. Johnston, to his eternal regret, turned down the job to take a similar position with Gino Vannelli, a Canadian pop star several leagues below Springsteen's status.

"Vannelli's going to be the biggest thing since Frank Sinatra," Johnston predicted.

"Maybe, but Springsteen will be bigger than Elvis before he's through," I told Johnston. I'm willing to amend my prediction now. Someday, Bruce will be bigger than the Babe.

—*Chuck Bauerlein*

YOU CAN LOOK
(BUT YOU BETTER NOT TOUCH)

Springsteen Collectibles

Another Tramp of Hearts: Washington, D.C., August 28, 1984.

THE ABCs OF THE BOSS

A Primer for Springsteen Collectors

Though he doesn't like nicknames, when it comes to record collecting it would be hard to call Bruce Springsteen anything but the Boss. With the exceptions of the Beatles and Elvis Presley, Springsteen is the most collected rock artist. And since both of those exceptions are no longer producing new records and only so much stuff can be dug out of the vaults, one would have to guess that at some point Bruce Springsteen may overtake both the Fab Four and the King to become the most collected artist in rock 'n' roll.

Lord knows Springsteen stuff already rivals all others in terms of price — there are at least a half dozen Springsteen records worth over $1,000. And considering that Springsteen's recording career only stretches back two decades, that's quite an accomplishment. Springsteen has only released nine official albums since he started recording back in 1973. Collecting the official albums is a snap (they're all still in print), but picking up all the non-LP B-sides, import CDs, magazines, promos and the like is where the challenge is.

Collecting the entire range of Springsteen collectibles — from magazine covers that bear his likeness to import 45s — is a lifelong quest, not unlike that for the Holy Grail, and only advised for those loaded with cash. But collecting any one single aspect of Springsteen's catalog is possible. In this chapter we've outlined 26 very different subcategories of Springsteen collecting — from Asbury Park memorabilia to Yugoslavian 45s — and outlined the material available in each category.

. . . . .

A IS FOR ASBURY PARK

Most true Springsteen fans know the real answer to the trivia question "Where was Bruce Springsteen born?" Though many identify Asbury Park, New Jersey, as Springsteen's hometown, he was actu-

ally born and raised about 15 miles to the west in the little township of Freehold. Still, in the Springsteen universe, Asbury Park is the spiritual hub.

Springsteen titled his first record *Greetings From Asbury Park, N.J.,* and he chose to reproduce a tourist greeting card for the cover. One of the first things any visitor to Asbury Park now usually picks up is a batch of the postcards made famous by that album cover. Before Springsteen's career started, the cards simply had some type about Asbury Park's many attractions on the back — now the cards plug Springsteen.

Many of the songs on Springsteen's first three records feature names of real places in the Jersey Shore area and in particular in Asbury Park where Springsteen spent much of his time. You can actually drive down Kingsley and Ocean avenues (mentioned in songs), get your fortune told by Madam Marie (from the song "Fourth of July, Asbury Park") and if you want to find Thunder Road all you need do is look for a fire road out on the bad side of town. Over in nearby Belmar you can even drive down E Street. Springsteen's material is created out of a real place and the area is filled with icons that have been worked into songs.

Crazed Springsteen fans have stolen so many street signs from the main drags that the town finally gave up even trying to keep them up. But even if you can't find a street sign, fans can find

A business card from the Castiles, 1966.

Rock'n Roll - Rhythm'n Blues

"The Castiles"

Management:
Gordon Vinyard

After 5 P.M.
(201) 462-6107

tons of tourist junk on the boardwalk. Not much of the stuff available mentions Springsteen but the place's name is enough to tip off other fans that you've been to Bruce mecca.

No trip to Asbury Park would be complete without a trip to the Stone Pony, the small Jersey club that has been a second home to Springsteen and the site of numerous unannounced jam sessions. Also essential is a visit to the Asbury Park Rock 'n' Roll Museum where archivists Billy Smith and Steve Bumball have the entire rich musical heritage of the Shore on display.

B IS FOR B-SIDES

Bruce Springsteen's official record releases number just nine albums at present and his output of 45s is only slightly higher. But since Springsteen is an extremely prolific songwriter and usually ends up with several hours of outtakes from every album, he frequently issues previously unreleased material on the B-sides of 45s. All of Springsteen's singles before 1980's "Hungry Heart" had album cuts on the B-sides but every release since then has featured a song not on the actual album. There were seven singles released from the *Born in the USA* album alone — if you add the seven non-LP B-sides you get another 22 minutes of material from those sessions. Finding these cuts is a great introduction for new collectors.

Springsteen also uses non-LP material as added tracks on twelve-inch singles and on CD singles. Unlike bootlegs, all of the B-side material features top-quality sound and for the most part is not too hard to find. Add together all of Springsteen's B-sides from the U.S. and overseas and you have at least two albums worth of previously unreleased material.

In the United States the most sought-after B-side is "Be True," the flip side of the 1980 release "Fade Away." Also hard to find is "Held Up Without a Gun," the flip side of "Hungry Heart," which also made it onto several overseas twelve-inches. All three singles from the *Tunnel of Love* album had new material on the B-sides including Springsteen's much-talked-about song, "Roulette," which was the flip of "One Step Up."

Overseas the rarities are many and sometimes prices can get steep. Though Springsteen didn't release any singles off *Nebraska* in the U.S. he did release a couple overseas and he threw a rockabilly song called "The Big Payback" on flip sides over

there. And even though Springsteen stuck 40 songs on his three album *Live* set, he still had plenty of material left over and live tracks of "For You," "Merry Christmas Baby" and "Incident on 57th Street" were featured on B-sides.

C IS FOR CD SINGLES

Springsteen collecting, like the rest of the collecting field, has really turned into CD collecting. All of Springsteen's albums are commercially available on CD, and a few rare gems exist. Japan issued a special live EP compact disc off the *Live 1975-85* album that included two non-LP songs: "Incident on 57th Street" and "For You." This was also issued on vinyl in Japan. Both songs were B-sides in England and Europe, but to hear these cuts on CD is a real treat. For the *Tunnel* tour, CBS also released a special promo-only CD sampler with two songs from the record, and versions of "Be True," "Roulette" and "Pink Cadillac."

This is really just the tip of the iceberg for Springsteen CDs; the list doesn't include all the various CDs with selected Springsteen cuts (like *We Are the World*'s "Trapped," the only version of that song on CD anywhere), nor does it include the CDs of cover songs (Johnny Cash's "Highway Patrolman" is a new CD) or the CDs of related artists (Southside Johnny's *Havin' a Party*). With the rate of growth in the CD field, some collectors are going CD-only and passing up all collectibles not issued in this format.

D IS FOR *DARKNESS* PICTURE DISC

Back before picture discs were an everyday item, CBS issued a promo picture disc of the *Darkness on the Edge of Town* album in the United States to radio stations and record stores. It remains one of the cornerstone items in the Springsteen discography. Exactly how many were made is unclear; there are even rumors of counterfeits. The original would be easy to tell, however, if one were smart enough to play the album (most people don't ever play picture discs, which leaves them wide open to counterfeiting): The official picture disc sounds almost as good as the plain album, with little of the hiss you find on the mass-produced picture discs by artists like Samantha Fox.

CBS in England went mad around the *Born in the USA* album and started issuing picture discs left and right. They came up with a pink Cadillac (for "Dancing in the Dark"), a jumping Bruce (for

"Cover Me"), and a flag (for "Glory Days"). Though these picture discs at first were a desired collectible, the market seems to be flooded with them at the moment, making their real value questionable. "Tunnel of Love" as a single was made into a picture disc in the shape of a postcard. Both the *Tunnel of Love* and *Born in the USA* albums were made into picture discs and sold in shops for a brief period.

. . . .

E IS FOR DAVE EDMUNDS

What does Dave Edmunds have in common with Bruce Springsteen? Well, one song at least — a distinction shared by dozens of artists, who, like Edmunds, have covered Springsteen songs. Edmunds chose Bruce's previously unreleased "From Small Things (Big Things One Day Come)" for his *D.E. 7th* album, and even released a single of the tune in the United States and England. A U.K. radio station even played the original Springsteen demo on a show on Edmunds' career, and that tape is a sought-after collectible.

Springsteen tunes have been covered by almost 100 other artists on record, and early in Springsteen's career he made more money from songwriting royalties than from his own recordings. The biggest hits were "Because the Night" by Patti Smith and "Blinded by the Light" by Manfred Mann, but there are dozens of others you've possibly never heard of (Johnny Cash doing "Johnny 99," Allan Clarke doing "If I Was the Priest," Half Japanese doing "Tenth Avenue Freeze-out").

Springsteen collectors seek out these cover songs — particularly the ones never issued by Springsteen himself — and that alone has fueled a whole field of Bruce collecting. Rhino Records even issued a whole album of Springsteen songs covered by other artists, calling it *Cover Me*. Springsteen's songwriting credits have been so numerous there's barely been a time over the last decade when a song he wrote *wasn't* in the Top 100.

. . . .

F IS FOR FANZINES

Springsteen is more than just a vinyl phenomenon; he's also the Boss when it comes to print. Dave Marsh's first biography of Bruce, *Born to Run,* was reportedly one of the best-selling rock biographies ever, and since then there have been no less than a dozen other major books on Springsteen. Most recommended are Robert Hilburn's coffee-table tome, titled *Springsteen,* Chris Hunt and Patrick

Humphries' *Blinded by the Light,* the original Marsh book, and, for sheer intimacy, Lynn Goldsmith's photo book, also titled *Springsteen.*

But books on the Boss don't seem to be enough. There are at least a dozen photocopied fanzines in almost that many countries and languages. In England, *Point Blank* and *Candy's Room* are the top fanzines, while *Thunder Road* was the first U.S. Bruce fanzine and a professional effort (though now defunct). Even the fanzines themselves — publications put together to cater to collectors — have become collectibles, with prices of up to $100 for the first edition of *Backstreets.*

. . . .

G IS FOR GOLD RECORDS

Gold records by Bruce Springsteen or any other artist should be rarer than hen's teeth, and, because of their rarity, only within the grasp of serious and wealthy collectors. Unlike most of the other items listed in this article, they really are *too* rare for the novice to really hope to collect.

The reason we note this field, however, is to illustrate that when an artist becomes as collectible as Bruce Springsteen, things sometimes go sour. In the past few years there have been a slew of Springsteen gold records on the market, a hundredfold more than common logic would suggest are available. Since most of these things are pressed in quantities of less than two dozen — and only given to those directly involved with making the record — it simply doesn't make sense for there to be so many of them around. The answer is simple:

The fanzine Thunder Road *is now a valuable collectible.*

they're fakes, and part of a growing counterfeit industry. The problem crops up when the value of something like a Springsteen gold record (or an acetate, a new popular item with bootleggers) far exceeds the cost to make up a fake one — and with Springsteen, that point came about three years ago. Let the buyer beware.

. . . . .

H IS FOR *THE HEAVYWEIGHTS*

The Heavyweights is one of the many promo or compilation albums that contain Springsteen songs. *The Heavyweights* is a two-record set issued by CBS in 1975, and happens to be the first U.S. compilation promo to include the Boss. These sorts of items are only of value to the serious collector, since they usually contain the album version of a song, though the packaging is different.

Other CBS promos include *Hitline 80* from the United States and *The Frontrunners* from England (both with one Bruce track). In the United States, CBS has also issued a couple of Bruce-only compilations, including *As Requested Around the World* in 1981 and the B-sides compilation in 1985. These are for-promotional-use-only records that are issued to radio stations and frequently end up being sold on the collectors' market.

. . . . .

I IS FOR INTERVIEWS

Not only do Springsteen collectors value every Bruce recording; they also value his every word. At least that's what you'd think after seeing the popularity of various interview discs. This field is of questionable legitimacy and only comes about because of a strange copyright law in England that says an artist can't own his own "talk." As a result, a large number of interview discs (most of them picture discs) have flooded the collectors' market in the United States and overseas during the past few years, many times repackaging the same interviews with different graphics to make another buck off the sucker consumers.

Great Britain has issued no less than four Springsteen interview picture discs (one in the shape of a motorcycle), and one would have to be a fanatic to sit down and listen to them all more than once (they also recycle material). There's even a Bruce interview CD.

. . . . .

J IS FOR JAPAN

When it comes to collecting Bruce Springsteen — an artist as American as apple pie itself — there is one country that stands out as the ultimate source of any Springsteen item. Strangely enough, that country is Japan.

Though Springsteen has only fronted one Japanese tour (during the *Born in the USA* jaunt), ever since *Greetings From Asbury Park, N.J.* came out in Japan in 1975 with an alternative wrap-around cover with a unique picture, Japanese graphic designers have apparently been unable to resist changing at least the graphics on every item they release. This makes Japan the source of many valued and interesting Bruce collectibles.

The real Japanese gem would be *The Last American Hero*, a compilation album issued in 1978 that at that point was the only official greatest-hits package yet done by CBS; it is one of the most valuable items in the entire Springsteen catalog.

The aforementioned *Live Collection* CDs and LPs are hot Japanese items, as are the many Japanese Springsteen 45s (almost all with unique graphic treatments). Japan was also the only country with the sense to issue "Born to Run" backed with "Backstreets," the strongest double A-sided single since "La Bamba"/"Donna." And when Japan released the CD of the *Nebraska* album, they somehow got a different copy of the master; early pressings include a different mix and an extended song.

. . . . .

K IS FOR *KILLER CUTS FROM THE RIVER*

While we're on the subject of Japanese collectibles, there's also *Killer Cuts From The River*, one of the best names for any Springsteen recording (the only better idea would be to have one called *Killer Cuts From Nebraska* and include "Johnny 99" and "Nebraska"). This is one of many Japanese promo albums, and it includes several tracks from *The River*.

Other weird foreign promos include *Rocktagon*, an Australian album that's octagon-shaped and includes one Bruce song; and *Dead End Street*, an Israeli promo 12-inch with three songs from a similarly titled film. The film itself is a real weirdo, surely the only time a Springsteen song ("Point Blank") is used as the soundtrack while a hooker performs sex acts on street corners. (See Suki Lahav interview for more on the film and record.)

. . . . .

L IS FOR LIVE RECORDS

No artist in recent history has been bootlegged more than Bruce Springsteen. Early in his career Springsteen took an almost nonchalant attitude

The rare Japanese 45s for "Born to Run" and "Badlands" came with unique picture sleeves.

toward boots (he's heard yelling, "Bootleggers, roll your tapes," at a couple of early shows), though later in his career he took a particularly hard stance, sending his personal lawyers out to bust notorious bootleggers. It has always been true that Springsteen's greatest moments have occurred live onstage, and some of that was captured on the early Bruce bootlegs. Stuff like *Live at the Bottom Line, Winterland,* and *You Can Trust Your Car* caught some of Springsteen's best shows while CBS waited 15 years to release a live record.

There are a handful of Springsteen bootlegs that are priceless, but there are another couple of hundred that are pure crap, and a complete waste of money. Shamefully, the bootleg industry practically tripped over itself in 1984 and 1985 trying to release as much bootleg product as possible, and even the hardcore fans got burned out.

The release of the official CBS *Live* album did little to stop bootlegging of the Boss, but tougher law-enforcement efforts have had some effect. Most serious Springsteen collectors these days won't touch boots, and the growing dollars spent on CDs may spell the end for bootleggers of Springsteen, on vinyl at least — bootleggers have now begun issuing Springsteen releases on CD.

· · · · ·

M IS FOR "MEETING ACROSS THE RIVER"

The trivia question behind "Meeting Across the River" is "What was the original name of that song, and how do we know?" The answer is "The Heist," and we know the alternate title because

early pressings of *Born to Run* came with a post-card-sized placard that listed the title as "The Heist." That early pressing is what has become known as the "script cover." This description refers to the different type used on the front cover for the very first promo pressings of the record send out. The type was script and looked as if Ralph Steadman drew it. The script cover also features no printed lyrics or credits, and the inside picture is larger. The printing on this version is also more sepia-toned, and the record inside the sleeve should be an advance test pressing. This advance pressing was sent out in early 1975 to radio stations and a few industry types; it has since gone on to become one of the rarest Springsteen items.

· · · · ·

N IS FOR *NO NUKES*

No Nukes features one of the only official Springsteen recordings not on CBS; it's on Asylum. Springsteen has songs on both the official three-album set of the benefit concert and on a special 12-inch promo of "Devil with a Blue Dress Medley." The 12-inch is rather common, as is the album, but they still are important collectibles and a must for any Springsteen fan.

· · · · ·

O IS FOR ODDITIES

What any collector considers collectible varies with that person's personality, and since there's such a wide range of Springsteen collectors, what they choose to collect can get pretty odd. There are people who rabidly collect ticket stubs, people who

The infamous script cover version of the promotional **Born to Run** *album.*

cover their jackets with buttons, people who cover the back of their cars with bumper stickers, and there are even a couple of collectors of Springsteen's classic '57 Chevy. (See ''The Ultimate Collectible'' later in this chapter.)

P IS FOR POSTERS

Like all megastars, Bruce Springsteen has had his mug on all sorts of posters. Most of them are promo posters, though, since Springsteen only licensed one official commercial poster prior to *Born in the USA* (that one is the Lynn Goldsmith shot of him needing a shave). Copyright laws in other countries are a little looser, and there have been literally dozens of commercially available posters overseas.

The early Springsteen posters, for gigs prior to his forming the E Street Band (with groups like Child, Earth, and Steel Mill) are probably the most valuable, although they are not elaborate in design. The early album promos are great, although finding an official and legitimate one is another matter altogether. Almost all the early promo posters have been bootlegged to death.

In recent years, several posters have established themselves as important ones to collectors, including the *Darkness* four-by-four (the giant square promo for the album); the *Playboy* promo poster (done to promote a 1976 article in the magazine); and the Tour 80/81 poster (featuring a picture of

Bruce with the band looking at his feet). For the last few Springsteen records CBS has gone poster-wild, and official Springsteen promo posters now number more than two dozen in the United States alone.

Q IS FOR Q MAGAZINE

Q is a British magazine that did a cover story on Springsteen once. There are collectors who make magazines and printed matter their sole field of collecting, and when you see how many magazines feature Springsteen on the cover, it boggles the mind. A fan compiled a list of magazines back in 1985 with Springsteen cover stories, and it included more than 500 publications at that point.

In the United States the most famous Springsteen magazine covers are the *Time* and *Newsweek* issues from the week of Oct. 27, 1975, when Springsteen became the first non-newsmaker to hit both newsweeklies' covers at the same time. It started a period of hype and backlash for Springsteen, but surprisingly, those very issues are now valued collector's items when they can be found in mint shape.

There are hundreds of other magazines that Bruce Tramps collect. A few of the classics are *Crawdaddy* (two Bruce cover stories: one in 1975 and one in 1978); *Musician* magazine (a valued Bruce cover story in 1980 and another in 1984); *Trouser Press* (they stuck a picture of Bruce's guitar on the cover); and *Creem* (three Bruce covers prior to 1985's media barrage). Bruce has even made the cover of the *National Inquirer* a couple of times, and after the first time he even mentioned it in the lyrics of ''Rosalita'' at the next show.

R IS FOR ''ROSALITA''

''Rosalita'' has always been one of Springsteen's concert staples, one of his most popular live songs. Surprisingly, though, it was never issued as a single in the United States. In fact, *no* 45s were issued off his second record. CBS did finally have the sense to go back and sticker the album with ''Contains 'Rosalita,' '' but even that didn't come until 1978.

But ''Rosalita'' was released in the Netherlands as a single in 1975, and it is one of the rarest of all Springsteen 45s. The Dutch also released a ''Rosalita'' 12-inch around the same time, and it too is a valued and hard-to-find item. The 45 picture sleeve

This poster was found plastered on a telephone pole in Paris. Unique and unusual posters like this are valuable collector's items. ▶

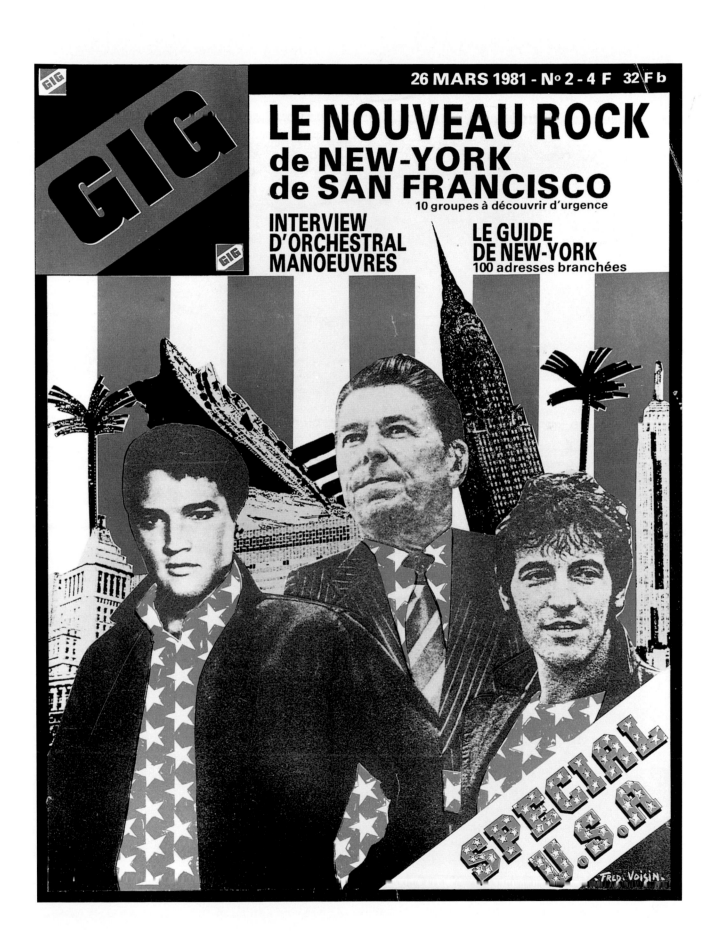

Holland was the only country to release "Rosalita" as a single. The 45 is also the only Bruce Springsteen picture sleeve without a picture on the cover.

extremely collectible. The all-time best Springsteen sheet would have to be that for "Badlands"; it features a sepia print of Bruce driving a car through the desert, which was reported to have also been considered at one point for the cover of *Darkness*.

The later sheets are much more common than the early ones, but are also collected by those who specialize in this field. Even better than sheet music, though, are the songbooks; every Springsteen songbook contains alternative photos, many used only in these books and nowhere else. Songbooks were issued for every album from *Born to Run* onward, and all are worth getting. In 1986, Columbia finally released a complete songbook of all of Springsteen's songs, titled *Bruce Springsteen Complete* (so that we could finally find out the lyrics to the second album) and that too is an essential item for any fan, especially anyone who would want to attempt to play any of Springsteen's music.

· · · · ·

T IS FOR TOUR BOOKS

Like songbooks, tour books are another one of those collectibles that many fans let slip away, and in Springsteen's case it's a shame. Bruce has issued several tour books, and all feature intimate photos and compelling design.

Though there were a few programs issued for individual shows prior to 1980, *The River* was the first tour that had an official tour book. There were two tour books released for *Born in the USA* and one for *Tunnel of Love*; all are recommended.

· · · · ·

U IS FOR UNRELEASED SONGS

Probably the largest single area of Springsteen collecting is the area of tape trading. Tape trading and bootlegging are two entirely different things: in the latter, profit is the only intent; in the former, usually no money ever trades hands and the intent is only to share material with other collectors. Both are illegal, and anyone who decides to collect in either way should think twice and consider the consequences.

That having been said, Springsteen tape trading is second only in popularity to trading Grateful Dead tapes. While Dead Heads concentrate on live shows, Bruce Tramps most value the many unreleased songs that either crop up in concert once in a blue moon, or the rare studio outtakes that somehow see the light of day. Since Springsteen records dozens of songs before weeding through them to make an album, the number and variety of outtakes

features only type — it's rather unusual for that reason alone — while the 12-inch cover features a live shot of Springsteen never before used.

England did make up for lost time in 1980, when CBS released a 12-inch there that contained "Born to Run," "The River," and "Rosalita." It's important because it used the famous portrait of Springsteen in front of a gas station for its cover (the same picture can be found on the cover of the bootleg *E Ticket*). The first pressing of this 12-inch was also one of the many Springsteen bloopers that some collectors like to specialize in: it listed the E Street Band in two places as the "East Street Band" and hence is rarer than the second pressing, which was corrected.

· · · · ·

S IS FOR SHEET MUSIC

Sheet music is a field of collecting that too few collectors even know exist. Musicians have been aware of sheet music for years (it was particularly big back in the fifties, when seemingly every household had its own sing-alongs), but only recently have collectors warmed up to these items.

Like many other sheets, all the Springsteen sheets feature some sort of alternative use of type, photo, or graphic to adapt the 45 art to the rectangular format. A few — including the early sheets for "Tenth Avenue Freeze-out," "Born to Run," and "Prove It All Night" — featuring completely different photos, which make the sheets

The "Dancing in the Dark" video made Bruce Springsteen an MTV staple.

would surprise many people. These tapes are usually traded through want lists and informal circles of fans; only when bootleggers get hold of them does money come into play. Usually by that point the quality of the tapes is so poor that they truly are a ripoff.

. . . .

V IS FOR VIDEO

Like most other rock artists of the modern age, Bruce Springsteen has chosen to make videos. The results have been mixed, but one thing is for sure: all of Springsteen's videos take some sort of creative chance. In January 1989, Springsteen released his first home video, an anthology of all his video clips, including three previously unreleased in the United States and two songs from the *No Nukes* film. With the proliferation of unauthorized videos in recent years, this release comes as no surprise. Below is a list of all of Springsteen's official videos as of March 1989:

"Rosalita" was shot July 8, 1978, in Phoenix, Arizona. Five songs in all were filmed by Columbia this night: "Prove It All Night," "Badlands," "Born to Run," and "The Promised Land," as well

as the title song. They were intended for promotional use, but only "Rosalita" has yet been released. The video was directed by Arnold Levine.

"The River" and "Thunder Road" were shot September 22, 1979, at the MUSE concert held at Madison Square Garden in New York City. The film, as released in 1980, also included an edited version of "Quarter to Three," which does not appear on the video anthology. The *No Nukes* film was directed by Danny Goldberg, Julian Schlossberg, and Anthony Potenza.

"Atlantic City" was Springsteen's first conceptual video and also the first to air on MTV, where it premiered in December 1982. Springsteen does not appear in the clip. The video was directed by Arnold Levine.

"Dancing in the Dark" was shot July 28 and 29, 1984, at the Civic Centre in St. Paul, Minnesota. The first day of shooting involved the conceptual footage of Bruce picking actress Courtney Cox out of the audience, and was shot in front of a crowd of extras. The second-day footage was shot during the show that night, from two consecutive performances of the song. This lip-synced video was

"Open All Night" 45 from Spain with non-LP B-side.

directed by noted filmmaker Brian DePalma.

"Born in the USA" was shot November 4, 1984, at the Sports Arena in Los Angeles, California. This performance clip, intercut with other images, suffers from poor lip-syncing despite its one-time rating as the most popular video of all time on MTV. This is the first of three videos to be directed by John Sayles.

"I'm on Fire" was shot in March 1985, in Los Angeles, and stands as the first purely conceptual video that Bruce appears in. He does not sing or lip-sync the song in the video but does his first real acting, playing a mechanic with an infatuation. Directed by John Sayles.

"Glory Days" was shot May 24, 27, and 28, 1985, in Hoboken, New Jersey, primarily at Maxwell's, a popular local bar. This video is a mix of conceptual footage and a lip-synced performance by the full E Street Band, including Little Steven. Directed by John Sayles.

"My Hometown" was shot in August 1985, at Giants Stadium, East Rutherford, New Jersey as a live-performance clip. Directed by Arthur Rosato.

"War" was shot September 30, 1985, at the Coliseum in Los Angeles, California. This live-performance clip was also directed by Arthur Rosato.

"Fire" was shot October 13, 1986, at the Shoreline Amphitheater in Mountain View, California. This live-performance clip is taken from the Bridge Benefit concert, arranged by Neil Young. This

acoustic version of "Fire" is not available on any other release. Footage was taken directly from the in-house video system, so the director is uncredited.

"Born to Run" was shot at various shows during the 1985 stadium tour. The video was originally intended as an exclusive for the BBC *Glory Days* documentary, but reportedly Springsteen's management liked the results so much they asked to release it in the United States as well.

"Brilliant Disguise" was shot in September 1987, on a soundstage in Sandy Hook, New Jersey. This clip features a live vocal performance by Springsteen, something almost unheard of on nonconcert videos. Shot in black and white and directed by Meiert Avis.

"Tunnel of Love" was shot November 16 and 17, 1987, in Asbury Park, New Jersey. Most of the footage was shot inside Palace Amusements, located right on the boardwalk. This video is a mix of lip-synced footage and black-and-white conceptual footage. An alternate edit of the video that does not have any intercut conceptual footage is known to exist. Directed by Meiert Avis.

"One Step Up" was shot in January 1988, in Wall Township and Asbury Park, New Jersey. Lip-sync footage was most likely shot at the *Tunnel* tour rehearsal space in Wall Township. The conceptual footage was shot at the Wonder Bar in Asbury Park. Directed by Meiert Avis.

"Vigilante Man" and "I Ain't Got No Home" were shot in January and February 1988, also on the soundstage in Wall Township, New Jersey. These live performances in a rehearsal setting are available exclusively on the *Folkways: A Vision Shared* documentary. The director is uncredited.

"Tougher Than the Rest" and "Born to Run" (acoustic) were both shot April 27 and 28, 1988, at the Sports Arena in Los Angeles, California. "Tougher Than the Rest" has black-and-white and color footage of both nights' performances, as well as shots of crowd members outside the show and couples posing in front of a backdrop set up in a room at the arena. Both videos were directed by Meiert Avis.

"Spare Parts" was shot July 9, 1988, at Bramall Lane Stadium in Sheffield, England. This live-performance clip was directed by Carol Dodds.

· · · ·

W IS FOR WEIRD PROMO ITEMS

In the last couple of decades, promo items have become as much a part of the record industry as vinyl. Even artists like Bruce Springsteen — who really needs little promotion to sell records — are targets for record company executives who think of new ways to fill up their T-shirt drawers.

The first Springsteen promo item of note was the *Born to Run* key chain, a nice cast-metal item issued back in 1975. Unfortunately, it was counterfeited and the originals are not easy to distinguish. Tour jackets were also issued for *Born to Run,* and again they were almost instantly counterfeited.

When *The River* came out, CBS issued a couple of different tour jackets and a neat cardboard cutout spelling Springsteen's name. *Born in the USA* saw the big promotional push, though. First there was a T-shirt, then a cap, and finally a blanket issued for "Cover Me." For the *Live* album, CBS issued a denim jacket, a coffee mug, and a laminated listening pass. And finally, for *Tunnel of Love,* CBS again issued two promo jackets, a promo bolo tie, not unlike the one Springsteen is wearing on the cover of the album, and a promo Swiss Army knife.

· · · · ·

X IS FOR "MERRY XMAS BABY"

"Merry Xmas Baby" is just one more of the numerous Springsteen B-sides that really make up the core of Springsteen collecting. This song was released as the B-side to "War" back in 1986. It's also included on the *Very Special Christmas* album.

This song followed the release of "Santa Claus Is Coming to Town," issued first as a tape to radio stations back in 1976, then on a children's album in 1980, and finally as the official B-side to "My Hometown" in 1985.

· · · · ·

Y IS FOR YUGOSLAVIA

Apart from 45s, the second-biggest area of Springsteen record collecting is foreign pressings of albums. Many times these pressings feature alternative graphics (and sometimes even different song order), and some are quite unusual and rare. Yugo-slavia is one of the stranger countries to release Springsteen records; officials there issued both *Nebraska* and *The River.* East Germany issued *Born in the USA* (the only communist country to officially release any Springsteen record). Greece issued *Born to Run* and *Darkness*; both feature badly reproduced cover graphics. Taiwan has to top all other countries; all pressings there are just a thin line away from pirate pressings. For *The River,* the Taiwanese chose to issue the two-record set with only one of the two records included, though the jacket lists all the lyrics to all the songs from both discs. The Filipino pressing of *The River* says "Include [sic] hit 'Hungry Heart.'"

The River seems to be the album that most countries had problems with; the first pressings from Brazil, the Netherlands, and the United Kingdom listed "Held Up Without a Gun" as being on the record; it wasn't.

· · · · ·

Z IS FOR ZERO

One of the trickiest Springsteen trivia questions is one that might confuse even Joel Whitburn: How many Bruce Springsteen singles have gone to Number 1? The answer is zero. Although Springsteen has had almost a dozen Top 10 hits, and sold more than 17 million copies of *Born in the USA,* he has yet to have one of his own records go to Number 1 (several songs he *wrote* have that distinction, but never his versions).

This may be one of the reasons Springsteen is so collected: record collectors always seem to seek out the underdogs, the cult figures, the artists with critical acclaim but without commercial success. Springsteen developed into a record-collecting phenomenon long before he was a moneymaking machine, which is why his hardcore fans take his music so seriously and collect his records with such fervor.

—Charles R. Cross

THE ULTIMATE COLLECTIBLE

....

Buying Bruce's '57 Chevy

Somewhere down Atlantic City way, it still cruises the haunted streets of a former glory town, sleek and shiny, yellow with red flames painted on its sides. It is *the car*: Bruce Springsteen's 1957 Chevy convertible. It was the inspiration for much of his early material and that being the case, it stands as some great mythic icon in the romantic dreams of Springsteen fans.

But it is not a dream; it exists, and Brian Rogers should know. For more than a decade Rogers cruised up and down the Jersey Turnpike in the very same car that was the machine behind "Jungleland," "Born to Run," "Racing in the Streets" and a host of others. He bought it in 1976 from Bruce himself for a mere $2,000, and though he was forced to sell it recently for financial reasons, for years he could live out the reality of being the Magic Rat.

"I bought it from him in 1976, just after *Born to Run* came out," Rogers remembers now, speaking from his home in New Jersey. "After that album came out, a lot of people started hassling him and he just had to sell it. People would follow him around and pull him over and stuff.

"Mostly they just wanted to meet him, but it came to a head when one girl put a pie on the seat. She just wanted to give it to him, but Bruce didn't see it and he jumped into the car and sat on it."

Soon after getting pie on his rear, Bruce sold the car to Rogers, who knew the band from growing up near Freehold and from trading car talk with Garry Tallent, who also at that time had a '57 Chevy. Rogers was already a big Springsteen fan, but he bought the car because it was a Chevy in great condition, not because it was Bruce's car.

"I'm a Chevy collector," he said. "I've had '57 Chevys as long as I can remember. And this one was in great shape. It had a 283, three carbs — it was a four-speed with a Hurst on the floor."

Bruce Springsteen's 1957 Chevy.

Drivin' in my car: Bruce Springsteen and Patti Scialfa, Rumson, N.J., 1988.

Though Rogers bought the car for its collectibility, he soon found that notoriety came with it. The car was featured in *Newsweek, Time* and *Crawdaddy,* and was even on a t-shirt. And though Bruce no longer owned it, Rogers found people still flagging the car down.

"A lot of people used to chase me down and stop me, thinking I was him. I used to have a beard and I look a little like him and people would insist I was him."

Rogers says some of his most magical experiences in the car came when he first heard songs like "Born to Run" over the radio. "The opening lines of 'Jungleland' were great to hear — and when 'Thunder Road' came on, I couldn't help but speed."

He was forced to sell the car recently because of financial woes. Strangely enough, the buyer — who paid $10,000 — was a Chevy collector who didn't even know who Bruce Springsteen was and couldn't have cared less. Rogers kept the original registration, with Bruce's signature, and a baseball cap he found in the car when he first bought it.

About three years ago, Rogers advertised the car in *Goldmine,* thinking he would sell it then. The highest offer he got at that time was $15,000 from a Springsteen collector in Texas, though hundreds of people inquired about the car. "Many people were very honest about it," he says, "and they said they couldn't afford it but they'd love to have a picture of it. I sent out about 200 pictures."

Rogers says he's known Bruce for years from growing up in the same town and being involved in bands together. He said that after selling the car Bruce never asked to take a spin in it again, but every time he saw Rogers he'd say, "Take care of my baby."

After Rogers sold the car, he found that his financial needs weren't so great and he says he'd like to buy the car back if he could find the owner again. "It pains me to talk about it," he said emotionally. "I swear that if I could, I'd buy it back this very minute. I love that car."

—*Charles R. Cross*

SPARE PARTS

Springsteen's Studio Sessions, 1966-88

Forced to Confess: New York, N.Y., March 1980. A River *cover outtake.*

SPARE PARTS

Springsteen's Studio Sessions, 1966-88

What follows is an attempt to document Springsteen's work in the studio from the beginning of his career to the present. No thorough or authorized documentation of Springsteen's recording sessions has been made public, so what's here has been pieced together from dozens of sources. We've done everything we can to ensure its accuracy and to correct errors perpetuated elsewhere.

Springsteen is one of the most prolific songwriters of the modern era. He's written over 1,000 songs; the recorded work on his nine Columbia albums is just the tip of the iceberg. Many of his songs have been recorded by other artists — "Because the Night" by Patti Smith, "The Fever" by Southside Johnny, and "Fire" by Robert Gordon — and there are hundreds of cover versions of Springsteen's songs, by artists as different as Johnny Cash and Air Supply. Looking back at the charts over the last decade, there has rarely been a time when one of Bruce Springsteen's songs wasn't in the Top 100, either in his own performance or a cover version. Until the release of *Born in the USA* it was said that Springsteen made more money from songwriting royalties than from sales of his records.

During the last decade, Springsteen has spent more time in the studio than almost any other artist. Several of his records have ended up taking years to record (the studio bill for *Darkness on the Edge of Town* was rumored to be over $250,000 in 1978 dollars). For all records since *Born to Run*, Springsteen and his producers have had to mull over recorded material that sometimes included three to four times the amount of music possible to release on a single record. And even when Springsteen put together a double record, *The River*, he didn't seem to find much economy of scale — that record alone had as many as 60 different songs

considered at various points for inclusion. For *Born in the USA*, which had 12 songs, Max Weinberg tells us the band recorded 80 tracks.

We have attempted to document both the songs released on Springsteen's albums and singles and the songs recorded but never released. There are two different kinds of unreleased songs, which we divide into two basic categories: outtakes and alternative tracks. Outtakes are completely recorded songs that were considered for release but did not make it onto a record. A good example of an outtake would be the song "Don't Look Back," which was written and considered for *Darkness* and then dropped off the record at the last minute, so late that early promotional material lists the song as being on the album. Alternative tracks include variant recordings, such as the rockabilly version of "You Can Look" that was recorded during *The River* sessions (it's essentially the same song as the released version but done with a different beat and nuance), as well as reference tracks or alternative mixes, which are songs that have already been recorded but that are remixed in the studio to create a different effect. For each record, there would be literally thousands of these different mixes. We've tried to indicate here only those that are dramatically different from the released version.

We also include under alternate tracks the many demos recorded both in the studio and with portable recording equipment. Demos are rough versions of a song, intended to demonstrate the song's lyrics, melody, and structure to other musicians. Some of these are hard to differentiate from studio outtakes.

When unclear about the recording history of a track, we've left it open rather than assign it to a session we're unsure of. We've left material out of these listings entirely, rather than list material we were uncertain about.

We are certain, however, that even these extensive listings represent only a small fraction of what has been recorded by Bruce Springsteen and the E Street Band. Particularly for the last two records, recording-session information is still rather sketchy, though with time we assume more of this data will come out. Sessions are listed roughly in chronological order. Where sessions were intended for a particular album, we list them under the name of that album. Whenever possible, we say where the sessions took place and the exact dates of the recordings. Under album sessions we list first the songs released from the session on albums, singles, and CDs; then we list outtakes and alternate tracks, with comments describing whatever we know about the songs or how they differ from released versions. Under each of these groupings, songs are listed alphabetically by title.

This listing is meant to provide insight and information about Springsteen's recording processes. Most of the material listed here is not available even through illegal bootleg channels. Please do not write us asking how you can obtain these songs. —*Charles R. Cross*

. . . . .

THE CASTILE SESSIONS
May 18, 1966: Bricktown, N.J., Mr. Music Inc.

- Baby I
- That's What You Get

This session produced acetate pressings of a 45, three of which are still known to exist. Both songs were co-written by Springsteen and bandmate George Theiss during the car ride to the studio.

THE STEEL MILL SESSIONS
February 22, 1970: San Francisco, Calif., Fillmore Recording Studios

- Goin' Back to Georgia
- He's Guilty (Send That Boy to Jail)
- The Train Song

All three songs are Springsteen originals, chosen from among the more than 50 Springsteen compositions performed by Steel Mill during its two-year existence (1970-71). Springsteen plays lead guitar and sings. The sound of all three is bluesy and hard rocking, reminiscent of the British sound of the late sixties and early seventies.

THE HAMMOND DEMOS
May 3, 1972: New York, N.Y., CBS Studios

- The Angel
- Arabian Night
- Cowboys of the Sea
- Does This Bus Stop at 82nd Street
- Growin' Up
- If I Was the Priest
- It's Hard to Be a Saint in the City
- Jazz Musician
  Contains some lyrics that would later appear in "Tenth Avenue Freeze-out."
- Mary Queen of Arkansas
- Southern Son
- Street Queen

- Two Hearts in True Waltz Time
  Considered for the third album.

This is Springsteen's solo audition tape, recorded for John Hammond. Springsteen plays acoustic guitar throughout the recording and piano on "Jazz Musician" and "If I Was the Priest."

LONDON PUBLISHING DEMOS
June or July 1972: New York, N.Y., Media Sound

- Arabian Night
- Circus Song
  This went by many titles and underwent many changes before it finally appeared on the second album; other titles include "Circus Town" and "Wild Billy's Circus Story."
- Cowboys of the Sea
- Henry Boy
- If I Was the Priest
- Marie
- No Need
- She's Leaving
- Song for the Orphans
  Included on an early song list for the third album.
- Southern Son
- Street Queen
- Tokyo
  Also referred to by fans as "Born to Win" and "And the Band Played."
- Vibes Man
  Would later evolve into "New York City Serenade."
- Visitation at Fort Horn
  This song also underwent many title changes, at various times referred to as "Vision at Fort Horn" and "The Visitation" and mistakenly called "American Tune"; it was in early consideration for the second and third albums and was included on early acetates of the first album but was removed in favor of "It's Hard to Be a Saint in the City."
- The Word
  Also known as "I Never Heard the Word on You" and incorrectly as "The Song."

The above tape of Bruce's solo acoustic originals was put together to sell his songs to other artists. In 1972 it surfaced in London in the hands of Intersong Music. Bruce cut demos of more than 60 songs in 1972, but only a handful have ever surfaced.

THE GREETINGS SESSIONS
June or July 1972: Blauvelt, N.Y., 914 Sound Studios

Released Tracks
- The Angel
- Blinded by the Light
  Also at one time called "Madman's Bummers."
- Does This Bus Stop at 82nd Street
- For You
- Growin' Up
- It's Hard to Be a Saint in the City
- Lost in the Flood
- Mary Queen of Arkansas
- Spirit in the Night

According to Vini Lopez, these sessions lasted only about a week, with the basic tracks laid down in a single day, probably in June or July of 1972. The band most likely recorded other songs during these sessions, but no further information is available.

1973 SESSIONS
May 1973: Richmond, Va., WGOE Studios

- The Fever
  Another Bruce original written as a publishing demo and eventually

Rehearsal, Bryn Mawr, Pa., February 25, 1974. ▶

recorded by Southside Johnny. Though a frequent concert favorite, the song was never considered for any album, but was included on a six-song acetate sent to Intersong in 1973. Danny Federici plays piano on this track. Two other songs (possibly "Bishop Dance" and "Thundercrack") were also cut during this one-day session.

THE WILD, THE INNOCENT SESSIONS

July and August 1973: Blauvelt, N.Y., 914 Sound Studios

Released Tracks
- The E Street Shuffle
- Fourth of July, Asbury Park (Sandy)
  This song grew out of many earlier songs, including "Casper" and "Glory Road."
- Incident on 57th Street
- Kitty's Back
- New York City Serenade
  Grew out of "New York Song" and became a serenade when David Sancious joined the E Street Band.
- Rosalita (Come Out Tonight)
- Wild Billy's Circus Story
  Grew out of the earlier "Circus Story" and "Circus Town."

Alternate Tracks
- Fourth of July, Asbury Park (Sandy)
  Instrumental mix.
- Kitty's Back
  Different take, with slight lyrical and arrangement alterations.
- Rosalita (Come Out Tonight)
  Instrumental mix.
- Zero and Blind Terry
  Instrumental mix.

Outtakes
- Santa Ana
  Also called "Contessa." Nice, mid-tempo love song, contains some lyrics that would later become "She's the One." Both "Santa Ana" and "Seaside Bar Song" were intended for inclusion on the second album, but the songs were vetoed by Columbia.
- Seaside Bar Song
  Also sent out as a publishing demo. Played live in 1973.
- Zero and Blind Terry
  This romantic opus was also considered for the third album.

These three songs, along with "The Fever," "Bishop Dance" and "Thundercrack" were pressed as an acetate in the U.S. for Intersong, an English music publisher. An article which appeared in the October 4, 1975 issue of *Music Week* (the European equivalent of *Billboard*) interviews Adrian Rudge, the man in charge of Springsteen for Intersong. He says that he first received tapes from Springsteen in December of 1972 (likely "The Publishing Demos") and set up a deal in January to handle Springsteen's songs in the U.K. and Europe. At that time in 1975, Rudge told *Music Week* that he had 43 Springsteen songs available for other artists to cover.

OTHER SONGS 1972 TO 1974

The songs listed below are titles that show up on general lists of songs catalogued during this period. Some may have been recorded, and some may be variant titles of other songs. They are part of the large body of tunes Springsteen wrote around the time of his signing with Columbia.
- Angel Baby
  Included on early song lists for the third album.
- Angel's Blues
  Considered for the second album.
- Architect Angel
  Also called "Saga of the Architect's Angel"; considered for both the second and third albums.
- Balboa vs. the Earthslayer
  Antiwar song, circa 1972, that Mike Appel wanted Bruce to sing before the Super Bowl. The Super Bowl declined the offer.

- Ballad of the Self-Loading Pistol
- Bishop Dance
  Played live frequently in 1972 and 1973. A live version was performed on a "King Biscuit Flower Hour" broadcast. Probably recorded in 1973.
- Calvin Jones and the Thirteenth Apostle
  Written around the time of the second album.
- Casper
  Probably written between the first and second albums; included some lyrics that would later be part of "Sandy."
- Cherokee Queen
  Evolved out of a Steel Mill song commonly called "Daddy Sing Me a Cradle Song."
- Full of Love
  Some of the lyrics are similar to those that later appeared in "Pink Cadillac."
- Funky Broadway
- Glory Road
  Very early version of lyrics that later become "Thunder Road."
- Harlem
- Here She Comes
  Also called "Here She Comes Walking" on some lists, it was considered for the third album. A version of the song resurfaced in 1980 as the introduction to "I Wanna Marry You" on *The River* tour.
- How the West Was Won
- Janey Needs a Shooter
  Considered for the third album and probably written in 1974. Never recorded for any album, though there is one known version from a rehearsal at Bruce's house with the band in late 1977 or early 1978. Released by Warren Zevon in a slightly rewritten version.
- Jennifer
  Possibly recorded for the first album.
- Keep on Goin'
- Lady and the Doctor
  Probably evolved from the Steel Mill Song "I Am the Doctor."
- Lonesome Train
- Over the Hills of St. Croix
  Evolved into "Zero and Blind Terry."
- Secret to the Blues
  Another revised version of a Bruce Springsteen Band song, then called "The Band's Just Boppin' the Blues." Played live in 1973.
- Shanghai
- Small Town
  From a titles list circa 1973.
- Still There
  Lyrically similar to songs from the *Darkness* era though likely written in 1974. Hand-written lyric sheet surfaced in 1988.
- Texas
- Thundercrack
  Considered for both the second and third albums. Often performed live in 1973 and 1974.
- War and Roses
  Considered as a title track for the third album.
- Wild Billy's Lullaby
  Included on a title sheet for the third album. It can only be speculated that this song continued the same story-line as "Wild Billy's Circus Story."
- You Mean So Much to Me
  Played live in 1973 and 1974, before Bruce gave it to Miami Steve for Southside's first album. Originally written for the Bruce Springsteen Band.

By 1974, Springsteen had a giant backlog of songs that could have been considered for any of the first three records. Appel's influence on Springsteen's writing in the early years was considerable as he tried to move Springsteen into an almost rock-opera mode of songwriting.

Philadelphia, Pa., July 16, 1981. ►

1974 SESSIONS
August 1974: Blauvelt, N.Y., 914 Sound Studios

Released Track
- Born to Run

  The first track recorded for Bruce's as-yet-untitled third album, with David Sancious on piano and Ernest "Boom" Carter on drums.

Alternative Track
- Born to Run

  At least four different mixes are known to exist that include strings, a female chorus, and one mix with a double-tracked lead vocal.

The work for the third record began to show the influence of Jon Landau, who first came into the project as a sort of editor for the songs. With Landau's influence the record, and perhaps Springsteen's career, changed forever.

When Springsteen first planned the third record he wrote a list of songs titled "New Album #3" which included "Angel Baby," "Architect Angel," "Thundercrack," "Vision at Fort Horn," "Two Hearts," "Here She Comes," "Glory Road," "Janey Needs a Shooter," and "Jungleland." Needless to say, it would have been a dramatically different record from the *Born to Run* that was eventually released.

After Springsteen wrote "Born to Run," the record changed in concept, format and style. Based on the idea that Bruce Springsteen might actually be able to write a hit record, CBS warmed up to the project and started the wheels in motion for the commercial push that started in early 1975. With less worry about the budget, Springsteen began to write in the studio and developed his habit of making every recording session stretch on until everyone involved reached the utter extremes of exhaustion. This style of recording meant cutting most songs live in the studio, then trying them as many different ways as possible. It was not uncommon for Springsteen to scrap an entire song but keep one line and add that to another new song. His style during this period was constantly to recycle and reassemble his material. While the resulting albums sound extremely finished and complete — both *Born to Run* and *Darkness* sound so mature and well thought out that it's easy to imagine they were recorded in one straight session — the technique was far from simple and involved literally years of studio work.

October 1974: Blauvelt, N.Y., 914 Sound Studios

Outtake
- A Love So Fine

  Recorded as an instrumental with new band members Max Weinberg on drums and Roy Bittan on piano. Considered for the third album.

THE BORN TO RUN SESSIONS
March–July 1975: New York, N.Y., Record Plant

Released Tracks
- Backstreets
- Jungleland
- Meeting Across the River
- Night
- She's the One
- Tenth Avenue Freeze-out
- Thunder Road

Alternative Tracks
- Backstreets

  Two rough takes exist with unfinished lyrics, one using the chorus "falling on the Backstreets." At least one alternative track was mixed with strings added.
- Jungleland

  One mix adds strings throughout the song. Another short rehearsal take of the ending adds a new piano part and vocals from Suki Lahav. This snatch of piano will be used on the *Born to Run* tour as an introduction to "Lost in the Flood."
- Meeting Across the River

  Multiple takes and mixes with varying amounts of horn.
- Night

  Rough take with double-tracked lead vocals.
- She's the One

  Early take included lyrics that later became "Backstreets."
- Thunder Road

  One complete take of Bruce playing the song in a slow acoustic arrangement. Another take, much like the album, had "Chrissie's" dress waving. One other alternate starts the song with more saxophone.

Outtakes
- Linda Let Me Be the One

  Probably the last song ruled out for inclusion on the album, it is a pleading, mid-tempo love song.
- Lonely in the Park
- Walking in the Street

  One very rough take is known to exist. The style is similar to that of "Thunder Road," but the lyrics are not finished.

Many of the songs listed in the "Other Songs 1973-74" section may also have been recorded for *Born to Run*. The third album had been in planning for over two years, and the idea for what should be included changed wildly over time. One list from 1974 includes nine potential titles for the third album: "American Summer," "War and Roses," "Up From the Street," "Sometimes at Night," "From the Churches to the Jails," "The Legend of Zero and Blind Terry," "The Hungry and the Hunted," "Between Flesh and Fantasy," and "Jungleland."

The original concept of the album was for it to represent one full day in the character's life, starting with an alarm clock going off. That version of the LP had its starting and ending with "Thunder Road," opening with an acoustic version and closing with the full band take. That concept of the LP was eventually scrapped, but the idea that it represents an entire day remains subtly; the record begins with the sound of the morning in "Thunder Road," and ends late in the evening in "Jungleland."

THE DARKNESS SESSIONS
June-November 1977: New York, N.Y., Atlantic Studios
November 1977-April 1978: New York, N.Y., Record Plant

Released Tracks
- Adam Raised a Cain
- Badlands

  Take 23.
- Candy's Room

  Take 42.
- Darkness on the Edge of Town

  Take 28.
- Factory

  Take 28.
- The Promised Land

  Take 5.
- Prove It All Night

  Take 49.
- Racing in the Street

  Take 46.
- Something in the Night

  Take 42.
- Streets of Fire

  Take 28.

Takes noted above are the ones included on the album. Obviously, considering that the version of "Racing in the Street" used was the 46th take, a tremendous number of alternate takes exist. For the alternate tracks below, we've noted the most significant variations.

Alternate Tracks
- Badlands

  One alternate mix with added guitar, one rough take with many unfinished lyrics. An early instrumental take had different guitar and saxophone parts.

Rehearsal with David Sancious, Bryn Mawr, Pa., February 25, 1974.

- Candy's Room
  Two different outtakes were combined to make the finished track. The music is from "The Fast Song," the words from "Candy's Boy," both recorded in late 1977 or early 1978.
- Darkness on the Edge of Town
  An early rough take was recorded at Atlantic Studios in the summer of 1977. Another take includes an added rockabilly-style guitar part.
- Factory
  One alternate take includes violin.
- The Promised Land
  Same take as the released track, but the guitar solo is mixed out. This mix appeared on some of the first acetates of the LP.
- Racing in the Street
  Two rehearsal takes: one with just Bruce's piano and vocals, and another full-band take that is close to the released track, but with many lyric changes.
- Something in the Night
  A rough take recorded at Atlantic Studios in the summer of 1977.
- Streets of Fire
  One rough take, similar to the released track, but with lyric differences in the final verse.

Outtakes
- The Ballad
  Often misidentified as "Castaway" or "La, La, La," instead of the actual working title. A slow, unfinished, sleepy tune.
- Because the Night
  Two very rough takes are known, at least one recorded at Atlantic Studios. Bruce never finished the song before he gave it to Patti Smith, but did finish it for performance on the 1978 tour.
- Bo Diddley Rocker
  Working title for an obviously Diddley-inspired song often called "Goin' Back."

- Candy's Boy
  A slow, organ-led song, the lyrics to which change slightly and become "Candy's Room."
- Don't Look Back
  Replaced on the album by the title track at the last moment. The song is listed on early promotional material describing the impending release of the record. The take that was to be used was Take 3, recorded March 1, 1978. One rough take includes different guitar parts, and an instrumental reference mix is also known.
- Don't Say No
  A rough rehearsal of a fast-paced tune, with unfinished lyrics.
- Drive All Night
  Much longer than the version that later appeared on *The River.* Another short rehearsal has Bruce humming a proposed string section over the finished track.
- English Sons
  Working title for a fast-paced song with driving vocals and guitars from Bruce. Often misidentified as "Endless Night."
- The Fast Song
  Two rough takes of the music that will eventually be used in "Candy's Room." Recorded in late June 1977.
- Fire
  A song Bruce wrote for Elvis Presley. (He went so far as to send a demo to Graceland.) Springsteen played the song on the *Darkness* tour.
- Frankie
  Played live for a short time on the 1976 tour, this song was also recorded for the *Born in the USA* LP.
- Get That Feeling
  Mid-tempo, Phil Spector-ish sounding tune.
- Hearts of Stone
  This track recorded by the E Street Band is given to Southside

Johnny. Vocals and solos are changed, but the basic track is left intact so that the released version is essentially Southside Johnny and the E Street Band.

- The Iceman
  Some of these lyrics will later be included in "Badlands." Recorded in late 1977.
- I Wanna Be with You
  One of the first tracks recorded for *Darkness* at Atlantic Studios.
- Let's Go Tonight
  A slow song that will inspire both "Factory" and "Johnny Bye Bye."
- Outside Lookin' In
  Another of the early songs recorded at Atlantic Studios.
- Preacher's Daughter
  Recorded in late 1977, this song is similar in tempo to the '78-tour live performance of "She's the One," which also included a few lyrics apparently lifted from "Preacher's Daughter."
- The Promise
  Originally titled "The Loser." Two versions exist: one rough rehearsal and one finished track. Seriously considered for the LP and perhaps for *The River* as well. Springsteen has said that this song is not about his legal battles around this time, as has been widely reported. Introducing this song in 1978, he said, "I wrote this soon after I wrote 'Born to Run,'" which would put the time frame well before the lawsuit. The song was copywritten in 1979.
- Rendezvous
  Another of the first tracks cut at Atlantic Studios. Played live (1976-81) and later recorded by Greg Kihn.
- Say Sons
  Working title for this rollicking song often incorrectly identified as "Down By the River." Ends with Bruce commenting, "This song should be one verse."
- Sherry Darling
  Two rough rehearsal takes. Later re-recorded for *The River*.
- Spanish Eyes
  Two rough takes of this unfinished slow tune.
- Talk to Me
  Recorded by Bruce and the E Street Band. Bruce then gives the song to Southside Johnny who re-recorded it with the Jukes.
- Taxi Cab
  A melancholy, unfinished song about driving through a city at night. Some lyrics appeared later in "Ramrod."
- The Way
  Six different reference mixes of this song exist, plus one finished take. The song was seriously considered for the record, and is similar in tempo and feel to "Factory." A few lyrics from this dirge-like, brooding love song appeared later in "The River."

The *Darkness* recording sessions represent Springsteen's most prolific period. These were the first sessions where Bruce came into the studio and worked out his songs, as well as writing new songs in the studio. Bits and pieces of many of the unreleased songs from these sessions were worked into other songs that appear on *Darkness* and *The River*. Alternate titles for the album itself included *Badlands* and *Racing in the Street*. Several different album cover designs were considered.

1978 BAND REHEARSALS
October 1978: Location unknown

- The Ties That Bind
  This song is worked out many times during this loose rehearsal, held during a one-month break on the *Darkness* tour. After an arrangement was decided upon, this song was played live at the first show following the break, November 1, 1978, Princeton, N.J.
- Tonight
  This song was worked out for five or six takes, but never really went anywhere. The song does not appear again at any time in the future.
- I'm Gonna Treat You Right

This song is also called "Wild Kisses." This is another song that was rehearsed but never played again.

1979 HOME DEMOS
1979: Holmdel, N.J.

- Chevrolet Deluxe
  Worked out for five or six takes. This is a sad epic not unlike "The River."
- Everybody's Looking for Somebody
- I Don't Know
- I Wanna Start a New Life
  Similar story to "Seeds," about packing up a life and moving away.
- Held Up Without a Gun
- Looking Out for Number One
  Strange lyrics about a "Mr. Outside."
- White Town
  There is a quirky reggae feel about this tune, which includes some lyrics that will appear in "Jackson Cage."
- You Gotta Fight
- You Can Look (But You Better Not Touch)

These demos show Bruce at home writing songs on acoustic guitar with a portable tape recorder. All the songs are in bits and pieces, not finished. "Chevrolet Deluxe" is being written over the course of multiple takes.

THE RIVER SESSIONS
April 1979-August 1980: New York, N.Y., The Power Station

Released Tracks

- Be True
  B-side of the "Fade Away" single.
- Cadillac Ranch
- Crush on You
- Drive All Night
  Although it cannot be confirmed, the primary recording of this version probably took place during the *Darkness* sessions, but it was likely remixed and finished during *The River* sessions.
- Fade Away
- Held Up Without a Gun
  B-side of the "Hungry Heart" single.
- Hungry Heart
- I'm a Rocker
- Independence Day
- I Wanna Marry You
- Jackson Cage
- Out in the Street
- Point Blank
- The Price You Pay
- Ramrod
- The River
- Sherry Darling
- Stolen Car
- The Ties That Bind
- Two Hearts
- Wreck on the Highway
- You Can Look (But You Better Not Touch)

Alternative Takes

- Be True
  Seven rehearsal takes include double-track vocal and a later sax solo.
- Cadillac Ranch
  Rehearsal take with slight lyric changes and more guitar in the ending. One mix added screeching tire sounds to the background and fade-out. Another starts with a siren.

- Crush on You
  Two rehearsal takes with slight lyric changes and different sax parts.
- Fade Away
  Multiple rough mixes with alternate backing vocals are known.
- Held Up Without a Gun
  Longer, unedited version of the released track.
- Hungry Heart
  An instrumental rough mix.
- I Wanna Marry You
  Three different (numbers 8, 9 and 22) rough mixes alter organ and rhythm guitar.
- Out in the Street
  Over nine different rehearsal takes, all very similar to the released track. There are changes in drums, organ, and vocals.
- Point Blank
  Four rehearsal takes, all featuring radically different music with alternate lyrics and a screaming guitar solo. This is an excellent example of the kind of experimenting that Bruce does in the studio.
- Ramrod
  Three or four rough mixes, one with double-tracked vocals.
- Stolen Car
  Often called "Son You May Kiss the Bride." Begins with just piano in an alternative arrangement with many lyric changes. Recorded in 1979.
- Two Hearts
  Alternate mix without back-up vocals from Miami Steve.
- You Can Look (But You Better Not Touch)
  Rockabilly version of the song.

Outtakes
- Cindy
  Mid-tempo love song that was seriously considered for the album.
- From Small Things (Big Things One Day Come)
  A full-band rockabilly number given to Dave Edmunds.
- I Wanna Be Where the Bands Are
  A searing, hook-laden pop song with a great guitar solo, back-up vocals and hand-clapping.
- Loose Ends
  One rehearsal take, "mix number one," was recorded in 1979. One finished take was seriously considered for the album. Mentioned by some members of the E Street Band as the strongest vocal track ever done by Springsteen in a recording session.
- Mary Lou
  This rehearsal take is an early version of what became "Be True." Recorded in 1979.
- Restless Nights
  Another finished take of a driving rocker with nice organ work.
- Rickie (Wants a Man of Her Own)
  Seriously considered for the record, and rumored to have been written for Rickie Lee Jones, it is not unlike "Sherry Darling" in style.
- Roulette
  Three takes including one that will be released on the B-side of the "One Step Up" single in 1988. This track was recorded in 1979, the first track in The River sessions, but was quickly dismissed until its surprise revival in 1988. One other rough take exists with a double-track vocal. One of Springsteen's hottest guitar solos.
- Slow Fade
  An early title for "Fade Away" with different lyrics.
- Take 'Em as They Come
  Three very polished rehearsal takes, one with an alternate verse, the other three with fades and finished endings.
- White Lies
  Often incorrectly identified as "Don't Do It to Me" or simply an alternate "Be True." The lyrics to this "Fiddler on the Roof"-sounding tune will evolve into "Be True."

The long River sessions can be divided into two sections. In 1979, Bruce finished a single record that was called "The Ties That Bind," a ten-song LP that included the outtakes of "Stolen Car," "Loose

Ends," "Cindy," "The Ties That Bind," "The Price You Pay," "Independence Day," and four other songs. A cover photo was shot and design work was begun. The record was set to roll in late 1979, but Bruce, for unknown reasons, was unhappy. He continued to write songs and the band continued to record. In the summer of 1980 it was decided that the new LP would be a two-record set.

THE NEBRASKA SESSIONS
January 3, 1982: Holmdel, N.J.

Released Tracks
- Atlantic City
- The Big Payback
  B-side of the "Open All Night" single in Europe.
- Highway Patrolman
- Johnny 99
- Mansion on the Hill
- My Father's House
- Nebraska
- Open All Night
- Reason to Believe
- State Trooper
- Used Cars

It's unclear whether "The Big Payback" was recorded on January 3, along with the rest of Nebraska or if it is from a later date. It must have been written around this time, as the sound is very similar to Nebraska.

Alternative Track
- My Father's House
  An alternative track with 32 extra seconds of synthesizer coda appeared on the first CD mix of this album as pressed in Japan. The CD was recalled as soon as information about the alternate track was reported in the United States.

Though Nebraska was Bruce Springsteen's simplest album to record — he recorded it at home with a Teac Tascam tape deck — its history is the most mysterious. Only Springsteen and Mike Batlin were at the sessions, if you can call them that, and neither has been forthright about what was recorded that day in early January. Springsteen clearly set out to record demos for a new rock record, and eventually, at a later recording date as yet unspecified, these songs were cut in full-band arrangements. But the more those involved listened to the full-band version, the more convinced everyone became that Springsteen's original demos were truer to the material. Sometime in late spring of 1982, Springsteen and Jon Landau pitched CBS with the idea of a solo acoustic album, and CBS, reportedly less than enthusiastic about the idea, allowed Bruce his creative masterpiece, knowing that his next record would be a rocker. Nebraska was rushed into production and released that September. Other titles that were considered for the LP include "Open All Night" and "January 3, 1982."

THE BORN IN THE USA SESSIONS
Early 1982 to April 1984: New York, N.Y., The Power Station and the Hit Factory

Released Tracks
- Bobby Jean
- Born in the USA
  Also recorded during the Nebraska sessions acoustically.
- Cover Me
- Dancing in the Dark
  The last track written for the record, reportedly after Landau's request for a hit single.
- Darlington County
- Downbound Train
  Also recorded acoustically during the Nebraska sessions.
- Glory Days
- I'm Goin' Down
- I'm on Fire

Seattle, Wash., October 24, 1980. ▶

- Janey, Don't You Lose Heart
  B-side of the "I'm Goin' Down" single.
- Johnny Bye Bye
  B-side of the "I'm on Fire" single. Originally written and performed on the '81 tour and called "Bye Bye Johnny." Co-credited to Chuck Berry, whose own song provided the title and first two lines. Grew out of the *Darkness* outtake "Let's Go Tonight."
- My Hometown
- No Surrender
  Early title was "Brothers Under the Bridges."
- Pink Cadillac
  B-side of the "Dancing in the Dark" single.
- Shut Out the Light
  B-side of the "Born in the USA" single.
- Stand on It
  B-side of the "Glory Days" single.
- Working on the Highway

Alternative Tracks
- Bobby Jean
  Unedited album version includes strange keyboard and the full count-in.
- Born in the USA
  First take is almost seven minutes long, with a long instrumental ending. Second take, used on the album, is edited down by about a minute. Bruce's "Oh my God no" lyric is mixed out.
- Cover Me
  Two different rehearsal takes, one without a lead guitar part, another with an extended guitar part that fades out.
- Dancing in the Dark
  Unedited take includes longer sax solo, and instead of fading out, a synthesizer coda finishes the song. Another rehearsal take includes Patti Scialfa on vocals.
- Darlington County
  Rehearsal takes include slight lyric changes and a different beginning and ending.
- Downbound Train
  Reference mix with more guitar and vocals in the middle section.
- Glory Days
  Alternate takes include an extra verse about Springsteen's father, which is edited from the finished track. Rehearsal takes have a full beginning and ending.
- I'm Goin' Down
  Rehearsal takes have full beginnings and endings.
- I'm on Fire
  Rehearsal takes are longer than the released track, but otherwise nearly identical to it.
- Janey Don't You Lose Heart
  Miami Steve on background vocals. The song ends with a 30-second synthesizer coda, much like that on the alternate "My Father's House."
- Pink Cadillac
  Unedited take is longer than the official track. Seriously considered for the LP, probably the last song left off the record.
- Working on the Highway
  Rehearsal take with complete ending and slight lyric changes.

Outtakes
- Child Bride
  Title from lyric sheet. Probably dates from early 1982.
- Cynthia
  Sweet, playful love song with double-tracked vocals.
- (Drop on Down and) Cover Me
  Driving and radical version of what would become "Cover Me." Same basic lyrics, but completely different music.
- Follow that Dream
  Loosely based on the Presley song, but with new lyrics and arrangement. Bruce may be playing all instruments.
- Frankie
  Two rehearsal takes, one with a sax solo, the other with harmonica. The song is slightly rewritten from the 1976 live version.

- Murder, Inc.
  Four different rehearsal takes with differing sax solos, guitar solos, and beginnings. The mix is very finished and may have been part of an album concept that was scrapped in 1983.
- My Love Won't Let You Down
  Relentless and driving rocker, with strong guitar. Two rehearsal takes with different beginnings.
- None But the Brave
  Sax-led rehearsal take with a ripping guitar solo.
- Protection
  Given to Donna Summer. Bruce plays guitar on her released version.
- Sugarland
  Song about the plight of a farmer who burns his fields out of frustration. Bruce may be playing all the instruments on this track. Performed only twice on the *Born in the USA* tour.
- This Hard Land
  This up-tempo, *Nebraska*-style song got serious consideration for the album. In 1984 Max Weinberg called it his favorite song the band had ever cut.

Much like the period of 1972 to 1974, early in Bruce's career, the period from 1982 to 1984 is blurry as to when songs were written. Since so little is known about the full-band recordings of the *Nebraska* songs, we are left with little solid information about what exactly were the actual *Born in the USA* sessions. The songs "Born in the USA" and "Downbound Train" are definitely from the batch of songs that ended up on *Nebraska*. The recording of those songs probably dates from early 1982. At the other extreme, both "No Surrender" and "Dancing in the Dark" were among the last songs recorded, sometime in early 1984.

THE TUNNEL OF LOVE SESSIONS
January–June 1987: Rumson, N.J.; Los Angeles, Calif., A&M Studios and Kren Studios; New York, N.Y., the Hit Factory

Released Tracks
- Ain't Got You
- All That Heaven Will Allow
- Brilliant Disguise
- Cautious Man
- Lucky Man
  B-side of the "Brilliant Disguise" single.
- One Step Up
- Spare Parts
- Tougher Than the Rest
- Tunnel of Love
- Two for the Road
  B-side of the "Tunnel of Love" single.
- Two Faces
- Valentine's Day
- Walk Like a Man
- When You're Alone

The sessions for *Tunnel of Love* still are unclear, primarily because Springsteen has done so few interviews in the past couple of years. Bruce has said that most of the record was recorded in his house. Pictures taken there show a basic home studio. He's also said that the two B-sides were all the extra material he was happy with; the fact that an older outtake, "Roulette," was used as the B-side to the third single from the album reinforces this.

Springsteen started recording this record in 1986, first in Los Angeles with noted country session players and then in New York, but what came out of those sessions is uncertain; security was extraordinarily tight. This is further clouded by the fact that, unhappy with those sessions, Springsteen moved the whole process of recording back into his house.

Penn State, February 19, 1975. ▶

PROVE IT ALL NIGHT

Springsteen's Performances, 1965-89

Tying Faith Between Our Teeth: Tacoma, Wash., May 5, 1988.

PROVE IT ALL NIGHT

Springsteen's Performances, 1965-89

Bruce Springsteen's live performances are his legacy. Though he sold 17 million copies of *Born in the USA* and has enjoyed record sales from all albums combined upwards of 30 million copies, his live shows have had the most enduring impact on his fans. At times the studio has been a difficult place for Springsteen, but onstage he acts at times as if he was born in the spotlight. No other rock performer in history has established a reputation for such searing stage shows, and no one has continued in that tradition for so long. Bruce Springsteen proves it all night, every night he gets on stage.

From the day he bought his first guitar, Bruce Springsteen began to establish his reputation as a player. Early in his career, back when he was performing in small Jersey Shore clubs like the Upstage, he was known more as a guitar player than a singer. At the time his reputation was as a Clapton-inspired lead guitarist, though the sound of those early groups seemed more influenced by the Allman Brothers. In early pictures from those days, Springsteen looked better onstage than he ever looked off — it was almost as if there were two different Bruce Springsteens and that by strapping a guitar on, Bruce became some sort of super version of his other self. Offstage he was always described as shy and thoughtful, while onstage he was as sure of himself as any young man could be.

Though it is not uncommon for artists to survive on their concert fees, what may be surprising about Bruce Springsteen is just how many years concert revenues were his major, and sometimes only source of income. Well into the recording of *Born to Run,* Springsteen and the E Street Band were forced to take time off from recording to play shows to make enough money to pay the rent. It was not uncommon, even as late as 1974, for band members to come back from a show with less than $100 in their pockets.

Even though money is no longer a problem for him, it still sometimes seems as if Bruce Springsteen *needs* to play live. During the times when the band isn't touring behind a record, Springsteen frequently makes surprise guest appearances in clubs. He seems perennially ready to strap on a guitar and shout out "Lucille," even if he's backed up by the rawest guitar band in the land. During the summer of 1982, right after recording *Nebraska* and at the point where he wasn't playing regularly with the E Street Band, Springsteen played in Shore clubs more than 40 times, almost as many dates as most bands schedule when they go out on paying tours. None of those appearances were scheduled, and Springsteen wasn't paid a dime for any of them. He played to crowds as small as 20 people, and the tradition continues to this day on the Jersey Shore.

What follows is the most complete list ever assembled of Springsteen's live performances, including information about what songs were performed. It would be impossible to print every known set list without turning this book into an encyclopedia, so we've given the basic set list for every tour, and noted significant changes. We've also given set lists for unusual or important shows.

You'll find noticeable differences between this list and lists that have appeared in other books. We've attempted to double-check all information to make this list as accurate as possible, relying on *Backstreets'* network of writers, collectors, and subscribers around the world to confirm exactly what was played at a particular show. Even this list, however, is nowhere near complete or totally accurate; we'd appreciate information or updated information other fans can provide. Write us.

1965 Woodhaven, N.J., Woodhaven Swim Club
The Castiles, managed by Tex Vinyard, play their first show ever. The group will play together until 1967. Other common venues for the

band are The Left Foot, a teen club in Freehold; The Surf 'n' See Club in Sea Bright, N.J.; and Le Teendezvous in New Shrewsbury, N.J. Bruce sings lead on "Eleanor Rigby," "My Generation," "Purple Haze" and Hendrix's "Fire." A wedding reception set list from '65 or '66 includes standards like "Summertime," "Sentimental Journey," "Never on Sunday," "In the Mood," and "Moon River." Contemporary songs on the list include "I Got You Babe," "Money," "Satisfaction," and "You've Lost That Loving Feeling."

4/22/66 Matawan, N.J., Matawan-Keyport Roller Dome
The Castiles participate, along with over 20 other area bands, in a "battle of the bands." Admission to the event is two dollars.

5/18/66 Bricktown, N.J., Mr. Music Inc., Brick Mall Shopping Ctr.
Bruce and the Castiles record "That's What You Get" and "Baby I," co-written by Springsteen and George Theiss during the car ride to the studio. At least three acetates of this recording are still known to exist.

7/29/66 Hazlet, N.J., Loew's 35 Drive-In
A newspaper article previewing the concert describes the event as "Dance night, tomorrow night at Loew's 35 Drive-In Theatre will help the theatre celebrate its tenth-anniversary.... Starting at 7 P.M. The Castiles, a local rock 'n' roll band, will provide music with a beat very different from other rock bands. Their uniqueness has made them great favorites with the teen set."

11/24/66 Freehold, N.J., Freehold Regional Dance

3/10/67 Freehold, N.J., Hullabaloo Club
The full name of the club is the Hullabaloo Scene Teen Dance Club.

6/9/67 Freehold, N.J., Freehold Regional High School
The Castiles play for the "Senior Farewell Dance."

11/3/67 Middletown, N.J., Hullabaloo Club
Bruce meets Steve Van Zandt here. Van Zandt's band, the Shadows, plays the next night. The Hullabaloo club bills itself as "a groovy kind of fun. Strictly for teenagers. With dancing, live entertainment and refreshments."

12/67 New York, N.Y., Cafe Wha?
The Castiles play a series of impressive sets here during December and part of January, but the group splits up soon after.

2/14/69 Long Branch, N.J., Italian American Men's Association
Bruce forms a short-lived new band called Earth. This show is their only known appearance under that name. The poster bills the show as "St. Valentine's Day Massacre Featuring Earth."

5/23/69 Ocean, N.J., Pandemonium
Bruce joins a new band formed by Danny Federici and Vini Lopez called Child, and this night they open for James Cotton. Bass player Vini Roslin joins the band a short time later. The band often plays here and continues to do so as Steel Mill until the Pandemonium burns down in 1970. One of the highlights of any Child show was their cover of Buffalo Springfield's "For What It's Worth."

6/1/69 Richmond, Va., Monroe Park
Set list is said to have included "Voodoo Chile," "Jennifer," a Springsteen original, and "Crown Liquor" written by Billy Chinnock. This was a rare afternoon show and was free.

6/13/69 Long Branch, N.J., The Auction

6/14/69 Long Branch, N.J., The Auction

7/15/69 Ocean, N.J., Pandemonium

7/20/69 Ocean, N.J., Pandemonium
The band reportedly becomes upset when the audience stops watching the show and instead watches television coverage of Neil Armstrong's first steps on the moon.

8/29/69 Sea Bright, N.J., Oceanside Surf Club

9/19-20/69 Richmond, Va., The Center

11/1/69 Richmond, Va., Virginia Commonwealth University

11/20/69 Richmond, Va., The Center
The band is billed as "Steel Mill — Formerly Child of N.J." Tickets are $2.00 and the performance includes a light show.

12/12/69 Long Branch, N.J., Monmouth College
The band hears of another band from Long Island also called Child and changes its name to Steel Mill. For this show the band is promoted as "Steel Mill — Child under an assumed name." The band now includes Springsteen, Federici, Lopez, and Roslin; Roslin will

soon be replaced by Steve Van Zandt. They are managed by Carl "Tinker" West, who quickly books them on a tour of California.

1/13/70 San Francisco, Ca., The Matrix
In a review in the *San Francisco Examiner*, Philip Elwood calls Steel Mill "the first big thing that's happened to Asbury Park since the good ship *Morro Castle* burned to the waterline off that Jersey beach in '34." Set includes "The War is Over," "Lady Walking Down by the River," "Jeannie, I Want to Thank You," "He's Guilty," and "The Train Song."

2/12/70 San Francisco, Ca., The Matrix

2/14/70 San Francisco, Ca., The Matrix

2/22/70 San Francisco, Ca., The Fillmore Record Studios
At the request of Bill Graham, Steel Mill enters the studio and records a three-song demo of "Goin' Back to Georgia," "The Train Song," and "He's Guilty." Graham likes the songs and makes an offer, which Tinker declines. The band returns to New Jersey, where they eventually add Robbin Thompson from Richmond as a second vocalist.

2/27-28/70 Richmond, Va., The Center
A partial set list exists: The Judge Song/Jeannie, I Want to Thank You/You Say You Love Me/California Blues/I Am the Doctor/Goin' Back to Georgia/America Under Fire/The War Is Over/On the Road/Sweet Melinda/Crown Liquor/Lady Walkin' Down by the River.

4/18/70 Ocean, N.J., Ocean County College
The band is promoted as "Steel Mill, Just Back from San Francisco."

4/24/70 Long Branch, N.J., Monmouth College

5/4/70 Long Branch, N.J., Monmouth College
Set includes "I Am the Doctor" and "He's Guilty."

5/16/70 Richmond, Va., Virginia Commonwealth University
Set includes "I Am the Doctor," "For What It's Worth," and "Sweet Melinda."

5/23/70 Richmond, Va., Virginia Commonwealth University

6/13/70 Bricktown, N.J., Ice Palace

6/21/70 Atlantic Highlands, N.J., Clearwater Swim Club

7/17-18/70 Asbury Park, N.J., The Sunshine Inn

7/27/70 Asbury Park, N.J., The Upstage Club

8/8/70 Long Branch, N.J., The Beachcomber
Steel Mill performs at the first annual "Nothing's Festival."

8/14/70 Richmond, Va., Marshall Street Parking Deck

9/11/70 Atlantic Highlands, N.J., Clearwater Swim Club
This show ends in a near riot when police pull the plug. Twenty-one people are arrested for drug use and other infractions, and the police force becomes the target of a petition drive calling for a probe of their tactics. The issue blossoms into a giant controversy, drawing lines between the liberal youth and conservative elders of the township. The issue dominates the local press for days. During the melee, Danny Federici allegedly assaults a police officer; however, he escapes arrest that night by disappearing into the crowd during a sing-a-long, hence his nickname "Phantom Dan."

9/19/70 Point Pleasant Beach, N.J., Beacon Beach
Steel Mill performs with others in a benefit concert to raise money for the legal fund of the 21 people arrested at the Clearwater Swim Club show. The benefit raises $200.

11/2/70 Richmond, Va., University of Richmond
Interesting early set of covers and originals: Do It With a Feeling/Cherokee Queen/Look to the River/Not Fade Away/When You Dance/Goin' Back to Georgia/Got My Mojo Working/It's All Over Now, Baby Blue.

11/20/70 Richmond, Va., The Center

11/27/70 Asbury Park, N.J., The Sunshine Inn
Billed as "Monmouth County's Biggest Concert Ever." Steel Mill is third on the bill behind Black Sabbath and Cactus.

1/12/71 Long Branch, N.J.

1/18/71 Sayreville, N.J., D'Scene
Twelve-song set lasting over two hours.

1/22-23/71 Asbury Park, N.J., The Upstage Club
Billed as Steel Mill's final shows.

Los Angeles, Calif., October 18, 1975. ▶

4/16-17/71 Asbury Park, N.J., The Upstage Club
Billed as the "Bruce Springsteen Jam Concert."
5/14/71 Asbury Park, N.J., The Sunshine Inn
First show as Dr. Zoom and the Sonic Boom, made up of Springsteen, Federici, Lopez, Van Zandt, David Sancious, and Garry Tallent, in a rotating lineup with numerous other Shore musicians, including Southside Johnny, Bobby Williams, Kevin Connair, Danny Gallagher, John Luraschi, Kevin Kavanough, Al Tellone, Johnny Waasdorp, and a group of female backup singers known as the Zoomettes. A banner above the stage identifies the band.
5/15/71 Union, N.J., Newark State University
7/10/71 Lincroft, N.J., Brookdale Community College
The unwieldy size of Dr. Zoom leads Bruce to trim down the band to what becomes "The Bruce Springsteen Band." The band is made up of the principal members of Dr. Zoom, joined at certain shows by the horn section of Harvey Cherlin and Bobby Feigenbaum and the backup vocals of Francine Daniels, Barbara Dinkins, and Delores Holmes. The band headlines the "Second Annual Nothing's Festival."
7/11/71 Asbury Park, N.J., The Sunshine Inn
The band opens for Humble Pie and receives a positive review from Joan Pikula in the *Asbury Park Evening Press.*
7/29/71 Sayreville, N.J., D'Scene
8/7/71 Asbury Park, N.J., The Sunshine Inn
9/71 Asbury Park, N.J., The Student Prince
The band plays here every Friday, Saturday, and Sunday night in September, with Springsteen billed as "That Sensational Soul Man." Sunday show features a happy hour and free buffet. Southside Johnny often sits in with the band here.
9/1/71 Long Branch, N.J., City Park
Billed as the Bruce Springsteen Blues Band. A partial set list exists, consisting mostly of covers: Little Queenie/Bright Lights, Big City/Ballad of Jesse James/Jumpin' Jack Flash/Festival/You Better Be Nice to Me/Route 66/The Night They Drove Old Dixie Down/Dance, Dance, Dance/Jambalaya.
10/23/71 Richmond, Va., University of Richmond, Keller Hall
10/31/71 Long Branch, N.J., National Guard Armory
12/17/71 New Brunswick, N.J., Rutgers University
Also on the bill were Southern Conspiracy and PowerHouse.
2/4/72 Richmond, Va., Back Door Club
2/14/72 Asbury Park, N.J., The Sunshine Inn
The band reportedly opens for Crazy Horse, though it is questionable whether this actually occurred.
2/16/72 Long Branch, N.J., Monmouth College
Billed as the "Save a Tree Concert."
2/26/72 Richmond, Va., Back Door Club
Set includes "Down to Mexico," "Something You Got," "All I Wanna Do Is Dance" and "I Remember."
4/15/72 New Brunswick, N.J., The Ledge, Rutgers University
Last known show as the Bruce Springsteen Band, though an undated poster from 1972 has the band playing a George McGovern benefit.
5/2/72 New York, N.Y., CBS Building
Bruce has his now-famous 15-minute audition with John Hammond, set up by Mike Appel, who has now become Springsteen's manager. Bruce ends up playing at least two hours and earns a recording session the next day. Appel later describes Bruce as "literally jumping in the air running down the street after the audition."
5/2/72 New York, N.Y., The Gaslight Club
Show is hastily arranged by John Hammond.
5/3/72 New York, N.Y., CBS Studios
Bruce lays down fourteen tracks and plays both acoustic guitar and piano. Mary Queen of Arkansas (twice)/Saint in the City/Jazz Musician (twice)/If I Was the Priest/Arabian Night/Growin' Up/Does This Bus Stop at 82nd Street/Two Hearts in True Waltz Time/Street Queen/The Angel/Southern Son/Cowboys of the Sea.
8/30/72 New York, N.Y., Max's Kansas City
Part of the show is recorded by "King Biscuit Flower Hour," and "Bishop Dance" is later broadcast on the very first King Biscuit broadcast. The song is later rebroadcast during the pre-concert

◀ *Lenox, Mass., September 23, 1975.*

special that aired before the Stockholm '88 *Tunnel* radio simulcast.
11/31/72 York, Pa.
Perhaps the first show with the new E Street Band lineup of Springsteen, Danny Federici, Clarence Clemons, Garry Tallent, and Vini Lopez.
12/72 New York, N.Y., Kenny's Castaways
12/7/72 New York, N.Y., Prison Concert
12/29/72 Dayton, Ohio
12/30/72 Columbus, Ohio
1/4-7/73 Bryn Mawr, Pa., The Main Point
Springsteen makes his first Main Point appearance opening for Travis Shook. Over the years this becomes one of his favorite venues of all time.
1/5/73 *Greetings From Asbury Park, N.J.* is released in the U.S.
1/8-10/73 Boston, Mass., Paul's Mall
1/10/73 Boston, Mass., WBCN Studios
Bruce does his first major radio interview and an acoustic set, a practice he will continue during the next two years. Satin Doll/Bishop Dance/Circus Song/Song for the Orphans/Does This Bus Stop at 82nd Street/Blinded By the Light.
1/16/73 Villanova, Pa., Villanova University
1/24/73 Chicago, Ill., The Quiet Knight
1/31-2/4/73 New York, N.Y., Max's Kansas City
2/10/73 Asbury Park, N.J., The Sunshine Inn
Billed as "New Jersey's Own Superstar."
2/11/73 South Orange, N.J., Seton Hall University
2/16/73 Long Branch, N.J., Monmouth College
3/2/73 Berkeley, Calif.
After opening one West Coast date for Paul Butterfield a week earlier, the E Street Band leaves that tour, picking up a few opening slots for Blood, Sweat and Tears.
3/3/73 Santa Monica, Calif., Santa Monica Civic
Opened for Blood, Sweat and Tears.
3/12/73 Boston, Mass., Oliver's
3/18/73 Kingston, R.I., University of Rhode Island
3/23/73 Providence, R.I.
3/24/73 Niagara, N.Y., Niagara University
3/29/73 Kutztown, Pa.
4/1/73 New Brunswick, N.J., Rutgers University
4/7/73 Norfolk, Va.
4/11/73 Atlanta, Ga., Poor Richard's
4/13/73 Villanova, Pa., Villanova University
4/18/73 Lincroft, N.J.
4/23/73 Hartford, Conn., Shaboo
4/24-25/73 Bryn Mawr, Pa., The Main Point
Part of this show is later broadcast on WMMR radio, Philadelphia. Set includes "New York Song," which will evolve into "New York City Serenade" when David Sancious joins the band. Partial set list: New York Song/Circus Song/Spirit in the Night/Does This Bus Stop at 82nd Street/Santa Ana/Tokyo/Thundercrack.
4/27/73 Athens, Ohio, Ohio University
4/28/73 College Park, Md., Field House, University of Maryland
Bruce and the band are on a triple bill opening for Chuck Berry and Jerry Lee Lewis. They also serve as Berry's back-up band. Springsteen recounted the story in the film about Berry called *Hail, Hail, Rock 'n' Roll,* saying that Berry came on and began playing without filling the band in on what number he was starting with. Springsteen described it as "total panic" as the band tried to figure out both what song and what key Berry was playing. At one point during the show Springsteen says Berry came over and told them "Play for that money boys," but Springsteen says the band wasn't getting paid for backing him. Tickets to the show were $5.50 and Springsteen's name was misspelled in the newspaper ads as was a frequent occurrence at this time.
5/1/73 Los Angeles, Calif., Ahmanson Theater
CBS Records convention, with many other artists. "Thundercrack" and "Circus Song" are shot for a promotional video. The live "Circus Song" later appears on a CBS Playback single.
5/5/73 Providence, R.I.
5/6/73 Amherst, Mass., University of Mass.

5/11/73 Columbus, Ohio, Ohio State University
5/12/73 Niagara, N.Y., Niagara University
5/26-28/73 Washington, D.C., Childe Harold
5/30/73 Fayetteville, N.C., Cumberland County Civic Center
First show opening for Chicago. Bruce will become so disillusioned during this tour that he refuses to play arenas again until 1976.
5/31/73 Richmond, Va., Alfa Studios
Acoustic set is recorded and later broadcast on WGOE radio, Richmond. Satin Doll/Does This Bus Stop at 82nd Street/Circus Song/Growin' Up/New York Song/You Mean So Much to Me.
5/31/73 Richmond, Va., Coliseum
Short opening set includes "Santa Ana," "Secret to the Blues," "Tokyo," "Thundercrack."
6/1/73 Hampton, Va., Coliseum
6/2/73 Bethesda, Md., WHFS radio studios
Five-song acoustic set: Satin Doll/Circus Song/New York Song/Growin' Up/Mary Queen of Arkansas.
6/2/73 Baltimore, Md., Civic Center
6/3/73 New Haven, Conn., Veterans Memorial Coliseum
6/6/73 Philadelphia, Pa., The Spectrum
6/8-9/73 Boston, Mass., Boston Gardens
6/10/73 Springfield, Mass., Civic Center
6/12/73 Binghamton, N.Y., Broome County Memorial Arena
Seven-song set, opening for Chicago. Spirit in the Night/Does This Bus Stop at 82nd Street/Over the Hills of St. Croix/Secret to the Blues/Take Me Out to the Ballgame/Seaside Bar Song/Thundercrack. "Over the Hills of St. Croix" will later evolve into "Zero and Blind Terry."
6/14-15/73 New York, N.Y., Madison Square Garden
Chicago tour ends.
6/22-24/73 Seaside Heights, N.J., Fat City
David Sancious's first shows with the band.
7/5-8/73 Bryn Mawr, Pa., The Main Point
7/18-23/73 New York, N.Y., Max's Kansas City
Seven-song set, now features Sancious on piano. The band co-headlines with Bob Marley and the Wailers. New York City Serenade/Sandy/Spirit in the Night/Does This Bus Stop at 82nd Street/Something You Got/Zero and Blind Terry/Thundercrack.
7/31/73 Roslyn, N.Y., My Father's Place
Terrific show, 60 minutes of which are broadcast on WLIR radio, Long Island, N.Y. Set includes "You Mean So Much to Me," written around 1971 and played then by the Bruce Springsteen Band. Sandy/New York City Serenade/Spirit in the Night/Does this Bus Stop at 82nd Street/Saint in the City/You Mean So Much to Me/Thundercrack.
8/1-2, 4/73 Asbury Park, N.J., Convention Center
8/14/73 Cherry Hill, N.J., Erlton Lounge
8/16/73 East Paterson, N.J., Mr. D's
8/20-26/73 Boston, Mass., Oliver's
8/31-9/2/73 Seaside Heights, N.J., Fat City
9/6/73 Franklin, Mass., Dean Junior College
9/7/73 University Park, Pa., Penn State University
9/8/73 Pittsburgh, Pa., University of Pittsburgh
9/14-16/73 Syracuse N.Y., Jabberwocky Club
9/22/73 Miami Beach, Fla.
9/28/73 Hampden, Va., Hampden-Sydney College
9/29/73 Waynesboro, Va., Waynesboro College
9/30/73 Stony Brook, N.Y., State University of New York
10/6/73 Villanova, Pa., Villanova University
10/13/73 Washington, D.C.
10/15-16/73 Boston, Mass., Oliver's
10/20/73 Rindge, N.H., Franklin Pierce College
10/26/73 Geneva, N.Y., Hobart College
10/29-31/73 Bryn Mawr, Pa., The Main Point
Roadie Al Tellone guests on baritone sax. The band plays three songs from the second album which has just been sent to radio stations. Sandy/New York City Serenade/Spirit in the Night/Does This Bus Stop at 82nd Street/E Street Shuffle/Growin' Up/Walking the Dog/

◄ *The Darkness tour, 1978.*

For You/Lost in the Flood/Saint in the City/Zero and Blind Terry/Blinded by the Light/Thundercrack.
11/3/73 Houlton, Maine, Rickler College
11/5/73 *The Wild, the Innocent and the E Street Shuffle* is released in the U.S.
11/6-10/73 New York, N.Y., Max's Kansas City
11/11/73 Trenton, N.J., Trenton State College
11/14-16/73 Roslyn, N.Y., My Father's Place
11/17/73 Manayunk, Pa., Roxy Theater
11/25/73 Amherst, Mass., Amherst College
11/30/73 Richmond, Va., The Mosque
12/1/73 Hamden, Conn., Quinnipiac College
12/6-8/73 Washington, D.C., Childe Harold
Forty-five minute live broadcast by WGTB radio, Washington, D.C., on 12/6/73, including the first known performances of "Let the Four Winds Blow" and "Kitty's Back." Set also includes "For You," "Walking the Dog," "E Street Shuffle" and "Does This Bus Stop at 82nd Street."
12/14/73 New Haven, Conn., Pine Crest
12/15/73 Garden City, N.Y., Nassau Community College
12/16/73 Hartford, Conn., Shaboo
12/17-18/73 Asbury Park, N.J., The Student Prince
12/20/73 Providence, R.I., Roger Williams College
12/21-22/73 Cherry Hill, N.J., Erlton Lounge
12/23/73 Cassville, N.J., Rova Farms
Outdoor festival appearance.
12/27-30/73 Bryn Mawr, Pa., The Main Point
1/5/74 Boston, Mass., Joe's Place
Terrific 14-song set includes the premier of "Rosalita." New York City Serenade/Spirit in the Night/Does This Bus Stop at 82nd Street/Walking the Dog/Saint in the City/Kitty's Back/Thundercrack/You Mean So Much to Me/Growin' Up/Let the Four Winds Blow/Zero and Blind Terry/Blinded by the Light/For You/Rosalita/Twist and Shout.
1/12/74 Parsippany, N.J., Joint in the Woods
Similar show to the above, but includes the only known performances of "Ring of Fire" and "634-5789."
1/19/74 Kent, Ohio, Kent State University
This show is believed to have included the first performance of "Incident on 57th Street."
1/25/74 Richmond, Va., The Mosque
"Rosalita" ends the set and will be played at nearly every show from now until 1984. Spirit in the Night/New York City Serenade/Blinded by the Light/Let the Four Winds Blow/Kitty's Back/For You/Rosalita/Twist and Shout. Poster advertises the show by saying "Brucie's back in town."
1/26/74 Norfolk, Va., Chrysler Theater
2/1/74 Cleveland, Ohio, Allen Theater
2/2/74 Springfield, Mass., Springfield College
2/7-9/74 Atlanta, Ga., Poor Richard's
2/12/74 Lexington, Ky., University of Kentucky
2/15/74 Toledo, Ohio, University of Toledo
2/17-18/74 Columbus, Ohio, The Agora
Vini Lopez's last shows with the band.
2/23/74 Cookstown, N.J., Satellite Lounge
Ernest "Boom" Carter becomes the E Street Band's new drummer.
2/25-27/74 Bryn Mawr, Pa., The Main Point
3/3-4/74 Washington, D.C., Gaston Hall, Georgetown University
110-minute show on 3/3/74 is broadcast live on WGTB radio, Washington, D.C. Wild Billy's Circus Story/New York City Serenade/Spirit in the Night/Walking the Dog/Sandy/E Street Shuffle/Saint in the City/Kitty's Back/For You/Rosalita.
3/7/74 Houston, Tex., Liberty Hall
3/8/74 Houston, Tex., KILT Studios
Acoustic set is recorded of "Something You Got" and "Satin Doll."
3/8-9/74 Houston, Tex., Liberty Hall
Performance on 3/9/74 is broadcast live on KILT radio, Houston. Same set as 3/3/74, but "Blinded by the Light" is played and "Sandy" is not.

3/10-11/74 Houston, Tex., Liberty Hall
Show on 3/11/74 opens with a rare version of "Mary Queen of Arkansas" followed by "The Fever." Clarence also takes center stage for the barroom classic "Gimme That Wine." Mary Queen of Arkansas/The Fever/Spirit in the Night/Gimme That Wine/E Street Shuffle/Something You Got/Saint in the City/Does This Bus Stop at 82nd Street/Kitty's Back/Ride on Sweet William/Thundercrack/For You/Rosalita.
3/14-16/74 Austin, Tex., Armadillo World Headquarters
3/18-21/74 Dallas, Tex., Mother Blues
3/24/74 Phoenix, Ariz., Celebrity Theater
4/5/74 Chester, Pa., Widener College
4/6/74 Pemberton, N.J., Burlington County College
4/7/74 South Orange, N.J., Seton Hall University
4/9/74 Boston, Mass., WBCN Studios
Forty-five minute acoustic set including the only known acoustic version of "Rosalita." Satin Doll/Does This Bus Stop at 82nd Street/Growin' Up/Wild Billy's Circus Story/Sandy/Rosalita.
4/9-11/74 Cambridge, Mass., Charlie's Bar
4/13/74 Richmond, Va., The Mosque
4/18/74 Long Branch, N.J., Monmouth College
4/19/74 New Brunswick, N.J., New Jersey State Theater
4/20/74 Collegeville, Pa., Ursinus College
4/26/74 Providence, R.I., Brown University
4/27/74 Storrs, Conn., University of Connecticut
4/28/74 Swarthmore, Pa., Swarthmore College
4/29/74 Allentown, Pa., Roxy Theater
5/4/74 Upper Montclair, N.J., Montclair State College
5/5/74 Kent, Ohio, Kent State University
5/6/74 Newtown, Pa., Bucks County Community College
5/9/74 Cambridge, Mass., Harvard Square Theater
This show is attended by Jon Landau and results in a rave review in *The Real Paper*, which includes the quote "I saw rock 'n' roll future and its name is Bruce Springsteen." CBS uses the quote in ads for *Born to Run.* Bruce adds "I Sold My Heart to the Junkman" to the regular set. Other sources claim both "Born to Run" and "She's the One" premiered here, but this cannot be confirmed. Partial set list: New York City Serenade/Spirit in the Night/I Sold My Heart to the Junkman/Does This Bus Stop at 82nd Street/Saint in the City/The E Street Shuffle/Kitty's Back/Rosalita.
5/10/74 Providence, R.I., Palace Theater
5/11/74 Rutherford, N.J., Fairleigh Dickinson University
5/12/74 Glassboro, N.J., Glassboro State College
5/14/74 Greeneville, Tenn., Tusculum College
5/24/74 Trenton, N.J., War Memorial
5/25/74 Radnor, Pa., Archbishop Carroll High School
5/28-29/74 Bryn Mawr, Pa., The Main Point
5/31/74 Columbus, Ohio, The Agora
6/1/74 Kent, Ohio, Kent State University
6/2/74 Toledo, Ohio, University of Toledo
6/3/74 Cleveland, Ohio, The Agora
Sixty minutes of the show are broadcast live on WMMS radio, Cleveland. Songs broadcast are Spirit in the Night/E Street Shuffle/Sandy/You Never Can Tell/Tokyo/Rosalita/Let the Four Winds Blow/I'm Ready.
6/13/74 Oklahoma City., Okla., Music Hall
6/14/74 Arlington, Tex., Texas Hall
A show the following night in Austin is cancelled.
6/16/74 Houston, Tex., Music Hall
6/19/74 Kansas City, Mo., Cowtown Ballroom
6/26-30/74 Memphis, Tenn., La Fayettes
7/5/74 St. Louis, Mo., Ambassador Theater
7/12-14/74 New York, N.Y., The Bottom Line
"Jungleland" premieres on 7/13/74 in a version much different from the final released version. The song is much longer and more jazz-styled, and omits the now-famous saxophone solo. Then She Kissed Me/Spirit in the Night/Does This Bus Stop at 82nd Street/E Street Shuffle/Saint in the City/No Money Down/Jungleland/Born to Run/Sandy/Kitty's Back/New York City Serenade/Rosalita.
7/16/74 Newark, Del., The Stone Balloon

7/19/74 Sedalia, Mo., outdoor show
7/25/74 Santa Monica, Calif., Civic Center
Opened for Dr. John.
7/26/74 San Diego, Calif.
7/27/74 Phoenix, Ariz., Celebrity Theater
7/28/74 Tucson, Ariz., Raceway
8/3/74 New York, N.Y., Central Park
Bruce opens for Anne Murray. Murray is greeted with boos and cries of "Bring back Bruce!"
8/9/74 Lenox, Mass., Tanglewood Music Festival
8/10/74 Port Chester, N.Y., Capitol Theater
8/12/74 Boston, Mass., Performance Center
8/13/74 Wilmington, Del.
8/14/74 Red Bank, N.J., Carlton Theater
David Sancious and Ernest Carter leave the band following this show.
9/8/74 Asbury Park, N.J., Stone Pony
Bruce and others guest with Southside Johnny.
9/18-19/74 Bryn Mawr, Pa., The Main Point
First shows for Max Weinberg and Roy Bittan with the E Street Band. Also joining the band on violin is Suki Lahav.
9/20/74 Philadelphia, Pa., Tower Theater
9/21/74 Oneonta, N.Y., State University
9/22/74 Union, N.J., Kean College
10/4/74 New York, N.Y., Avery Fisher Hall
"She's the One" is the third song to be performed live from the as-yet-untitled third album. At this point the song still contains some lyrics that will later become "Backstreets." Incident on 57th Street/Spirit in the Night/Does This Bus Stop at 82nd Street/Cupid/Saint in the City/Lost in the Flood/She's the One/Jungleland/A Love So Fine/Kitty's Back/New York City Serenade/Rosalita/Sandy/Quarter to Three.
10/5/74 Reading, Pa., Allbright College
10/6/74 Worcester, Mass., Clark University
10/11/74 Gaithersburg, Md., Shady Grove Music Fair
Martin Mull opens the show.
10/12/74 Princeton, N.J., Alexander Hall, Princeton University
Similar set to 10/4/74, with "A Love So Fine" as the encore.
10/18/74 Passaic, N.J., Capitol Theater
Again, similar to the basic set of 10/4/74, but with the addition of Ben E. King's "Spanish Harlem."
10/19/74 Schenectady, N.Y., Union College
Show includes "Spanish Harlem" and "Lost in the Flood."
10/20/74 Carlisle, Pa., Dickinson College
10/25/74 Hanover, N.H., Dartmouth College
10/26/74 Springfield, Mass., Springfield College
10/27/74 Millersville, Pa., Pennsylvania State College
10/29/74 Boston, Mass., Music Hall
11/1-2/74 Philadelphia, Pa., Tower Theater
11/6-7/74 Austin, Tex., Armadillo World Headquarters
Posters say "The Lone Star Comes Back to Texas."
11/8/74 Corpus Christi, Tex., Ritz Theater
11/9/74 Houston, Tex., Music Hall
11/10/74 Dallas, Tex., Sportatorium
11/15/74 Eaton, Pa.
11/16/74 Washington, D.C., Gaston Hall, Georgetown University
11/17/74 Charlottesville, Va., University of Virginia
11/21/74 Blackwood, N.J., Camden Community College
11/22/74 West Chester, Pa., West Chester State College
11/23/74 Salem, Mass., Salem State College
11/29-30/74 Trenton, N.J., War Memorial Building
Great set, including the premiere of Dylan's "I Want You." Incident on 57th Street/Spirit in the Night/Does This Bus Stop at 82nd Street/I Want You/Growin' Up/Saint in the City/E Street Shuffle/Jungleland/Kitty's Back/New York City Serenade/Rosalita/Sandy/A Love So Fine/Wear My Ring Around Your Neck/Quarter to Three.
12/6/74 New Brunswick, N.J., New Jersey State Theater
12/7/74 Geneva, N.Y., Hobart College
12/8/74 Burlington, Vt., University of Vermont
2/5/75 Bryn Mawr, Pa., The Main Point
Benefit concert for WMMR radio, Philadelphia. Tremendous 18-song

New York, N.Y., 1975.

set includes the premiere of "Thunder Road," which at the time was called "Wings for Wheels." Incident on 57th Street/Mountain of Love/Born to Run/E Street Shuffle/Thunder Road/I Want You/Spirit in the Night/She's the One/Growin' Up/Saint in the City/Jungleland/Kitty's Back/New York City Serenade/Rosalita/Sandy/A Love So Fine/For You/Back in the USA.

2/6-7/75 Chester, Pa., Widener College
2/18/75 Cleveland, Ohio, John Carroll University
2/19/75 University Park, Pa., Penn State University
2/20/75 Pittsburgh, Pa., University of Pittsburgh
2/23/75 Westbury, N.Y., Westbury Music Fair
Encores include "Wear My Ring Around Your Neck."
3/1/75 Syracuse, N.Y., Syracuse University
3/2/75 Stony Brook, N.Y., State University of New York
3/7/75 Baltimore, Md., Painters Mill Music Fair
3/8-9/75 Washington, D.C., Constitution Hall
Suki Lahav plays her last shows with the E Street Band.

· · · · ·

BORN TO RUN TOUR

7/20/75 Providence, R.I., Palace Theater
Miami Steve Van Zandt plays his first show with the E Street Band, on the first show of the *Born to Run* tour. Incident on 57th Street/Spirit in the Night/Tenth Avenue Freeze-out/Growin' Up/Saint in the City/E Street Shuffle/Born to Run/Thunder Road/New York City Serenade/Kitty's Back/Rosalita/Sandy/A Love So Fine/Sha La La/Quarter to Three.
7/22/75 Geneva, N.Y., Geneva Theater
Same set at 7/20/75, but "She's the One" replaces "Thunder Road." Soundcheck includes "Needles and Pins," "You Really Got Me," "Cry to Me," "Let the Four Winds Blow," "Soothe Me," and "Higher and Higher."

7/23/75 Lenox, Mass., Music Inn
Similar set to the preceding night, with the addition of "Thunder Road" and Clarence Clemons's "Gimme That Wine," as well as an unknown instrumental. A rare afternoon appearance.
7/25-26/75 Kutztown, Pa., Keystone Hall, Kutztown State College
7/28-29/75 Washington, D.C., Carter Barron Amphitheater
Set includes "Sandy," "Carol," and "A Love So Fine" in the encores.
8/1/75 Richmond, Va., The Mosque
Set includes "Up on the Roof" and "Quarter to Three" in the encores.
8/2/75 Norfolk, Va., Chrysler Theater
8/8/75 Akron, Ohio, Civic Theater
Set includes "Then She Kissed Me," "Up on the Roof" and an encore of "Sandy," "A Love So Fine," "Havin' a Party," "Carol," and "Quarter to Three."
8/9/75 Pittsburgh, Pa., Syria Mosque
8/10/75 Canton, Ohio, Civic Theater
Set includes "Up on the Roof."
8/13-17/75 New York, N.Y., The Bottom Line
Bruce gives five nights of shows, with two shows per night. On 8/14/75, a 14-song set includes "Then She Kissed Me" and the premiere of "Night." The show on 8/15/75 is broadcast live on WNEW radio, New York City. Perhaps the most famous show Bruce ever gave. Tenth Avenue Freeze-out/Spirit in the Night/Then She Kissed Me/Growin' Up/Saint in the City/E Street Shuffle/Every Time You Walk in the Room/She's the One/Born to Run/Thunder Road/Kitty's Back/Rosalita/Sandy/Quarter to Three. On 8/16/75, another great set includes "Then She Kissed Me," "It's Gonna Work Out Fine," "Sha La La," "Every Time You Walk in the Room" and "Up on the Roof." The show on 8/17/75 is the same set as 8/16/75, but without "Sha La La" and "Up on the Roof."
8/21-23/75 Atlanta, Ga., Electric Ballroom
Seventeen-song set on 8/21/75 includes "Does This Bus Stop at 82nd

Street" for the first time on the tour.

9/1/75 *Born to Run* is released in the U.S.

9/6/75 New Orleans, La., Performing Arts Center

9/7/75 New Orleans, La., Ya Ya Lounge

9/11/75 Arlington, Tex., Texas Hall

9/12/75 Austin, Tex., Municipal Auditorium
Encores include "Save the Last Dance for Me."

9/13-14/75 Houston, Tex., Music Hall
Seventeen-song set on 9/13/75 includes Manfred Mann's "Pretty Flamingo." Incident on 57th Street/Tenth Avenue Freeze-out/Spirit in the Night/Pretty Flamingo/Growin' Up/Saint in the City/E Street Shuffle/She's the One/Born to Run/Thunder Road/Kitty's Back/Jungleland/Rosalita/Sandy/Quarter to Three/Carol/Lucille.

9/16/75 Dallas, Tex.

9/17/75 Oklahoma City, Okla., Music Hall

9/20/75 Grinnell, Iowa, Grinnell College

9/21/75 Minneapolis, Minn., Guthrie Theater
Set includes "Pretty Flamingo" and "Backstreets."

9/23/75 Ann Arbor, Mich., Hill Auditorium, University of Michigan
Nineteen-song set opens with "Thunder Road" and closes with encores of "Detroit Medley," "Sandy," "Quarter to Three," "Carol," and "Twist and Shout."

9/25/75 Chicago, Ill., City Auditorium

9/26/75 Iowa City, Iowa, University of Iowa

9/27/75 St. Louis, Mo., Ambassador Theater

9/28/75 Kansas City, Mo., Memorial Hall

9/30/75 Omaha, Neb., University of Nebraska

10/2/75 Milwaukee, Wis., Uptown Theater
Famous "bomb scare" show. "Meeting Across the River" premieres. Seven songs are played before the band leaves the stage because of a bomb threat. After a break, they return after apparently spending most of the time in a bar, for what can only be described as a very loose second set. Meeting Across the River/Tenth Avenue Freeze-out/Spirit in the Night/Pretty Flamingo/She's the One/Born to Run/Thunder Road/Little Queenie/E Street Shuffle/Saint in the City/Sha La La/Kitty's Back/Jungleland/Rosalita/Detroit Medley/Sandy/Quarter to Three.

10/4/75 Detroit, Mich., Michigan Palace
Six-song encore of "Detroit Medley," "Sandy," "Ain't Too Proud to Beg" (sung for the only time as a duet with Steve), "Quarter to Three," "Little Queenie," and "Twist and Shout."

10/11/75 Red Bank, N.J., Carlton Theater

10/16/75 Los Angeles, Calif., The Roxy
Bruce plays four nights, with two shows per night.

10/17/75 Los Angeles, Calif., The Roxy
Early set broadcast live on K-WEST radio, Los Angeles, includes "Pretty Flamingo" and "Goin' Back." Late show includes "It's Gonna Work Out Fine" and "Every Time You Walk in the Room."

10/18/75 Los Angeles, Calif., The Roxy
First show of the night is one of the 16 source concerts for *Live 1975-85*. The opening number, "Thunder Road," is played by Bruce, alone on piano. Thunder Road/Tenth Avenue Freeze-out/Spirit in the Night/E Street Shuffle/Every Time You Walk in the Room/She's the One/Born to Run/Sandy/Backstreets/Kitty's Back/Jungleland/Rosalita/Goin' Back/Carol. Late set includes "Pretty Flamingo."

10/19/75 Los Angeles, Calif., The Roxy

10/25/75 Portland, Ore., Paramount Theater

10/26/75 Seattle, Wash., Paramount Theater
Sixteen-song set includes encores of "Detroit Medley," "For You," "Quarter to Three," "Carol," and "Twist and Shout."

10/29/75 Sacramento, Calif., Memorial Auditorium

10/30/75 Oakland, Calif., Paramount Theater

11/1/75 Santa Barbara, Calif., University of California

11/3-4, 6/75 Phoenix, Ariz.

11/9/75 Tampa, Fla., Jai Alai Pavilion
Fifteen-song set includes "Growin' Up."

11/11/75 Miami, Fla., Jai Alai Pavilion

◀ *Philadelphia, Pa., May 26, 1978.*

11/18/75 London, England, Hammersmith Odeon
Bruce's first European show ever includes "Lost in the Flood" for the first time since 10/74.

11/21/75 Stockholm, Sweden, Konserthuset

11/23/75 Amsterdam, The Netherlands, R.A.I. Building

11/24/75 London, England, Hammersmith Odeon
Twenty-two song set is Bruce's longest to date. Footage from this show is later included in the BBC's "Glory Days" special in 1987. The show was described by Peter Gabriel as the second greatest concert he had ever seen, second only to Otis Redding. Thunder Road/Tenth Avenue Freeze-out/Spirit in the Night/Lost in the Flood/She's the One/Born to Run/Growin' Up/Saint in the City/Pretty Flamingo/Backstreets/Sha La La/Jungleland/Rosalita/Sandy/Wear My Ring Around Your Neck//Detroit Medley/For You/Every Time You Walk in the Room/ Quarter to Three/Twist and Shout/Carol/Little Queenie.

12/2-3/75 Boston, Mass., Music Hall
Set on 12/2/75 includes "Lost in the Flood," "Santa Claus," and "Party Lights." "Pretty Flamingo" and "For You" are both included in the 12/3/75 set.

12/5-6/75 Washington, D.C., McDonough Gym, Georgetown University

12/10/75 Lewisburg, Pa., Bucknell University, Davis Gym

12/11/75 South Orange, N.J., Seton Hall University
An eight-song encore includes "Party Lights," "Santa Claus," "Wear My Ring Around Your Neck," and "Twist and Shout."

12/12/75 Greenvale, N.Y., C.W. Post College
Set includes "It's My Life," "For You," "Sha La La," and "Santa Claus" which will later be released on the *In Harmony 2* LP and as the B-side of "My Hometown."

12/16/75 Oswego, N.Y., State University of New York

12/17/75 Buffalo, N.Y., Kleinhans Music Hall

12/19/75 Montreal, Quebec, Place des Arts

12/20/75 Ottawa, Ontario, National Arts Centre

12/21/75 Toronto, Ontario, Seneca College

12/27-28/75 Philadelphia, Pa., Tower Theater

12/30-31/75 Philadelphia, Pa., Tower Theater
Bruce plays "Tenth Avenue Freeze-out" in a slowed-down piano version. Show opens for the first time with "Night." 12/30/75 set: Night/Tenth Avenue Freeze-out/Spirit in the Night/Does This Bus Stop at 82nd Street/It's My Life/She's the One/Born to Run/It's Gonna Work Out Fine/Growin' Up/Saint in the City/Backstreets/ Mountain of Love/Jungleland/Rosalita/Sandy/Detroit Medley/ Thunder Road/Wear My Ring Around Your Neck/Quarter to Three. A similar 18-song set on 12/31/75 includes "Pretty Flamingo" and "Twist and Shout."

3/21/76 Asbury Park, N.J., Stone Pony
Tour rehearsal.

3/25/76 Columbia, S.C., Township Auditorium
First show of the "Chicken Scratch" tour, named for the unorthodox itinerary the tour follows.

3/26/76 Atlanta, Ga., Fox Theater

3/28/76 Durham, N.C., Duke University

3/29/76 Charlotte, N.C., Oven's Auditorium

4/1/76 Athens, Ohio, Ohio University

4/2/76 Louisville, Ky., McAlly Theater

4/4/76 East Lansing, Mich., Michigan State University
Eighteen-song set includes "Frankie," which will be recorded for both *Darkness* and *Born in the USA*, but not released on either album. Night/Tenth Avenue Freeze-out/Spirit in the Night/It's My Life/ Thunder Road/She's the One/Born to Run/Frankie/Meeting Across the River/Backstreets/Growin' Up/Saint in the City/Jungleland/ Rosalita/Raise Your Hand/Sandy/Detroit Medley/Quarter to Three.

4/5/76 Columbus, Ohio, Ohio Theater

4/7/76 Cleveland, Ohio, Allen Theater
Same set as 4/4/76, but "Incident on 57th Street" replaces "Meeting Across the River," and Bruce adds "Blinded by the Light" for the first time since 4/74.

4/8/76 Cleveland, Ohio, John Carroll University
Last known performance of "Every Time You Walk in the Room."

Bryn Mawr, Pa., February 5, 1975.

4/9/76 Hamilton, N.Y., Colgate University
Identical set to 4/7/76.
4/10/76 Wallingford, Conn., Paul Mellon Arts Center
Bruce speaks fondly of John Hammond before playing "Growin' Up" at this show, which is played at Hammond's request. Set includes "Pretty Flamingo."
4/12/76 Johnstown, Pa., Memorial Auditorium
4/13/76 University Park, Pa., Recreation Hall, Penn State University
Encores include "Raise Your Hand," "Quarter to Three" and "Twist and Shout."
4/15/76 Pittsburgh, Pa., Syria Mosque
4/16/76 Meadville, Pa., Allegheny College
4/17/76 Rochester, N.Y., University of Rochester
4/20/76 Johnson City, Tenn., Freedom Hall
4/21/76 Knoxville, Tenn., Civic Auditorium
4/22/76 Blacksburg, Va., Burrus Auditorium
4/24/76 Boone, N.C., Appalachian State University
4/26/76 Chattanooga, Tenn., Tivoli Theater
4/28/76 Nashville, Tenn., Grand Ol' Opry
4/29/76 Memphis, Tenn., Ellis Auditorium
Eddie Floyd guests on "Knock on Wood" and "Raise Your Hand." It is after this show that Bruce and Steve take a cab to Graceland, and Bruce jumps the fence in an attempt to meet Elvis Presley.
4/30/76 Birmingham, Ala., Municipal Auditorium
5/3/76 Little Rock, Ark., Robinson Auditorium
5/4/76 Jackson, Miss., Municipal Auditorium
5/6/76 Shreveport, La., Municipal Auditorium
5/8/76 Baton Rouge, La., Louisiana State University
5/9-10/76 Mobile, Ala., Municipal Auditorium

5/11/76 Auburn, Ala., Auburn University
5/13/76 New Orleans, La., Municipal Auditorium
Set includes "Mississippi Queen."
5/28/76 West Point, N.Y., Eisenhower Hall, U.S. Military Academy
5/30/76 Asbury Park, N.J., Stone Pony
Bruce guests with Southside on "Havin' a Party."
8/1-3/76 Red Bank, N.J., Monmouth Arts Center
Bruce and the E Street Band are joined by the Miami Horns (Rick Gazda, Earl Gardner, Bob Malach, Bill Zacagni, and Louis Parente) for this second tour of '76 and the '77 tour. They will regularly play on "Tenth Avenue Freeze-out," "Raise Your Hand," and "You Can't Sit Down." Sixteen-song set on 8/1/76 includes the premieres of "Something in the Night" and "Rendezvous." Night/Rendezvous/Spirit in the Night/It's My Life/Thunder Road/She's the One/Born to Run/Something in the Night/Backstreets/Tenth Avenue Freeze-out/Jungleland/Rosalita/Raise Your Hand/Sandy/She's Sure the Girl I Love/You Can't Sit Down. The 8/2/76 set is the same as 8/1/76, but without "She's Sure the Girl I Love." A 15-song set on 8/3/76 includes "The Promise" for the first time.
8/5-7/76 Red Bank, N.J., Monmouth Arts Center
Same as 8/2/76, with the addition on 8/7/76 of "Growin' Up" and "Quarter to Three."
8/21/76 Waterbury, Conn., Palace Theater
Same set as 8/2/76.
9/4/76 Asbury Park, N.J., Stone Pony
Bruce guests with Southside Johnny on "Havin' a Party."
9/26/76 Phoenix, Ariz.
"Growin' Up" is added in the encores, expanding the standard 8/2/76 show to 16 songs.
9/29-30/76 Santa Monica, Calif., Civic Center
On 9/29/76 "The Promise" replaces "Growin' Up" in the encores, and "Born to Run" closes the show, replacing "You Can't Sit Down" in a 15-song set. "Growin' Up" is added in a 16-song set on 9/30/76. The same set will be played for the next nine shows.
10/2/76 Oakland, Calif., Paramount Theater
10/3/76 Santa Clara, Calif., Santa Clara University
10/5/76 Santa Barbara, Calif., County Bowl
10/9/76 South Bend, Ind., Notre Dame University
10/10/76 Oxford, Ohio, Miami University
10/12/76 New Brunswick, N.J., Rutgers University
10/13/76 Union, N.J., Wilkins Theater, Kean College
10/16/76 Williamsburg, Va., William and Mary University
10/17-18/76 Washington, D.C., Georgetown University
"You Can't Sit Down" is included in the encores.
10/25/76 Philadelphia, Pa., The Spectrum
Bruce's first headlining arena date, but only after an exhaustive two-hour-plus soundcheck. Night/Rendezvous/Spirit in the Night/It's My Life/Thunder Road/She's the One/Something in the Night/Backstreets/Growin' Up/Tenth Avenue Freeze-out/Jungleland/Rosalita/Sandy/A Fine, Fine Girl/Raise Your Hand/The Promise/Born to Run.
10/27/76 Philadelphia, Pa., The Spectrum
This show was originally scheduled for 10/26, but Clarence was involved in filming for his cameo in *New York, New York*. Set includes both "Incident on 57th Street" and "A Fine, Fine Girl."
10/28-30/76 New York, N.Y., The Palladium
On 10/29/76, "Quarter to Three" with special guest Gary "U.S." Bonds replaces "A Fine, Fine Girl." The set on 10/30/76 is the same as 10/25/76, with special guest Patti Smith on "Rosalita."
11/2/76 New York, N.Y., The Palladium
Previous night's set is rearranged slightly.
11/3-4/76 New York, N.Y., The Palladium
"Mona" is played for the first time on 11/3/76 as an intro to "She's the One." The Beach Boys's "Be True to Your School" is transformed by Bruce into "Be True to Your Band" as a segue to "Rosalita." "A Fine, Fine Girl" is also included in a 15-song set. The set on 11/4/76 is broadcast on WCOZ radio, Boston, at a later date. Bruce and the E

Asbury Park, N.J., July 31, 1987. ▶

Street Band are joined for this set by Ronnie Spector, who sings on "Baby I Love You," "Walking in the Rain," and "Be My Baby." First known version of the Animals' "We Gotta Get Outta This Place" by Springsteen and the E Street Band.

11/26/76 New York, N.Y., The Bottom Line
Bruce guests with Patti Smith on piano and guitar, during both her early and late shows. Both sets include "Gloria" and "My Generation."

2/7/77 Albany, N.Y., Palace Theater

2/8/77 Rochester, N.Y., Auditorium Theater
Show opens for the first time with "Something in the Night." Sound-check includes first ever version of "Don't Look Back" as well as another new song, "Action in the Streets," played later that evening and featuring the Miami Horns. "Action in the Streets" belongs to the family of very similar songs that also includes "A Love So Fine" and later "Paradise by the C." All share the same basic style and melody. Something in the Night/Rendezvous/Spirit in the Night/It's My Life/Thunder Road/Mona/She's the One/Tenth Avenue Freeze-out/Action in the Streets/Backstreets/Jungleland/Rosalita/Sandy/ Raise Your Hand/The Promise/Born to Run.

2/9/77 Buffalo, N.Y., Kleinhans Music Hall

2/10/77 Utica, N.Y., Memorial Auditorium

2/12/77 Ottawa, Ontario, Civic Centre
This show also opens with "Something in the Night."

2/13/77 Toronto, Ontario, Maple Leaf Gardens Concert Bowl
"Night" opens the show, and "Something in the Night" is moved to the middle of the set. "The Promise" and "Sandy" are taken out of the encores, and "Growin' Up" is added to the set.

2/15/77 Detroit, Mich., Masonic Temple Auditorium
Show again opens with "Something in the Night." "Raise Your Hand" and "Growin' Up" are left out of the set.

2/16/77 Columbus, Ohio, Franklin County Veterans Memorial Auditorium

2/17/77 Cleveland, Ohio, Richfield Coliseum
Ronnie Spector and Flo and Eddie guest on "Baby, I Love You," "Walking in the Rain," "Say Goodbye to Hollywood," and "Be My Baby." Ronnie Spector later records "Say Goodbye to Hollywood" with the E Street Band. This 17-song set also includes the first 1977 appearance of "Quarter to Three."

2/19/77 St. Paul, Minn., Civic Centre
Short and standard 13-song set.

2/20/77 Madison, Wisc., Dane County Coliseum

2/22/77 Milwaukee, Wisc., Milwaukee Arena
14-song set.

2/23/77 Chicago, Ill., Auditorium Theater
"The Promise" and "Quarter to Three" are played in the encores.

2/25/77 Lafayette, Ind., Purdue University

2/26/77 Indianapolis, Ind., Convention Center
A 13-song set.

2/27/77 Cincinnati, Ohio

2/28/77 St. Louis, Mo., Fox Theater
Standard 14-song set.

3/2/77 Atlanta, Ga., Civic Center

3/4/77 Jacksonville, Fla., Auditorium

3/5/77 Orlando, Fla., Jai Alai Fronton
"Sandy" returns to the encores.

3/6/77 Miami, Fla., Jai Alai Fronton

3/10/77 Toledo, Ohio, Centennial Arena
First in-concert performance of "Don't Look Back," which replaces "Rendezvous." "Growin' Up" is also included in a 14-song set.

3/11/77 La Trobe, Pa., St. Vincent's College
"Sandy" and "Rendezvous" both return to a 15-song set that closes with "Twist and Shout."

3/13/77 Baltimore, Md., Towson State College
"Don't Look Back" replaces "Rendezvous," as it will for the remainder of the '77 tour. "Something in the Night" is left out of the set.

3/14/77 Poughkeepsie, N.Y., Mid-Hudson Civic Center
"Something in the Night" replaces "It's My Life" in a 13-song set.

3/15/77 Binghamton, N.Y., Broome County Veterans Arena
"It's My Life" replaces "Something in the Night."

3/18/77 New Haven, Conn., Veterans Memorial Coliseum
3/19/77 Lewiston, Maine, Central Maine Youth Center
3/20/77 Providence, R.I., Alumni Hall, Providence College
3/22-25/77 Boston, Mass., Music Hall
Bruce brings back "The Promise" and "You Can't Sit Down" in a 16-song set on the first night of four that many consider to be among the finest shows of his career. The second night is another excellent 15-song set that includes "Growin' Up," "Incident on 57th Street," and "Little Latin Lupe Lu" which is played for the first time. On 3/24/77, surprises continue as Bruce brings back "Saint in the City" for the first time since 5/27/76. The 17-song set closes with a terrific cover of Jackie Wilson's "Higher and Higher," previously played only in a soundcheck on 7/22/75. The final night is another candidate for greatest show ever. The Miami Horns play on "Tenth Avenue Freeze-out," "Rosalita," and the final four songs of the encores. The set list speaks for itself: Night/Don't Look Back/Spirit in the Night/Incident on 57th Street/Thunder Road/Mona/She's the One/Tenth Avenue Freeze-out/Action in the Streets/Saint in the City/Backstreets/Jungleland/Rosalita/Born to Run/Quarter to Three/Little Latin Lupe Lu/You Can't Sit Down/Higher and Higher.

4/17/77 Asbury Park, N.J., Stone Pony
Bruce guests with Southside Johnny.

5/12-13/77 Red Bank, N.J., Monmouth Arts Center
Bruce, Steve Van Zandt and Ronnie Spector front the Asbury All-Star Revue on 5/12/77. Bruce backs up Steve, taking vocals on "The Fever" and sharing vocals on "I Don't Wanna Go Home" and "Havin' a Party." The E Street Band and Bruce play "Thunder Road," "Rendezvous," "Backstreets," and "Born to Run." At the early show on 5/13/77, Bruce and the E Street Band play "Thunder Road." At the late show they perform "Thunder Road" and "Higher and Higher." Bruce also sings "Amen" with Miami Steve and duets with Ronnie Spector on "You Mean So Much to Me."

9/4/77 Asbury Park, N.J., Stone Pony
Bruce joins the Shots onstage, playing guitar on "Funky Broadway" and "Further on Up the Road."

9/13/77 Asbury Park, N.J., Stone Pony
Bruce guests with Southside Johnny and then brings out the E Street Band for "Thunder Road," "Mona," "She's the One," and "Born to Run."

10/13/77 Asbury Park, N.J., Stone Pony
Bruce guests with Southside Johnny for a five-song set of "Down in the Valley," "Ain't Too Proud to Beg," "Soothe Me," "Let the Good Times Roll," "Carol."

12/2/77 New York, N.Y., NYU Loeb Student Center
Bruce joins Robert Gordon and Link Wray for "Heartbreak Hotel."

12/30/77 New York, N.Y., CBGB's
Bruce joins Patti Smith on "Because the Night."

12/31/77 Passaic, N.J., Capitol Theater
Bruce first joins Southside Johnny and the Jukes for "Havin' a Party," "Higher and Higher," "Little Latin Lupe Lu," and "You Can't Sit Down." Later he brings on the E Street Band for "Back-streets," "Born to Run," and "Quarter to Three." "Backstreets" includes for the first time a new song often called "Sad Eyes," which will later evolve into "Drive All Night." The middle section of "Back-streets," including these new lyrics, will become a favorite of fans on the next tour.

5/19/78 Asbury Park, N.J., Paramount Theater
Tour rehearsal includes most of the new set, plus assorted covers including the Rolling Stones' "Satisfaction" and "Heart Full of Soul."

. . . . .

DARKNESS ON THE EDGE OF TOWN TOUR
For song counts on this tour, "Mona/Not Fade Away/Gloria/She's the One" will be counted as one song. "Detroit Medley" consists of "Devil With the Blue Dress," "Jenny Take a Ride," "Good Golly Miss Molly," and "C.C. Rider," and will be counted as one song. On the tour, 118

Philadelphia, Pa., May 26, 1978.

shows are played. Each show now includes an intermission between two sets, designated by "//."

5/23/78 Buffalo, N.Y., Shea Theater
Soundcheck includes "Is That All to the Ball, Mr. Hall." First show of the *Darkness* tour includes nine songs off the new album and four songs not available on any release. "Prove It All Night" features a beautiful instrumental beginning not on the album, which makes this song one of the highlights of this tour. "The Promise" is played solo by Bruce on piano. Besides songs from the new record, the instrumental "Paradise by the C" and "Fire" premiere here also. Badlands/Night/Something in the Night/For You/Thunder Road/Spirit in the Night/Prove It All Night/Racing in the Street/Candy's Room/ Promised Land//Paradise by the C/Fire/Darkness/Streets of Fire/Mona/She's the One/Adam Raised a Cain/Backstreets/Rosalita/The Promise/Born to Run/Tenth Avenue Freeze-out/You Can't Sit Down.

5/24/78 Albany, N.Y., Palace Theater
"Spirit in the Night" is moved to the front of the first set, where it will remain for the rest of the tour. "Streets of Fire" is left out of the set, as is "You Can't Sit Down."

5/26-27/78, Philadelphia, Pa., The Spectrum
During "Spirit in the Night" on 5/26, Bruce not only enters the crowd, but finishes in a seating section on the second level of the Spectrum. Later in the set, Bruce swings from a rope ladder that leads to the overhead lighting rig. "Growin' Up," "Saint in the City," and "You Can't Sit Down" return to the 22-song set. On 5/27/78, "Jungleland" closes the first set, and "Candy's Room" is not played. Soundcheck includes two versions of "Lucille" and "Jungleland."

5/29-31/78 Boston, Mass., Music Hall
On 5/30/78, "Because the Night" is added to the encores, "You Can't Sit Down" is left out. "Candy's Room" also returns. On 5/31/78, "Quarter to Three" closes the show.

6/1/78 Annapolis, Md., U.S. Naval Academy
6/3/78 Uniondale, N.Y., Nassau Coliseum
"Sandy" and "Quarter to Three" close out the encores.
6/5/78 Toledo, Ohio, Centennial Arena
6/6/78 Indianapolis, Ind., Convention Center
6/6/78 Darkness on the Edge of Town is released in the U.S.
6/8/78 Madison, Wisc., Dane County Coliseum
"Jungleland" returns, and "Saint in the City" and "The Promise" are left out of a 20-song set.
6/9/78 Milwaukee, Wisc., Milwaukee Arena
"Darkness" replaces "Something in the Night." The set now looks like this: Badlands/Night/Spirit in the Night/Darkness/For You/Promised Land/Prove It All Night/Racing in the Street/Thunder Road/Jungleland//Paradise by the C/Fire/Adam Raised a Cain/Mona/She's the One/Growin' Up/Backstreets/Rosalita/Born to Run/Tenth Avenue Freeze-out/Quarter to Three.
6/10/78 Bloomington, Minn., Met Center
6/13/78 Iowa City, Iowa, University of Iowa
6/14/78 Omaha, Neb., Music Hall
"The Promise" returns to the encores.
6/16/78 Kansas City, Mo., Municipal Auditorium
6/17/78 St. Louis, Mo., Kiel Opera House
6/20/78 Morrison, Colo., Red Rocks Amphitheater
Five-song encore of "The Promise," "Born to Run," "Tenth Avenue Freeze-out," "I Fought the Law," and "Quarter to Three."
6/24/78 Portland, Ore., Paramount Theater
Twenty-one song set again includes "The Promise."
6/25/78 Seattle, Wash., Paramount Theater
Twenty-two song set with "I Fought the Law" in the encores.
6/26/78 Vancouver, British Columbia, Queen Elizabeth Theatre
6/29/78 San Jose, Calif., Performing Arts Center

Austin, Tex., November 9, 1980. ▶

6/30-7/1/78 Berkeley, Calif., Community Theater
"Darkness" is dedicated to *Mystery Train* author Greil Marcus. "Paradise by the C" and "Prove It All Night" are recorded for "The King Biscuit Flower Hour." These songs were to be released as a promotional 12-inch disc, but it was never pressed.

7/5/78 Los Angeles, Calif., The Forum
The 21-song set includes "Because the Night" in the encores.

7/7/78 Los Angeles, Calif., The Roxy
Broadcast live on KMET radio, Los Angeles, this is one of the 16 source concerts for *Live 1975-85*. "Rave On," "Point Blank," "Independence Day," and "Heartbreak Hotel" are all premiered in a devastating set. Rave On/Badlands/Spirit in the Night/Darkness/Candy's Room/For You (included as the live B-side to "Fire" from *Live 1975-85*)/Point Blank/Promised Land/Prove It All Night/Racing in the Street/Thunder Road//Paradise by the C/Fire/Adam Raised a Cain/Mona/She's the One/Growin' Up/Saint in the City/Backstreets/Heartbreak Hotel/Rosalita/Independence Day/Born to Run/Because the Night/Raise Your Hand/Twist and Shout.

7/8/78 Phoenix, Ariz., Veterans Memorial Coliseum
"Raise Your Hand" and "Because the Night" are both included in the encores. This show is filmed for promotional use and "Rosalita" is released as a video in 1984.

7/9/78 San Diego, Calif., Sports Arena
Long first set includes "I Fought the Law" and "Candy's Room." "Mona/Not Fade Away/Gloria" segues into "She's the One."

7/12/78 Dallas, Tex., Convention Center
"The Promise" returns to the encores.

7/14/78 San Antonio, Tex., Municipal Auditorium
"The Fever" makes a surprise appearance for the first time since 3/74. "Candy's Room" and "The Promise" are also included in a 23-song set.

7/15/78 Houston, Tex., Hofheinz Pavilion
"The Fever" is played in the first set and "Candy's Room" in the second set. This will be the final performance of "The Promise."

7/16/78 New Orleans, La., The Warehouse

7/18/78 Jackson, Miss., Civic Center
Twenty-song set.

7/19/78 Memphis, Tenn., Ellis Auditorium

7/21/78 Nashville, Tenn., Municipal Auditorium
"Factory" premieres. "Saint in the City" returns to the second set.

7/28/78 Miami, Fla., Jai Alai Fronton
Show opens for the first time with "Summertime Blues." The second set opens with "Heartbreak Hotel" and includes "I Fought the Law."

7/29/78 St. Petersburg, Fla., Bayfront Civic Center Auditorium
Unusual 20-song set includes covers of Buddy Holly's "Oh Boy" and "Around and Around." Oh Boy/Badlands/Spirit in the Night/Darkness/Factory/Promised Land/Prove It All Night/Racing in the Street/Thunder Road/Jungleland//Paradise by the C/Sandy/Around and Around/Not Fade Away/She's the One/Growin' Up/Backstreets/Rosalita/Born to Run/Because the Night/Quarter to Three.

7/31/78 Columbia, S.C., Municipal Auditorium

8/1/78 Charleston, S.C., Municipal Auditorium

8/2/78 Charlotte, N.C., Charlotte Coliseum

8/4/78 Charleston, W.Va., Civic Center
Show again opens with "Oh Boy" and includes the premiere of "Sherry Darling," which will later be included on *The River.*

8/5/78 Louisville, Ky., Louisville Gardens
"Sweet Little Sixteen" is included in the first set.

8/7/78 Kalamazoo, Mich., Wings Stadium

8/9/78 Cleveland, Ohio, The Agora
Broadcast live on WMMS radio, Cleveland, for its tenth anniversary. Also rebroadcast on some specially selected FM stations not included on any of the '78 tour simulcasts. "Growin' Up" includes the now-famous "I was a teenage werewolf" story. "Summertime Blues" cranks open the 22-song set, which ends with encores of "Raise Your Hand" and "Twist and Shout,"

8/10/78 Rochester, N.Y., War Memorial
"Summertime Blues" opens the first set, "Sweet Little Sixteen" opens

◄ *Austin, Tex., November 9, 1980.*

in the second set in this particularly hot show.

8/12/78 Augusta, Maine, Civic Center.

8/14/78 Hampton, Va., Hampton Roads Coliseum
"High School Confidential" opens the 21-song set that again includes "Sweet Little Sixteen."

8/15/78 Landover, Md., Capital Centre
"Summertime Blues" opens Springsteen's most famous unauthorized video, recorded from the closed-circuit television system in the Capital Centre's luxury boxes and arena big-screen.

8/18-19/78 Philadelphia, Pa., The Spectrum
Strange soundcheck for the 8/18 set includes "The Harder They Come," "Save the Last Dance for Me," and "The Fever," the only song of the three that will be played later in the show. A 22-song set on that date opens with "Summertime Blues" and includes special guest Gary Busey on "Rave On" and "Quarter to Three." On 8/19/78, Gary Busey again joins Bruce for "Rave On." Bruce starts the show for the first time with "Good Rockin' Tonight," in a 23-song set that also includes "Heartbreak Hotel" and "Sweet Little Sixteen."

8/21-23/78 New York, N.Y., Madison Square Garden
The 8/21 show is the same as 8/19/78, but "Summertime Blues" opens the show, and "Paradise by the C" replaces "Rave On" to open the second set. These are Bruce's first shows in Madison Square Garden as the headliner. On 8/22, "Candy's Room" is played in the second set, and "Streets of Fire" enters the first set following "Badlands," where it will appear in most of the remaining shows on the tour. The final night's 25-song set includes "High School Confidential," "Heartbreak Hotel," "Saint in the City," and a visit from Bruce's mother during the encores.

8/25/78 New Haven, Conn., Veterans Memorial Coliseum
A 24-song set includes "It's Gonna Work Out Fine."

8/25/78 New Haven, Conn., Toad's Place
Bruce and Clarence guest with Beaver Brown.

8/26/78 Providence, R.I., Civic Center
A 24-song set opens with "Summertime Blues."

8/28/78 Pittsburgh, Pa., Stanley Theater
Hank Williams' "I Heard That Lonesome Whistle" is played for the first and only time.

8/30/78 Cleveland, Ohio, Richfield Coliseum

8/31/78 Cleveland, Ohio, The Agora
Bruce joins Southside Johnny for "The Fever," "I Don't Wanna Go Home," and "Havin' a Party."

9/1/78 Detroit, Mich., Masonic Temple Auditorium
A 23-song set includes the first performance of Bob Dylan's "Chimes of Freedom." This song will reappear ten years later on the European leg of the *Tunnel of Love Express* tour, as well as the Amnesty International Human Rights Now tour. "Lost in the Flood" is also played for the last time to date.

9/3/78 Saginaw, Mich., Civic Center
Another great 25-song set includes the first appearance of "It's My Life" on the *Darkness* tour, as well as the first known version of "I Don't Wanna Hang Up My Rock 'n' Roll Shoes" and "Good Rockin' Tonight."

9/5/78 Columbus, Ohio, Veterans Memorial Auditorium
A 22-song set again includes "It's My Life."

9/6/78 Chicago, Ill., Uptown Theater
A 23-song set.

9/9/78 South Bend, Ind., Notre Dame University
A 22-song set includes first performance of the Swinging Medallions' "Double Shot of My Baby's Love" and "Louie, Louie." "Sandy" is also added to the second set.

9/10/78 Cincinnati, Ohio, Riverfront Coliseum

9/12/78 Syracuse, N.Y., War Memorial Auditorium
Typical set for this part of the tour: Badlands/Streets of Fire/Spirit in the Night/Darkness/Heartbreak Hotel/Factory/Promised Land/Prove It All Night/Racing in the Street/Thunder Road/Jungleland//Paradise by the C/Fire/Candy's Room/Saint in the City/Sandy/Not Fade Away/Gloria/She's the One/Backstreets/Rosalita/Born to Run/Because the Night/Quarter to Three.

9/13/78 Springfield, Mass., Civic Center

Bryn Mawr, Pa., July 6, 1973.

9/15-17/78 New York, N.Y., The Palladium
An unusual 23-song set on 9/15 includes "Something in the Night" for the first time, and the last "Adam Raised a Cain" until Worcester 2/25/88. The first set opens for the only time with "Darkness," and the second set opens with "Kitty's Back," played for the first time since Philadelphia 12/27/75. "Tenth Avenue Freeze-out" also returns to the encores, and "I Fought the Law" is added to the first set. On 9/16 "Point Blank" and "Independence Day" are played for the first time since Los Angeles 7/7/78. They will be included in the set for the rest of the tour. "Incident on 57th Street" is played for the first time since Boston 3/25/77, and the "Detroit Medley" is also played for the first time on this tour. "You Can't Sit Down" closes the show. On 9/17 a 24-song set includes "Meeting Across the River" for the first time since 1976. Badlands/Streets of Fire/Spirit in the Night/Darkness/Independence Day/Factory/Promised Land/Prove It All Night/Racing in the Street/Thunder Road/Meeting Across the River/Jungleland//Kitty's Back/Fire/Candy's Room/Because the Night/Point Blank/Not Fade Away/She's the One/Incident on 57th Street/Rosalita/Born to Run/Tenth Avenue Freeze-out/Detroit Medley/Quarter to Three.

9/19/78 Passaic, N.J., Capitol Theater
Show is broadcast live on WNEW radio, New York City. Similar set to 9/17/78, but without "Factory" or "Incident on 57th Street" and the addition of "Sandy" as the first encore. Show closes with "Raise Your Hand" instead of "Quarter to Three."

9/20-21/78 Passaic, N.J., Capitol Theater
Truly remarkable soundcheck before the show on 9/20/78. "The Ties That Bind" is played in a completely different arrangement that will not be played again. Also included is Hank Williams's "Wedding Bells," which will never be performed in concert. The evening show includes "Incident on 57th Street," "Kitty's Back," "Santa Claus," and "It's My Life," played for the final time. Unusual soundcheck on

9/21/78 includes "Wedding Bells," "I Walk the Line," "Guess Things Happen That Way," and two other songs believed to be called "Hey Porter," and "Go Away." The 24-song set includes "Meeting Across the River," "The Fever" and "Incident on 57th Street."

9/25/78 Boston, Mass., Boston Gardens
9/29/78 Birmingham, Ala., Boutwell Auditorium
A 23-song set again includes "The Fever" and closes with the "Detroit Medley." "Paradise by the C" is played for the final time on the 1978 tour.

9/30/78 Atlanta, Ga., Fox Theatre
A 23-song set is broadcast live across the southeast. "Night Train" enters the second set, replacing "Paradise by the C," which won't appear again for 10 years, until its surprising revival in Rotterdam, Holland 8/29/88. The show opens with "Good Rockin' Tonight" and closes with "Raise Your Hand."

11/1/78 Princeton, N.J., Jadwin Gym, Princeton University
Soundcheck includes "Thunder Road," "Badlands," "Prove It All Night," and "Promised Land." "The Ties That Bind" is played for the first time, as the fourth song in the set. The arrangement is completely different from the Passaic soundchecks of a month earlier, and similar to the final form that will appear on *The River* LP.

11/2/78 Landover, Md., Capital Centre
"The Ties That Bind" and "Detroit Medley" are both included in a 21-song set.

11/4/78 Burlington, Vt., University of Vermont
11/5/78 Durham, N.H., University of New Hampshire
11/7/78 Ithaca, N.Y., Cornell University
11/8/78 Montreal, Quebec, The Forum
A 21-song set.

11/10/78 Olean, N.Y., St. Bonaventure University
11/12/78 Troy, N.Y., Rensselaer Polytechnic Institute
Soundcheck includes "Badlands," "High School Confidential," "I

New York, N.Y., November 27, 1980.

Don't Wanna Hang Up My Rock 'n' Roll Shoes," "Darkness," and "Promised Land." This 23-song set includes "Sandy" in the encores and "Rave On" opens the second set.

11/4/78 Utica, N.Y., Utica Memorial Auditorium
"Rave On" opens the show, "High School Confidential" opens the second set, and "Louie, Louie" is played in the encores.

11/16/78 Toronto, Ontario, Maple Leaf Gardens
A 22-song set opens for the first time with "Reddy Teddy." "The Ties That Bind" opens the second set as it will for most of the remaining shows on the tour.

11/17/78 East Lansing, Mich., Michigan State University

11/18/78 Oxford, Ohio, Miami University

11/20/78 Champaign, Ill., University of Illinois
A 22-song set, typical of this part of the tour: Badlands/Streets of Fire/Spirit in the Night/Darkness/Independence Day/Promised Land/Prove It All Night/Racing in the Street/Thunder Road/Jungleland//Saint in the City/The Ties That Bind/Fire/Candy's Room/Because the Night/Point Blank/Mona/She's the One/Backstreets/Rosalita/Born to Run/Detroit Medley/Quarter to Three.

11/21/78 Evanston, Ill., Northwestern University
A 22-song set.

11/25/78 St. Louis, Mo., Kiel Opera House
Second set opens with "For You," and "Tenth Avenue Freeze-out" returns to the encores.

11/27/78 Milwaukee, Wisc., Milwaukee Arena
Second set opens with "The Ties That Bind," followed by "Santa Claus." "Santa Claus" will be played at all remaining shows on the tour.

11/28/78 Madison, Wisc., Dane County Coliseum
"High School Confidential" opens a 23-song set.

11/29/78 St. Paul, Minn., Civic Center
"Tenth Avenue Freeze-out" and "Detroit Medley" in the encores.

12/1/78 Norman, Okla., Lloyd Noble Center, University of Oklahoma
A 24-song set includes "Heartbreak Hotel," "Factory," and "Saint in the City."

12/3/78 Carbondale, Ill., Southern Illinois University

12/5/78 Baton Rouge, La., Louisiana State University

12/7/78 Austin, Tex., University of Texas
"The Fever" returns to the second set.

12/8/78 Houston, Tex., The Summit
"Badlands" kicks off an excellent 25-song set that closes with "You Can't Sit Down."

12/9/78 Dallas, Tex., Convention Center

12/11/78 Boulder, Colo., University of Colorado

12/13/78 Tucson, Ariz., Community Center
Home stretch of the *Darkness* tour is a streak of superb shows, including this 26-song set that closes with "Quarter to Three."

12/15-16/78 San Francisco, Calif., Winterland
Broadcast live on 12/15/78 across the West Coast, a 25-song set includes one of the most passionate performances of "Backstreets" ever. "Fire," recorded live here on 12/16/78, is included on *Live 1975-85*. Terrific follow-up show to the previous night's radio broadcast. Set includes "Good Rockin' Tonight," "Rendezvous" (played for the first time since 5/12/77), "Santa Claus," and "The Fever."

12/19/78 Portland, Ore., Paramount Theater
A 26-song set includes "Good Rockin' Tonight," "Rendezvous," "Rave On," and "Quarter to Three."

12/20/78 Seattle, Wash., Seattle Center Arena
"Pretty Flamingo" is played in the first set for the first time since

5/27/76. Bruce and the band return to the stage 15 minutes after the show appears to end. The stage is already partly disassembled. Undaunted, Bruce plugs in and plays "Rave On" and "Twist and Shout" for the remaining and duly amazed crowd. Badlands/Streets of Fire/Rendezvous/Spirit in the Night/Darkness/Independence Day/Promised Land/Prove It All Night/Pretty Flamingo/Thunder Road/Jungleland//The Ties That Bind/Santa Claus/Fire/Candy's Room/Because the Night/The Fever/Mona/She's the One/Backstreets/Rosalita/Born to Run/Detroit Medley/Tenth Avenue Freeze-out/Quarter to Three/Rave On/Twist and Shout.

12/27-28/78 Pittsburgh, Pa., Stanley Theater
A new song, "Ramrod," opens the 26-song set on the second night, which includes first-set performances of "Sandy" and "Factory," and second-set performances of "Saint in the City" and "Rave On."

12/30/78 Detroit, Mich., Cobo Hall
A 24-song set.

12/31/78-1/1/79 Cleveland, Ohio, Richfield Coliseum
Twenty-eight-song New Year's special includes "Rendezvous," "Pretty Flamingo," "Rave On," "Auld Lang Syne" and "Good Rockin' Tonight." Final night of the *Darkness* tour (1/1/79) is Bruce's longest to date, clocking in at three and a half hours and 31 songs. This will be the final performance to date of "The Fever," "Meeting Across the River," and "Streets of Fire." Rave On/Badlands/Rendezvous/Spirit in the Night/Darkness/Factory/Streets of Fire/Heartbreak Hotel/Promised Land/Prove It All Night/Racing in the Street/Thunder Road/Meeting Across the River/Jungleland//For You/Saint in the City/Santa Claus/I Fought the Law/The Fever/Fire/Candy's Room/Because the Night/Point Blank/Mona/She's the One/Backstreets/The Last Time/Rosalita/Born to Run/Detroit Medley/Tenth Avenue Freeze-out/Quarter to Three.

3/14/79 Asbury Park, N.J., The Fast Lane
Bruce joins Robert Gordon on "Heartbreak Hotel" and "Fire."

4/13/79 Asbury Park, N.J., The Fast Lane
Bruce guests with Beaver Brown.

4/15/79 Asbury Park, N.J., The Fast Lane
Bruce guests with Beaver Brown on four songs.

5/27/79 Asbury Park, N.J., Paramount Theater
Bruce again guests with Robert Gordon on "Fire" and "Heartbreak Hotel."

9/22-23/79 New York, N.Y., Madison Square Garden
Bruce and the E Street Band perform at the MUSE anti-nuclear benefit concert. Jackson Browne guests both nights on "Stay." Bruce debuts "The River," which will become the title track of his next record. The "Detroit Medley" is recorded and later released on the *No Nukes* soundtrack album. Prove It All Night/Badlands/Promised Land/The River/Sherry Darling/Thunder Road/Jungleland/Rosalita/Born to Run/Stay/Detroit Medley/Rave On. Same set on 9/23/79, but without "Rave On." Footage from this night will be included in the *No Nukes* film.

10/5-6/79 Asbury Park, N.J., The Fast Lane
Bruce guests with Beaver Brown on "Rosalita" and "Twist and Shout."

3/1/80 Asbury Park, N.J., Stone Pony
Bruce guests with David Johansen.

· · · · ·

THE RIVER TOUR
For this tour, the "Detroit Medley" will count as one song and will consist of "Devil with the Blue Dress," "Jenny Take a Ride," "C.C. Rider," "Good Golly Miss Molly," and "I Hear a Train," after the 10/9/80 Detroit show. "Here She Comes/I

Tacoma, Wash., May 5, 1988.

Wanna Marry You" will be counted as one song. "No Money Down/Cadillac Ranch" will be counted as one song.

10/3/80 Ann Arbor, Mich., Crisler Arena
First show of *The River* tour. Bruce plays 11 songs from *The River*, which will not be released for over two weeks. Bob Seger closes the show with Bruce on "Thunder Road," which had also been played earlier in the set. Born to Run/Prove It All Night/Tenth Avenue Freeze-out (with new sax solo)/Wreck on the Highway/Darkness/Jackson Cage/Promised Land/Out in the Street/Racing in the Street/The River/Thunder Road/Badlands//Cadillac Ranch/I Wanna Marry You/Crush on You/Ramrod/Point Blank/Stolen Car/Because the Night/Backstreets/Rosalita/Jungleland/Detroit Medley/Thunder Road.

10/4/80 Cincinnati, Ohio, Riverfront Coliseum
A 27-song set opens with "Prove It All Night" and also includes "Independence Day," "Factory," and "The Ties That Bind."

10/6-7/80 Cleveland, Ohio, Richfield Coliseum
"Two Hearts" is added to the first set on 10/6/80. "You Can Look" is added to the second set on 10/7/80. "Two Hearts" is left out of an otherwise identical 28-song set.

10/9/80 Detroit, Mich., Cobo Hall
A 27-song set. "Wreck on the Highway" is moved to late in the second set.

10/10-11/80 Chicago, Ill., Uptown Theater
"Stolen Car" returns to a 28-song set on 10/10/80, and a new song "Here She Comes," which can be traced back to the early seventies, is used for the first time to introduce "I Wanna Marry You" on 10/11/80. A 31-song set includes "For You," "Good Rockin' Tonight," "You Can Look," and "Raise Your Hand."

10/13/80 St. Paul, Minn., Civic Centre
A 30-song set.

10/14/80 Milwaukee, Wisc., Milwaukee Arena
Another 30-song set includes "In the Midnight Hour."

10/17/80 *The River* is released in the U.S.

10/17-18/80 St. Louis, Mo., Kiel Opera House
A 33-song set on 10/18/80 including the premieres of "Hungry Heart," "Drive All Night," and "I'm a Rocker." It was in St. Louis and not Denver that Bruce meets a fan while watching Woody Allen's *Stardust Memories* and ends up going home with him to meet his family. Badlands/Out in the Street/Tenth Avenue Freeze-out/Darkness/Factory/Independence Day/Racing in the Street/Two Hearts/Jackson Cage/Promised Land/The River/Prove It All Night/Thunder Road//Good Rockin' Tonight/Cadillac Ranch/Fire/Sherry Darling/Here She Comes/I Wanna Marry You/The Ties That Bind/Wreck on the Highway/Point Blank/Crush on You/Ramrod/Hungry Heart/Drive All Night/Rosalita/Jungleland/Born to Run/I'm a Rocker/Detroit Medley.

10/20/80 Denver, Colo., McNicholls Arena

10/23/80 Seattle, Wash., Old Timer's Cafe
Bruce guests with the Lost Highway Band.

10/24/80 Seattle, Wash., Seattle Center Coliseum
A 29-song set includes a silent "Cadillac Ranch," as Bruce's microphone is dead. "Raise Your Hand" closes the show. "Good Rockin' Tonight" is played to the early arriving crowd who see the last part of the soundcheck. *Backstreets #1* handed out free to the first 10,000 fans.

10/25/80 Portland, Ore., Coliseum
Great set includes the only live performance of "On Top of Old Smokey," played in honor of Mount St. Helens, as well as rare versions of "I'm a Rocker" and "Prove It All Night" as the show opener.

10/27-28/80 Oakland, Calif., Coliseum
A 30-song set on 10/27/80 includes "I'm a Rocker" in the encores. A 32-song set on 10/28/80 opens with "Good Rockin' Tonight." For the first time, the dark trio of "Wreck on the Highway," "Stolen Car," and "Point Blank" are played in sequence.

10/30-11/1/80 Los Angeles, Calif., Sports Arena
A 31-song set on 10/30/80 opens with "Born to Run." The wild Halloween show opens with "Haunted House" and Bruce in a coffin.

"The Price You Pay" is debuted in the first set, and the second set includes "Outer Limits" and "No Money Down" as an introduction to "Cadillac Ranch." On 11/1/80 "Fade Away" premieres in the second set and Jackson Browne joins Bruce in the encores for "Sweet Little Sixteen."

11/3/80 Los Angeles, Calif., Sports Arena
"Growin' Up" makes its first appearance on the *River* tour in a 28-song set that again includes "The Price You Pay." The version of "The Price You Pay" performed on the tour includes a new verse not included on the recorded LP track.

11/5/80 Tempe, Ariz., Arizona State University Activities Center
One day after the election of Ronald Reagan for President, Bruce begins the show by saying, "I don't know what you guys think about what happened last night, but I think it's pretty frightening. You guys are young, there's gonna be a lot of people depending on you comin' up, so this is for you." "Badlands" from this night is included on *Live 1975-85*. This set is a good example of the shows on the first leg of the *River* tour. Of note: The inclusion of "Jackson Cage," and "Crush on You," which will be played very infrequently on the rest of the tour, and the linkage of "Stolen Car," "Wreck on the Highway," and "Point Blank," in what would have to be considered the most depressing segment of any Springsteen show ever. Born to Run/Prove It All Night/Tenth Avenue Freeze-out/Darkness/Independence Day/Factory/Jackson Cage/Two Hearts/Promised Land/Out in the Street/Racing in the Street/The River/Badlands/Thunder Road//No Money Down/Cadillac Ranch/Hungry Heart/Fire/Candy's Room/Sherry Darling/Here She Comes/I Wanna Marry You/The Ties That Bind/Stolen Car/Wreck on the Highway/Drive All Night/Point Blank/Crush on You/Ramrod/You Can Look/Backstreets/Rosalita/I'm a Rocker/Jungleland/Detroit Medley.

11/8/80 Dallas, Tex., Reunion Arena
A 31-song set opens with "Born to Run." Second set opens with "Yellow Rose of Texas."

11/9/80 Austin, Tex., Frank Erwin Center
A 33-song set includes "The Price You Pay," "Waltz Across Texas," and "Yellow Rose of Texas." The show opens with "Prove It All Night," followed by "Two Hearts."

11/11/80 Baton Rouge, La., LSU Assembly Center
A 28-song set with "The Price You Pay."

11/14-15/80 Houston, Tex., The Summit
"In the Midnight Hour" is played fourth in a 30-song set on 11/14/80. A 31-song set on 11/27/80 includes "The Price You Pay." On 11/28/80, a 33-song set includes the first *River* tour performance of "Sandy" in out/Darkness/Independence Day/Factory/Two Hearts/Out in the Street/Promised Land/Racing in the Street/The River/Prove It All Night/Thunder Road//No Money Down/Cadillac Ranch/Hungry Heart/Fire/Candy's Room/Because the Night/Fade Away/Stolen Car/Growin' Up/Wreck on the Highway/Point Blank/The Ties That Bind/Ramrod/Crush on You/Backstreets/Rosalita/Born to Run/Jungleland/Detroit Medley.

11/20/80 Chicago, Ill., Rosemont Horizon
A 29-song set includes "The Price You Pay," "Growin' Up," and "Drive All Night."

11/23-24/80 Landover, Md., Capital Centre
A 29-song set with "I'm a Rocker" in the encores on 11/23/80. "You Can Look" is moved to the first set on 11/24/80 in a 32-song concert that opens with "Prove It All Night." "Fade Away" and "Growin' Up" are both included in the second set.

11/27-28/80 New York, N.Y., Madison Square Garden
A 31-song set on 11/27/80 includes "The Price You Pay." On 11/28/80 a 33-song set includes the first *River* tour performance of "Sandy" in the encores. "Mystery Train" is included in the "Detroit Medley." "Ramrod" includes a few lyrics that will later evolve into "Open All Night."

11/30-12/1/80 Pittsburgh, Pa., Civic Arena
On 11/30/80 "Growin' Up" is included in a 32-song set. On 12/1/80, the first set includes "You Can Look" and "The Price You Pay," while the second set features "Fade Away" and the first 1980 appearance of "For You."

Tacoma, Wash., October 17, 1984.

12/2/80 Rochester, N.Y., War Memorial
A 31-song set includes "For You," "Sandy," and "I'm a Rocker."
12/4/80 Buffalo, N.Y., War Memorial Auditorium
A 34-song set includes "The Price You Pay," "I Fought the Law,"
"For You," "Stolen Car," "Drive All Night," and "Santa Claus."
12/6/80 Philadelphia, Pa., The Spectrum
A 34-song set includes "Sandy," "Point Blank," and "I'm a Rocker."
12/8-9/80 Philadelphia, Pa., The Spectrum
Another 34-song set on 12/8/80 includes "Growin' Up." A 35-song set
the night after the murder of John Lennon on 12/9/80. Bruce opens
the show with a few comments about Lennon, explaining why he felt
he should go on and play that night. "Rendezvous" is played for the
first time since 1/1/79. 12/9/80 set: Born to Run/Out in the Street/
Tenth Avenue Freeze-out/Darkness/The Price You Pay/Indepen-
dence Day/Two Hearts/Prove It All Night/Promised Land/Racing in
the Street/The River/Badlands/Thunder Road//Cadillac Ranch/
Sherry Darling/Hungry Heart/Fire/Candy's Room/Because the
Night/Sandy/For You/Stolen Car/Wreck on the Highway/Point
Blank/Rendezvous/ Ramrod/You Can Look/Drive All Night/Rosali-
ta/Santa Claus/ Jungleland/I'm a Rocker/Detroit Medley/Twist
and Shout.
12/11/80 Providence, R.I., Civic Center
Same set as 12/9/80, but "Crush on You" and "Backstreets" replace
"You Can Look" and "Drive All Night," and "Twist and Shout" is
not played.
12/12/80 Hartford, Conn., Civic Center
"Fade Away" is included in a 33-song set that opens with "Prove It
All Night."
12/15-16/80 Boston, Mass., Boston Gardens
A 32-song set on 12/15/80. A great 34-song set on 12/16/80 includes
the first *River* tour performance of "Spirit in the Night." Also included
are "I Fought the Law," "Sandy," "Growin' Up," "For You," and

"Drive All Night." "Crush on You" makes its last appearance to date.
12/18-19/80 New York, N.Y., Madison Square Garden
Bruce returns to New York for two more shows, a month after his first
two *River* shows there. "Who'll Stop the Rain" premieres in a 35-song
set on 12/18/80 that again includes "I Fought the Law." A 34-song set
on 12/19/80 includes "Fade Away" and "Raise Your Hand."
12/28-29/80 Uniondale, N.Y., Nassau Coliseum
Show opens on 12/28/80 with the premiere of "Merry Christmas
Baby," the first of many surprises that will occur over these three
nights. Flo and Eddie join the band for "Hungry Heart," and that,
along with "Because the Night," are the songs from this night included
on *Live 1975-85*. "This Land is Your Land" is credited on *Live 1975-85*
liner notes to this night, but it is actually taken from the following
night. "Who'll Stop the Rain" and "Santa Claus" are also included in
this 33-song set. The show on 12/29/80 is the last to include "Incident
on 57th Street," and one of the few shows that links it to "Rosalita" as
they appear on the second album. "Incident" becomes one of the two
live B-sides from *Live 1975-85*. The show opens with a rare version of
"Night," in a 35-song set. "Darkness" and "You Can Look" from this
night are included on *Live 1975-85*.
12/31/80 Uniondale, N.Y., Nassau Coliseum
The longest show Springsteen and the E Street Band have ever
played, clocking in at four hours and 38 songs, this also was one of the
best. Rarities include "Night," "Rendezvous," "Fade Away," "The
Price You Pay," "Spirit in the Night," "Held Up Without a Gun," "In
the Midnight Hour," and "Auld Lang Syne," all done infrequently at
best, or never before this show in a few cases. Night/Prove It All
Night/Spirit in the Night/Darkness/Independence Day/Who'll Stop
the Rain/This Land Is Your Land/Promised Land/Out in the Street/
Racing in the Street/The River/Badlands/Thunder Road//Cadillac
Ranch/Sherry Darling/Hungry Heart/Merry Christmas Baby/Fire/
Candy's Room/Because the Night/Sandy/Rendezvous/Fade Away/

The Price You Pay/Wreck on the Highway/Two Hearts/Ramrod/ You Can Look/Held Up Without a Gun/In the Midnight Hour/ Auld Lang Syne/Rosalita/Santa Claus/Jungleland/Born to Run/Detroit Medley/Twist and Shout/Raise Your Hand.

1/20-21/81 Toronto, Ontario, Maple Leaf Gardens
After almost three weeks off, the *River* tour's second leg opens with a 32-song set that includes "Who'll Stop the Rain," "Sandy," "For You," and "I'm a Rocker." The concert on 1/21/81 is another 32-song set: Night/Out in the Street/Tenth Avenue Freeze-out/Darkness/Independence Day/Who'll Stop the Rain/Prove It All Night/Two Hearts/ Promised Land/The Price You Pay/The River/Badlands/Thunder Road//No Money Down/Cadillac Ranch/Sherry Darling/Hungry Heart/Fire/You Can Look/Sandy/Growin' Up/Fade Away/Stolen Car/Wreck on the Highway/Candy's Room/Ramrod/Backstreets/ Rosalita/I'm a Rocker/Jungleland/Born to Run/Detroit Medley/Raise Your Hand.

1/23/81 Montreal, Quebec, The Forum
"Night" opens a 31-song set that also includes "Because the Night," "The Ties That Bind" and "Drive All Night" in the second set.

1/24/81 Ottawa, Ontario, Civic Centre
"I Fought the Law" and "Sandy" are included in a 31-song set.

1/26/81 South Bend, Ind., Notre Dame University
"Out in the Street" opens a 32-song set. "Double Shot of My Baby's Love " and "Louie, Louie" start the second set.

1/28/81 St. Louis, Mo., Checkerdome
"Night" kicks off a 29-song set including "Fade Away," "The Price You Pay," and "For You."

1/29/81 Ames, Iowa, Hilton Coliseum
"Jackson Cage" is included in the first set.

2/1/81 St. Paul, Minn., Civic Centre

2/2/81 Madison, Wis., Dane County Coliseum
Five-song encore of "I'm a Rocker," "Jungleland," "Born to Run," "Detroit Medley," and "Twist and Shout."

2/5/81 Kansas City, Mo., Kemper Arena
"I Fought the Law" and "Because the Night" are played in a 29-song set that features "Kansas City" in the encores.

2/7/81 Champaign, Ill., University of Illinois
"Here She Comes/I Wanna Marry You" returns to a 30-song set.

2/12/81 Mobile, Ala., Municipal Auditorium
"This Land Is Your Land" is played for the first time since the Nassau Coliseum shows in December.

2/13/81 Starkville, Miss., Mississippi State University
A 28-song set includes "Fade Away," "For You," and "Sandy" in the second set.

2/15-16/81 Lakeland, Fla., Civic Center
Twenty-eight song sets are played both nights. The set on 2/16/81 includes "Good Rockin' Tonight" and "High School Confidential" in the "Detroit Medley." Show opens with "Born to Run."

2/18/81 Jacksonville, Fla., Coliseum
"This Land Is Your Land" returns to a 27-song set.

2/20/81 Hollywood, Fla., Sportatorium
Bruce plays a 27-song set that includes "The Price You Pay," "Fade Away," and "Because the Night."

2/22/81 Columbia, S.C., Carolina Coliseum
A 28-song set.

2/23/81 Atlanta, Ga., The Omni
"Fade Away" is included in a 28-song set.

2/25/81 Memphis, Tenn., Mid-South Coliseum

2/26/81 Nashville, Tenn., Municipal Auditorium
A 27-song set.

2/28/81 Greensboro, N.C., Greensboro Coliseum
"Racing in the Street" is played in the second set of a 28-song set.

3/2/81 Hampton, Va., Hampton Roads Coliseum
"Ramrod" opens the second set of a 28-song show that opens with "Prove It All Night."

3/4/81 Lexington, Ky., Rupp Arena
A 12-song first set includes "This Land Is Your Land" and "Who'll Stop the Rain."

◄ Oakland, Calif., October 21, 1984.

3/5/81 Indianapolis, Ind., Market Square Arena
Final show of the second leg of the tour. The band will take a month off before going on to Europe. Prove It All Night/Out in the Street/ Tenth Avenue Freeze-out/Darkness/Factory/Independence Day/ Who'll Stop the Rain/Two Hearts/Promised Land/This Land Is Your Land/The River/Badlands/Thunder Road//Cadillac Ranch/Sherry Darling/Hungry Heart/Fire/You Can Look/Fade Away/Because the Night/Stolen Car/Racing in the Street/Candy's Room/Ramrod/Rosalita/I'm a Rocker/Jungleland/Born to Run/Detroit Medley.

4/7/81 Hamburg, West Germany, Congress Centrum
Bruce and the E Street Band kick off their first European tour and play their first show ever in Germany.

4/9/81 West Berlin, Germany, ICC Halle
A 27-song set. Factory/Prove It All Night/Out in the Street/Tenth Avenue Freeze-out/Darkness/Independence Day/Who'll Stop the Rain/Two Hearts/Promised Land/This Land Is Your Land/The River/Badlands//Thunder Road/Cadillac Ranch/Sherry Darling/ Hungry Heart/Fire/You Can Look/Wreck on the Highway/Racing in the Street/Backstreets/Ramrod/Rosalita/Born to Run/Detroit Medley/Rockin' All Over the World, Twist and Shout.

4/11/81 Zurich, Switzerland, Hallenstadion
A 26-song set opens again with "Factory." Identical set to the preceding show with the omission of "Twist and Shout."

4/14/81 Frankfurt, West Germany, Festhalle
Another 26-song set, with "Point Blank" replacing "Wreck on the Highway."

4/16/81 Munich, West Germany, Olympiahalle
A 25-song set includes "The Ties That Bind" and "Wreck on the Highway."

4/18-19/81 Paris, France, Palais Des Sports
"Candy's Room" and "I Can't Help Falling in Love" are added to a 27-song set on 4/18/81. The second show opens for the first time with "Follow That Dream," a song originally performed by Elvis Presley and now rewritten by Bruce, incorporating part of Roy Orbison's "In Dreams" and some original lyrics. The 28-song set also includes "Because the Night," "Point Blank," "I Can't Help Falling in Love," and "Sweet Soul Music."

4/21/81 Barcelona, Spain, Palacio de Deportes
"Factory" again opens the show. A 26-song set.

4/24/81 Lyon, France, Palais des Sports
"Follow That Dream" opens a 25-song set.

4/26/81 Brussels, Belgium, Vorst National
Second set of the show includes "Stolen Car" and "Fire."

4/28-29/81 Rotterdam, Holland, Sportspaleis Ahoy
"Candy's Room" and "Point Blank" return to a 27-song set on 4/28/81. Bruce's frightening cover of Creedence Clearwater Revival's "Run Through the Jungle" starts an exceptional show on 4/29/81. The song is the first indication of the kind of material that Bruce will release the following year on the *Nebraska* LP. The arrangement of "Run Through the Jungle" is similar to 1984 performances of "State Trooper." Run Through the Jungle/Prove It All Night/The Ties That Bind/Darkness/Independence Day/Factory/Who'll Stop the Rain/ Two Hearts/Out in the Street/Thunder Road/This Land Is Your Land/The River/Promised Land/Badlands//Cadillac Ranch/Sherry Darling/Hungry Heart/Fire/You Can Look/Wreck on the Highway/ Racing in the Street/Backstreets/Candy's Room/Rosalita/Born to Run/Detroit Medley/I'm a Rocker/Rockin' All Over the World.

5/1/81 Copenhagen, Denmark, The Forum
Bruce sings "Hungry Heart" with the Danish group Malurt.

5/2/81 Copenhagen, Denmark, Brondby-Hallen
A 30-song set opens with "Follow That Dream," and also includes "Candy's Room," "Because the Night," and "Point Blank" in the second set.

5/3/81 Gothenberg, Denmark, Scandinavium
"Run Through the Jungle" and "I Can't Help Falling in Love" are included in a 25-song set.

5/5/81 Oslo, Norway, Drammenshallen

5/7-8/81 Stockholm, Sweden, Johnanneshovg Isstadion
A 27-song set on 5/7/81 opens with "Follow that Dream." On 5/8/81, a superb 31-song set opens with "Run Through the Jungle," which,

regrettably, is not played again. The second set includes "Point Blank," "Wreck on the Highway," and "I Can't Help Falling in Love" in the encores.

5/11/81 Newcastle, England, Newcastle City Hall
Bruce's first U.K. appearance since 1975.

5/13-14/81 Manchester, England, Apollo Theatre
"Johnny Bye Bye" premieres in the first set of a 29-song show on 5/13/81 that also features the first European performance of "The Price You Pay." The 24-song set on 5/14/81 is the shortest of the European tour.

5/16-17/81 Edinburgh, Scotland, Playhouse Theatre
"The Ties That Bind" opens a 26-song set on 5/17/81 that again includes "Johnny Bye Bye."

5/20/81 Stafford, England, New Bingley Hall
A 27-song set opens with "Prove It All Night."

5/26-27/81 Brighton, England, Brighton Centre
A 26-song set is played on 5/26/81. On 5/27/81, encores include "Jungleland" for the first time on the European tour. "Born to Run" opens the first set, which also includes "The Price You Pay."

5/29-30, 6/1-2/81 London, England, Wembley Arena
On the first night of six in London, Bruce's reworking of Jimmy Cliff's "Trapped" premieres. "Jackson Cage," "Trapped," "Because the Night," and "Jungleland" are included in a 28-song set on 5/30/81. The third show opens with "The Ties That Bind." The 27-song set includes "Follow That Dream," "Johnny Bye Bye," and "Trapped" in sequence in the first set. A 27-song set on 6/2/81 includes "I Fought the Law" in the encores.

6/4-5/81 London, England, Wembley Arena
Final night in London is a 31-song set that includes "Jole Blon" for the first time. Born to Run/Prove It All Night/Out in the Street/Follow That Dream/Darkness/Independence Day/Johnny Bye Bye/Two Hearts/Who'll Stop the Rain/Promised Land/This Land Is Your Land/The River/I Fought the Law/Badlands//Thunder Road/Hungry Heart/You Can Look/Cadillac Ranch/Sherry Darling/Jole Blon/Fire/Because the Night/Here She Comes/I Wanna Marry You/Point Blank/Candy's Room/Ramrod/Rosalita/I'm a Rocker/Jungleland/I Can't Help Falling in Love/Detroit Medley.

6/7-8/81 Birmingham, England, International Arena
Pete Townshend joins Bruce on guitar in the 6/7/81 set for "Born to Run" and the "Detroit Medley." "Drive All Night" and "I Wanna Marry You" are also included in the 27-song set. On 6/8/81, the final 29-song set of the European tour closes with "Rockin' All Over the World."

6/14/81 Los Angeles, Calif., Hollywood Bowl
Bruce joins Jackson Browne and Gary U.S. Bonds for the "Survival Sunday" anti-nuclear benefit. This Land Is Your Land/Promised Land/Jole Blon/Hungry Heart/Brother John Is Gone.

6/15/81 San Francisco, Calif., Old Waldorf
Bruce joins Gary U.S. Bonds at his own show, playing on "Jole Blon," "This Little Girl," "Quarter to Three," "School's Out," and "New Orleans."

7/2-3/81 East Rutherford, N.J., Brendan Byrne Arena
Bruce and the E Street Band open this brand-new arena with a 29-song set. Tom Waits's "Jersey Girl" is played for the first time, and many songs make their U.S. premieres. 7/2/81 set: Born to Run/Prove It All Night/Out in the Street/Darkness/Independence Day/Johnny Bye Bye/Two Hearts/Who'll Stop the Rain/Promised Land/This Land Is Your Land/The River/Badlands/Thunder Road//You Can Look/Cadillac Ranch/Sherry Darling/Jole Blon/Hungry Heart/Wreck on the Highway/Follow That Dream/Racing in the Street/Ramrod/Rosalita/I'm a Rocker/Jungleland/Jersey Girl/I Don't Wanna Go Home/Detroit Medley/Rockin' All Over the World. The 28-song set on 7/3/81 includes a guest appearance from Gary U.S. Bonds on "This Little Girl." "Summertime Blues" is also played in the first set.

7/5-6/81 East Rutherford, N.J., Brendan Byrne Arena
"Sandy" is added to a four-song encore on 7/5/81, in a 28-song set that opens with "Thunder Road." "Independence Day," "Cadillac Ranch," and "Racing in the Street" from 7/6/81 are later included on *Live 1975-85*.

7/8-9/81 East Rutherford, N.J., Brendan Byrne Arena
"Two Hearts" and "Candy's Room" from 7/8/81 are later included on *Live 1975-85*. A four-song encore on 7/8/81 includes "Jersey Girl," which will later appear as the B-side of "Cover Me" and as the closing song on *Live 1975-85*.

7/11/81 Red Bank, N.J., Big Man's West
Bruce and the E Street Band open Clarence's new club. Summertime Blues/Jole Blon/Ramrod/Around and Around/You Can't Sit Down/Cadillac Ranch.

7/13/81 Philadelphia, Pa., The Spectrum
A 27-song set.

7/15-16/81 Philadelphia, Pa., The Spectrum
A 26-song set is played on 7/15/81. The 7/16/81 set consists of 25 songs, with "Hungry Heart" as the second set opener.

7/18-19/81 Philadelphia, Pa., The Spectrum
A 26-song set on 7/18/81 includes "Candy's Room" and "Point Blank." The show of 7/19/81 is the only show of the five at the Spectrum with significant set changes. "Factory," "For You," "I Fought the Law," "Sandy," and "Growin' Up" are all played in a 25-song set.

7/29-30/81 Cleveland, Ohio, Richfield Coliseum
Southside Johnny guests both nights on "I Don't Wanna Go Home." The 26-song set on 7/29/81 includes "For You." An excellent 28-song set on 7/30/81 opens with "Rockin' All Over the World" and closes with "Twist and Shout."

8/4-5/81 Landover, Md., Capital Centre
The "Detroit Medley" now includes "Spotlight on the Big Man," a tribute to Clarence, to the tune of "Sweet Soul Music." The show on 8/4/81 is a 26-song set. A 27-song set on 8/5/81 opens with "Rockin' All Over the World" and also includes "Jackson Cage," "Wreck on the Highway" and "Twist and Shout."

8/6/81 Washington, D.C., Bayou Club
Bruce jumps onstage with Robbin Thompson's band for "Carol."

8/7/81 Landover, Md., Capital Centre
Final night's 27-song set includes "Summertime Blues," "Sandy," and "Twist and Shout."

8/11-12/81 Detroit Mich., Joe Louis Arena
A 29-song set on 8/11/81 includes "For You." On 8/12/81, Mitch Ryder guests on "Detroit Medley."

8/16-17/81 Morrison, Colo., Red Rocks Amphitheater
Bruce lets part of the crowd in for a soundcheck of "Hungry Heart," "Prove It All Night" and "Rockin' All Over the World" on 8/16/81. During the show, "Sea Cruise" is played for only the second time. Bruce's first outdoor show since he played here in 1978. On 8/17/81, a 27-song set includes "Summertime Blues" and "For You."

8/20-21/81 Los Angeles, Calif., Sports Arena
The show on 8/20/81 is a benefit for Vietnam veterans. A short speech by Vietnam veteran Bobby Muller is followed by one of Bruce's most passionate sets ever. During "The River," Bruce is overcome with emotion and stops singing. The beautiful "Ballad of Easy Rider" is played for the only time. Who'll Stop the Rain/Prove It All Night/The Ties That Bind/Darkness/Johnny Bye Bye/Independence Day/Trapped/Two Hearts/Out in the Street/Promised Land/The River/This Land is Your Land/Badlands/Thunder Road/Hungry Heart/You Can Look/Cadillac Ranch/Sherry Darling/Jole Blon/Wreck on the Highway/Racing in the Street/Candy's Room/Ramrod/Rosalita/Jungleland/Ballad of Easy Rider/Born to Run/Detroit Medley/Twist and Shout. The set on 8/21/81 consists of 26 songs.

8/23-24/81 Los Angeles, Calif., Sports Arena
A 28-song set on 8/23/81 includes "Stolen Car" and the only *River* tour performance of "Rave On." On 8/24/81, Tom Waits joins Bruce for "Jersey Girl," in a 28-song set that includes "Follow That Dream" and "Growin' Up."

8/27-28/81 Los Angeles, Calif., Sports Arena
The set of 8/27/81 consists of 27 songs. The 28-song final night is another exceptional set. Bruce's only performance of Woody Guthrie's "Deportee (Plane Wreck at Los Gatos)." Also Creedence's "Proud Mary" debuts. Other highlights include "Rockin' All Over

Cleveland, Ohio, December 31, 1978. ▶

the World," "I Fought the Law," and a killer "Quarter to Three."

9/2/81 San Diego, Calif., Sports Arena
A 30-song set again closes with "Quarter to Three," and also includes "Jackson Cage," "Follow That Dream," "Growin' Up," and "I'm a Rocker."

9/5/81 Pasadena, Calif., Perkin's Cow Palace
Bruce joins the Pretenders for an encore of "Higher and Higher."

9/8/81 Chicago, Ill., Rosemont Horizon
A 26-song set.

9/10-11/81 Chicago, Ill,. Rosemont Horizon
"Out in the Street" opens a 27-song set on 9/10/81 that includes the only *River* tour appearance of "Mona/She's the One." The song will not be played at all on the *Born in the USA* tour, but will be included in every *Tunnel of Love* tour set. A great 28-song set on 9/11/81 includes "Saint in the City" for the first time since 1/1/79. The set also includes "Jersey Girl," "For You," "I Wanna Marry You," and "Drive All Night," and closes with "Twist and Shout."

9/13-14/81 Cincinnati, Ohio, Riverfront Coliseum
A 27-song set on 9/13/81 ends with "Twist and Shout." The final night of the *River* tour on 9/14/81 is also Miami Steve's final performance with the E Street Band and the band's last show for 33 months. Rockin' All Over the World/Prove It All Night/The Ties That Bind/Darkness/Follow That Dream/Independence Day/Trapped/Two Hearts/Who'll Stop the Rain/Out in the Street/The Promised Land/The River/This Land is Your Land/Badlands/Thunder Road//Hungry Heart/Saint in the City/Cadillac Ranch/Sherry Darling/Proud Mary/Johnny Bye Bye/Racing in the Street/Ramrod/Rosalita/I'm a Rocker/Jungleland/Born to Run/Detroit Medley/Quarter to Three.

. . . . .

1982 TOUR OF NEW JERSEY

1/5/82 Asbury Park, N.J., Stone Pony
Bruce guests with the Lord Gunner Group on "In the Midnight Hour" and "Jole Blon." This is the first of over 40 guest appearances Bruce will make during 1982.

1/12/82 New Brunswick, N.J., Royal Manor North
Bruce joins Nils Lofgren onstage for "Lucille" and "Carol."

2/20/82 Red Bank, N.J., Big Man's West
Bruce joins Beaver Brown on "Ain't That a Shame," "Money," and "You Can't Sit Down."

4/9-11/82 Red Bank, N.J., Big Man's West
Bruce guests with Beaver Brown on "Twist and Shout" on 4/9/82, and on "Lucille," "Jersey Girl," "Jole Blon," and "Twist and Shout" on 4/10/82. On 4/11/82, Bruce guests with John Eddie on "Long Tall Sally," "Rockin' All Over the World," "Proud Mary," and "Carol."

4/16/82 Red Bank, N.J., Big Man's West
Bruce joins Clarence and the Red Bank Rockers.

4/25/82 Asbury Park, N.J., Stone Pony
Bruce guests with Cats on a Smooth Surface.

5/2/82 Asbury Park, N.J., Stone Pony
Bruce joins Cats for "Long Tall Sally" and "Twist and Shout."

5/8/82 Asbury Park, N.J., The Fast Lane
Bruce and Beaver Brown perform "Jole Blon," "Jersey Girl," "Lucille," and "Around and Around."

5/16/82 Red Bank, N.J., Big Man's West
Bruce again joins Clarence and the Red Bank Rockers for "Tenth Avenue Freeze-out."

5/23/82 Asbury Park, N.J., The Fast Lane
Bruce joins Cats on "Carol," "Long Tall Sally," and "Twist and Shout."

5/29/82 Red Bank, N.J., Big Man's West
Bruce and Southside join Beaver Brown on "Little Latin Lupe Lu," "Summertime Blues," "Around and Around," and "High School Confidential."

6/6/82 Asbury Park, N.J., Stone Pony
Bruce guests with Cats on a Smooth Surface.

6/12/82 New York, N.Y., Central Park
Bruce joins Jackson Browne for "Promised Land" and "Running on

Empty" at this giant event, the Rally for Disarmament.

6/12/82 Red Bank, N.J., Big Man's West
After playing with Jackson Browne earlier in the day, Bruce drives to Jersey and guests with Sonny Kenn on "Walking the Dog," "Route 66," and "Carol."

6/13/82 Asbury Park, N.J, Stone Pony
Bruce joins Cats on "Heartbreak Hotel," "Around and Around," "Lucille," "Kansas City," and "Twist and Shout."

6/20/82 Asbury Park, N.J., Stone Pony
Bruce again joins Cats for a six-song set. Come On, Let's Go/Little Latin Lupe Lu/Sweet Little Sixteen/Around and Around/Lucille/Twist and Shout.

6/26/82 Red Bank, N.J., Big Man's West
Billy Chinnock calls Bruce onstage for "Lucille."

6/27/82 Red Bank, N.J., Big Man's West
Bruce comes onstage for "Tenth Avenue Freeze-out" with Clarence and the Red Bank Rockers.

7/17/82 Red Bank, N.J., Big Man's West
Bruce guests with the Iron City Houserockers on "Mony Mony," "Shout," Chuck Berry's "Johnny Bye Bye" and "Whole Lotta Shakin' Going On."

7/23/82 Freehold, N.J., Monmouth County Fair
Bruce joins Sonny Kenn for "Sweet Little Sixteen," "Long Tall Sally," "Carol," "Shake," and "Land of 1000 Dances."

7/23/82 Asbury Park, N.J., The Fast Lane
Later in the evening, Bruce joins the Stray Cats for "Twenty Flight Rock," "Be Bop a Lula" and "Long Tall Sally."

7/25/82 Asbury Park, N.J., Stone Pony
Eight-song set with Cats on a Smooth Surface includes "From Small Things," written and recorded for *The River* and later given to and recorded by Dave Edmunds. Come On Let's Go/From Small Things/Ramrod/Lucille/Around and Around/The Wanderer/Long Tall Sally/Twist and Shout.

7/31/82 Red Bank, N.J., Big Man's West
Bruce joins Sonny Kenn for "Sweet Little Sixteen," "Ready Teddy," "Rip It Up," "Around and Around," and "Sweet Little Rock 'n' Roller."

8/1/82 Asbury Park, N.J., Stone Pony
Bruce joins Cats for a six-song set: Rip It Up/Come On Over to My Place/Come On Let's Go/Lucille/Around and Around/Twist and Shout.

8/6-7/82 Red Bank, N.J., Big Man's West
Bruce joins Beaver Brown for "Ready Teddy," "Lucille," "Jersey Girl," and "Twist and Shout" on 8/6/82, and for six songs on 8/7/82: Ready Teddy/From Small Things/Jersey Girl/Lucille/Do You Wanna Dance/Twist and Shout.

8/8/82 Asbury Park, N.J., Stone Pony
Bruce plays for the third straight night, this time for eight songs with Cats. Bruce plays a snatch of a new song titled "On the Prowl," which will later evolve into "Downbound Train." Ready Teddy/From Small Things/Come On Let's Go/Come On Over to My Place/Around and Around/Lucille, including On the Prowl/Twist and Shout.

8/13/82 Farmingdale, N.J., Tower Recording Studio
Bruce rehearses with Cats for the Stone Pony anniversary show in two days.

8/15/82 Asbury Park, N.J., Stone Pony
Seven-song set with Cats includes a long "Detroit Medley." Ready Teddy/From Small Things/Around and Around/Jersey Girl/You Can Look/Havin' a Party/Detroit Medley including "Shake" and "Sweet Soul Music."

8/31/82 Wall, N.J., Jon Jon's
Bruce plays with Cats.

9/4/82 Red Bank, N.J., Big Man's West
Bruce joins Beaver Brown on "From Small Things," "Come On Let's Go," and "Lucille."

9/18/82 Red Bank, N.J., Big Man's West
Dave Edmunds calls Bruce onstage for six songs: From Small Things/Johnny B. Goode/Lucille/Let's Talk About Us/Carol/Bama Lama Bama Loo.

Tacoma, Wash., October 17, 1984.

9/19/82 Asbury Park, N.J., Stone Pony
Superb 12-song set with Cats: Ready Teddy/From Small Things/
Come On Let's Go/Lucille/Come On Over to My Place/Around and
Around/Havin' a Party/Jersey Girl/Wooly Bully/Louie, Louie/High-
Heeled Sneakers/Twist and Shout.
9/21/82 New York, N.Y., Peppermint Lounge
Bruce again joins Dave Edmunds for "From Small Things."
9/25/82 Asbury Park, N.J., Stone Pony
Six-song set with Cats: Ready Teddy/From Small Things/Come On
Over to My Place/Around and Around/Lucille/Twist and Shout.
9/29/82 Westwood, N.J., On Broadway
Bruce guests with Billy Rancher and the Unreal Gods.
10/3/82 Asbury Park, N.J., Stone Pony
Fourteen-song set is probably Bruce's longest guest appearance ever.
"Open All Night" premieres, and "On the Prowl" is now a separate,
complete song. Bruce and Cats probably had another rehearsal in the
days before this show. From Small Things/Come On Let's Go/Around
and Around/Open All Night/Jersey Girl/On the Prowl/Do You
Wanna Dance/Lucille/Wooly Bully/Louie, Louie/Rock Baby Rock/
Come On Over to My Place/Havin' a Party/Twist and Shout.
10/4/82 *Nebraska* is released in the U.S.
11/27/82 Los Angeles, Calif., Club Lingerie
Bruce guests with Jimmy and the Mustangs.
12/3/82 Palo Alto, Calif., The Keystone
Bruce guests with Clarence and the Red Bank Rockers on "Lucille"
and "From Small Things."
12/31/82 New York, N.Y., Harkness House
Bruce and others jam following Little Steven's wedding. Jole Blon/
I'm a Rocker/Hungry Heart/Save the Last Dance for Me/Rockin' All
Over the World/Shout.
1/8/83 Red Bank, N.J., Big Man's West
Closing night of Big Man's West, Bruce plays on "Rockin' All Over
the World" and "Lucille."

4/24/83 Asbury Park, N.J., Stone Pony
Bruce joins Cats for "From Small Things," "Around and Around,"
"Lucille," and "Twist and Shout."
4/27/83 Asbury Park, N.J., Stone Pony
Bruce guests with the Diamonds on "Lucille" and "Long Tall Sally."
6/18/83 Asbury Park, N.J., Stone Pony
Bruce again plays with the Diamonds.
7/10/83 Asbury Park, N.J., Stone Pony
Bruce and Cats play five songs.
7/16/83 Neptune, N.J., The Headliner
Bruce guests with Midnight Thunder.
8/2/83 New York, N.Y., Madison Square Garden
Bruce and Jackson Browne duet on "Stay," "Running on Empty,"
and "Sweet Little Sixteen."
8/14/83 Asbury Park, N.J., Stone Pony
Bruce plays six songs with Cats on a Smooth Surface: Ready Teddy/
Around and Around/Jersey Girl/Lucille/Twist and Shout/Ain't That
Lovin' You Baby.
8/19/83 Long Branch, N.J., Brighton Bar
Bruce joins John Eddie on "Blue Suede Shoes," "Rockin' All Over
the World," "Ain't That Lovin' You Baby," "Jersey Girl," and
"Carol."
11/6/83 Asbury Park, N.J., Stone Pony
Bruce joins Cats for a late set.
12/28/83 Red Bank, N.J., Monmouth Arts Center
Bruce lends a hand at La Bamba's "Holiday Hurrah" jam session,
playing "From Small Things," "Santa Claus," and "Twist and
Shout."
1/8/84 Asbury Park, N.J., Stone Pony
After failing to win the early-evening joke contest, Bruce joins Cats
for "Lucille" and "Carol."
1/14/84 New Brunswick, N.J., Patrix
Bruce joins John Eddie for five songs, including his first performance

of "Boom Boom" which becomes a staple on the European leg of the *Tunnel of Love Express* tour: Rockin' All Over the World/Ain't Too Proud to Beg/Boom Boom/Proud Mary/Twist and Shout.

3/25/84 Asbury Park, N.J., Stone Pony
Bruce plays "I'm Bad, I'm Nationwide" and "Lucille" with Cats.

4/8/84 Asbury Park, N.J., Stone Pony
Another guest appearance with Cats. Bruce plays on "Proud Mary," "Dirty Water," "I'm Bad, I'm Nationwide," and "Lucille."

4/13/84 Philadelphia, Pa., Ripley Music Hall
Bruce joins Clarence and the Red Bank Rockers for "Fire" and "Rockin' All Over the World."

4/21/84 Mount Ivy, N.Y., Expo
Bruce again guests with Clarence and the Red Bank Rockers.

4/22/84 Asbury Park, N.J., Stone Pony
Bruce joins Cats on "I'm Bad, I'm Nationwide," "Little Latin Lupe Lu," and "Jersey Girl."

5/19/84 Asbury Park, N.J., Stone Pony
Bruce jumps onstage with Clarence and his band for four songs: Fire/Midnight Hour/Lucille/Twist and Shout.

5/26/84 Asbury Park, N.J., Xanadu
Bruce premieres "Dancing in the Dark," guesting with Bystander.

6/1/84 Asbury Park, N.J., Stone Pony
Bruce makes another appearance with John Eddie, joining him on "I'm Bad, I'm Nationwide," "Proud Mary," "Bright Lights, Big City," and "Carol."

6/4/84 *Born in the USA* is released in the U.S.

6/8/84 Asbury Park, N.J., Stone Pony
The E Street Band minus Patti, but with Nils, makes a surprise appearance as a warm-up for the upcoming tour. "Darlington County," "Glory Days," "My Hometown" and "Born in the USA" all make their live debut. Thunder Road/Out in the Street/Prove It All Night/Glory Days/The River/Darlington County/Dancing in the Dark/Promised Land/My Hometown/Born in the USA/Badlands/Born to Run.

6/10/84 Asbury Park, N.J., Stone Pony
Bruce and Nils guest with Cats on "Gloria," "Boom Boom," "We Gotta Get Outta This Place," "The Last Time" and "Rockin' All Over the World."

6/21/84 Lancaster, Pa., The Village
An abbreviated E Street Band gives one final warm-up performance, which includes Max Weinberg playing on a drum machine during "Dancing in the Dark." Out in the Street/Prove It All Night/Glory Days/Hungry Heart/Dancing in the Dark/Rosalita.

. . . . .

BORN IN THE USA TOUR

For this tour, the "Detroit Medley" will be counted as one song. "Travelin' Band" will be counted as one song when it doesn't appear in the "Detroit Medley." "Do You Love Me" will be counted as one song, though it is included in the middle of "Twist and Shout."

6/29/84 St. Paul, Minn., Civic Centre
Bruce and the E Street Band begin their first tour in over two and a half years. Set includes eight songs from *Born in the USA* and five songs from *Nebraska*. Patti Scialfa's first show with the E Street Band. "No Surrender" is played with the full band, and "Dancing in the Dark" is played twice for the filming of the video. The Rolling Stones' "Street Fightin' Man" also debuts. Thunder Road/Prove It All Night/Out in the Street/Johnny 99/Atlantic City/Mansion on the Hill/The River/No Surrender/Glory Days/Promised Land/Used Cars/My Hometown/Born in the USA/Badlands//Hungry Heart/Dancing in the Dark/Cadillac Ranch/Sherry Darling/Highway Patrolman/I'm on Fire/Fire/Working on the Highway/Bobby Jean/Backstreets/Rosalita/I'm a Rocker/Jungleland/Born to Run/Street Fightin' Man/Detroit Medley.

◄ *Chicago, Ill., July 17, 1984.*

Seattle, Wash., October 24, 1980.

7/1-2/84 St. Paul, Minn., Civic Centre
A 32-song set on 7/1/84 includes the premieres of "Pink Cadillac," "Open All Night," "Reason to Believe," and "Nebraska." Other changes from the first night are "Ramrod" and "Darlington County." The set on 7/2/84 includes the final, full-band version of "No Surrender." Both "Cover Me" and "Downbound Train" premiere here, but, strangely, "Downbound Train" will not be played again during the next 31 shows. "Racing in the Street" and "Twist and Shout" are also played for the first time in 1984. One of the shortest shows of the U.S. tour.

7/5-6/84 Cincinnati, Ohio, Riverfront Coliseum
Six songs from *Nebraska* are included in a 28-song set on 7/5/84. "Cover Me" will not be played in the next 19 shows. A 27-song set on 7/6/84 opens with "Thunder Road."

7/8-9/84 Cleveland, Ohio, Richfield Coliseum
"Born to Run" opens a 28-song set on 7/8/84 that includes "Open All Night," complete with a story about Bruce being pulled over while driving without a license. "Darkness" is included on 7/9/84, along with "Nebraska" and "Racing in the Street" in a 28-song set. "No Surrender" is played acoustically for the first time, as it will be for the rest of the tour. During the first two months of the tour, "Racing in the Street" and "Backstreets" will be interchanged on successive nights.

7/12-13/84 East Troy, Wisc., Alpine Valley Music Theater
A new song, "Man at the Top," premieres, with Bruce introducing it as a "song for an election year." It features beautiful, gospel-tinged backup vocals from Clarence, Nils, and Patti. Twenty-seven song set. On 7/13/84, "Thunder Road" opens a 27-song set with "Darkness" in the first set.

7/15/84 Chicago, Ill., Rosemont Horizon
A 28-song set includes "Nebraska," "Open All Night," and "Atlantic City."

7/17-18/84 Chicago, Ill., Rosemont Horizon
"Born in the USA" opens the show on 7/17/84 and is followed by "Tenth Avenue Freeze-out" for the first time in 1984. "Because the Night" is also included in the second set. On 7/18/84, "Thunder Road" opens the show for the last time in a 29-song set that ends with "Twist and Shout."

7/21/84 Montreal, Quebec, The Forum
First show to include "Do You Love Me" following "Twist and Shout." Born in the USA/Tenth Avenue Freeze-out/Out in the Street/Atlantic City/Johnny 99/The River/Prove It All Night/Glory Days/Promised Land/Used Cars/My Hometown/Badlands/Thunder Road//Hungry Heart/Cadillac Ranch/Dancing in the Dark/Sherry Darling/No Surrender/Because the Night/Pink Cadillac/Fire/Bobby Jean/Backstreets/Rosalita/Jungleland/Born to Run/Street Fightin' Man/Twist and Shout/Do You Love Me/Detroit Medley (including "I Hear a Train").

7/23-24/84 Toronto, Ontario, Exhibition Stadium Grandstand
Twenty-eight song set on 7/23/84. On 7/24/84, a 26-song set opens with "Badlands" and includes the first 1984 appearance of "Trapped." First outdoor shows of the tour.

7/26/84 Toronto, Ontario, Exhibition Stadium Grandstand
"My Father's House" premieres in a 27-song set. It will be performed infrequently on the rest of the tour. "Who'll Stop the Rain" and "Ramrod" are also included in the show, which opens with "Badlands."

7/27/84 Saratoga Springs, N.Y., Performing Arts Center
"Who'll Stop the Rain" opens this rain-soaked outdoor show.

7/30-31/84 Detroit, Mich., Joe Louis Arena
"Born in the USA" becomes the consistent show opener from here on. A 29-song set on 7/30/84 includes the first 1984 appearance of "Independence Day." "Trapped" and "Growin' Up" are included in a 28-song set on 7/31/84.

8/5-6/84 East Rutherford, N.J., Brendan Byrne Arena
First nights of ten in New Jersey. "Growin' Up" is again played on 8/5/84, and a five-song encore includes "Jersey Girl" for the first time in 1984. A 30-song set on 8/6/84 includes "Nebraska" and "No Surrender," which will later appear on *Live 1975-85*. "Spirit in the Night" makes its 1984 debut. It will only appear in selected East Coast shows.

8/8-9/84 East Rutherford, N.J., Brendan Byrne Arena
A 30-song set on 8/8/84 again includes "Spirit in the Night" and "Jersey Girl." On 8/9/84, J. T. Bowen guests on "Woman's Got the Power" in a 29-song set.

8/11-12/84 East Rutherford, N.J., Brendan Byrne Arena
"Spirit in the Night" is moved to the second half of a 30-song set on 8/11/84 that also includes "Because the Night." John Entwistle guests on "Twist and Shout." "The River" is included in the first set on 8/12/84. Southside Johnny joins the band for "Twist and Shout."

8/16-17/84 East Rutherford, N.J., Brendan Byrne Arena
A 30-song set on 8/16/84 includes "Johnny Bye Bye" for the first time in 1984. The tempo of the song is increased from the 1981 version. An excellent 31-song set on 8/17/84 includes the premiere of "I'm Goin' Down" and the first 1984 appearance of "Follow That Dream." "Cover Me" also returns in the second set.

8/19-20/84 East Rutherford, N.J., Brendan Byrne Arena
A 31-song set on 8/19/84 includes the rarely played "My Father's House" and the premiere of "State Trooper," the final song from *Nebraska* to be played live. "Reason to Believe" later appears on *Live 1975-85*. The 33-song set on 8/20/84 is one of the best on the tour. Little Steven and the Miami Horns guest at this final night of ten in New Jersey. The horns lend their support on "Tenth Avenue Freeze-out," which later appears on *Live 1975-85*. Little Steven joins on "Two Hearts," and in the encores everyone combines for one of the highlights of the entire tour, a marvelous cover of Dobie Gray's "Drift Away." Born in the USA/Out in the Street/Spirit in the Night/Atlantic City/Johnny 99/Highway Patrolman/I'm Goin' Down/Darlington County/Glory Days/Promised Land/My Hometown/Darkness/Badlands/Thunder Road//Hungry Heart/Dancing in the Dark/Cadillac Ranch/Tenth Avenue Freeze-out/No Surrender/Cover Me/Prove It All Night/Pink Cadillac/Growin' Up/Bobby Jean/Back-

streets/Rosalita/Jungleland/Two Hearts/Drift Away/Born to Run/Detroit Medley (including "Travelin' Band")/Twist and Shout/Do You Love Me.

8/22/84 Asbury Park, N.J., Stone Pony
Bruce guests with La Bamba and the Hubcaps, returning the favor for their appearance with him as the Miami Horns.

8/23/84 Long Branch, N.J., Brighton Bar
Bruce guests with Mama Tried.

8/25-26/84 Landover, Md., Capital Centre
A 31-song set on 8/25/84 includes "I'm Goin' Down" and "Who'll Stop the Rain." On 8/26/84, at the request of a fan, Bruce plays "Be True" for the first and only time on the *Born in the USA* tour. The song will later become a staple on the U.S. leg of the *Tunnel of Love Express* tour. Also included this night are "Spirit in the Night," "Trapped," and "Growin' Up."

8/28-29/84 Landover, Md., Capital Centre
A 32-song set is played on 8/28/84 during which Bruce forgets the lyrics to "Independence Day." "Wooly Bully" is played for the first time in a five-song encore. The second set on 8/29/84 includes "Follow That Dream," "Because the Night," and "Growin' Up."

9/3/84 Asbury Park, N.J., Stone Pony
Bruce guests with John Eddie on "Travelin' Band," "Proud Mary," "I'm Bad, I'm Nationwide" and "Twist and Shout."

9/4-5/84 Worcester, Mass., The Centrum
A 30-song set on 9/4/84 includes "Trapped" and "I'm Goin' Down." The 29-song set on 9/5/84 includes the first appearance of "Downbound Train" since the third show of the tour.

9/7-8/84 Hartford, Conn., Civic Center
A 31-song set is played on 9/7/84. "Rave On" is performed in the encores, in honor of Buddy Holly's birthday. Born in the USA/Out in the Street/Tenth Avenue Freeze-out/Atlantic City/Johnny 99/Highway Patrolman/I'm Goin' Down/Darlington County/Glory Days/Promised Land/My Hometown/Trapped/Badlands/Thunder Road//Hungry Heart/Dancing in the Dark/Cadillac Ranch/Sherry Darling/Downbound Train/I'm on Fire/Cover Me/Pink Cadillac/Bobby Jean/Racing in the Street/Rosalita/Rave On/Jungleland/Born to Run/Detroit Medley (including "Travelin' Band")/Twist and Shout/Do You Love Me. A 30-song set on 9/8/84 includes "Spirit in the Night" and "State Trooper" in the first set.

9/11-12/84 Philadelphia, Pa., The Spectrum
A 30-song set is played on the first of six nights in Philly, perhaps the best multiple-night stand of the tour. On 9/12/84 another 30-song set includes "Spirit in the Night," "State Trooper," "Nebraska," "Point Blank" (for the first time on the tour), and "Trapped."

9/14-15/84 Philadelphia, Pa., The Spectrum
Soundcheck on 9/14/84 includes "Darkness," "Born in the USA," "Tenth Avenue Freeze-out," and "Working on the Highway." The 31-song set includes "Point Blank," "My Father's House," and "Jersey Girl," as well as a guest appearance by the Miami Horns on "Tenth Avenue Freeze-out." "I'm Bad, I'm Nationwide" is played on 9/15/84 for the only time with the E Street Band, in a show that includes rare performances of "State Trooper" and "Candy's Room."

9/17-18/84 Philadelphia, Pa., The Spectrum
Soundcheck on 9/17/84 includes "Born in the USA" and "Independence Day." The 30-song set that night includes "Independence Day" and "Candy's Room." Final night set: Born in the USA/Out in the Street/Spirit in the Night/Atlantic City/State Trooper/Reason to Believe/I'm Goin' Down/Darlington County/Glory Days/Promised Land/Point Blank/I Fought the Law/Badlands/Thunder Road//Hungry Heart/Dancing in the Dark/Cadillac Ranch/Candy's Room/I'm on Fire/Cover Me/Growin' Up/Bobby Jean/Jersey Girl/Rosalita/Santa Claus/Jungleland/Born to Run/Detroit Medley/Twist and Shout/Do You Love Me.

9/21-22/84 Pittsburgh, Pa., Civic Arena
A 30-song set on 9/21/84 includes "Reason to Believe" and "Mansion on the Hill." On 9/22/84, a 31-song set includes "Who'll Stop the Rain" and closes with "Santa Claus."

9/24-25/84 Buffalo, N.Y., War Memorial Auditorium
A 29-song set with three songs from *Nebraska* is played on 9/24/84. The final show of the first leg of the tour includes the last 1984 perfor-

Asbury Park, N.J., May 19, 1984.

mance of ''Spirit in the Night'' and ''State Trooper.''
10/7/84 Asbury Park, N.J., Stone Pony
Five-song set with Cats.
10/15/84 Vancouver, British Columbia, PNE Coliseum
Bruce has to stop the show to calm an unruly crowd that has rushed the stage.
10/17/84 Tacoma, Wash., Tacoma Dome
A 31-song set includes ''Follow That Dream'' in a six-song encore.
10/19/84 Tacoma, Wash., Tacoma Dome
Energetic 32-song set following a one-day delay due to Bruce's bout with the flu. ''Rosalita'' is not played for the first time since 1974; instead, ''Born to Run'' closes the second set. ''Wooly Bully'' and ''Santa Claus'' are included in the encores. Born in the USA/Out in the Street/Darlington County/Atlantic City/Johnny 99/Highway Patrolman/Prove It All Night/Who'll Stop the Rain/Glory Days/Promised Land/My Hometown/Point Blank/Badlands/Thunder Road//Sherry Darling/Hungry Heart/Dancing in the Dark/Cadillac Ranch/No Surrender/I'm on Fire/Cover Me/Growin' Up/Bobby Jean/Backstreets/Born to Run/I'm a Rocker/Street Fightin' Man/Wooly Bully/Follow That Dream/Detroit Medley (including ''Travelin' Band'')/Twist and Shout/Do You Love Me.
10/21-22/84 Oakland, Calif., Coliseum
A 34-song set on 10/21/84 includes five songs from *Nebraska*: ''Atlantic City,'' ''Johnny 99,'' ''Reason to Believe,'' ''Mansion on the Hill,'' and

''State Trooper.'' ''Rosalita'' returns to the set. ''Shut Out the Light'' premieres in a stark acoustic arrangement during a 33-song set on 10/22/84 that also includes ''Stolen Car,'' ''Growin' Up,'' and ''Darkness.'' ''Stolen Car'' is played for the first time since 1981. Show closes with ''Santa Claus.''
10/25-26/84 Los Angeles, Calif., Sports Arena
Seven-concert series opens with a 34-song set with an eight-song encore. Second night (10/26/84) is a 32-song set.
10/28-29/84 Los Angeles, Calif., Sports Arena
A 33-song set is played on 10/28/84, with ''Badlands'' as the second song of the first set. The concert on 10/29/84 is the only 1984 appearance of ''Night,'' in a 30-song set that also includes ''Candy's Room'' and does not include ''Rosalita.''
10/31/84 Los Angeles, Calif., Sports Arena
Halloween special opens with ''High School Confidential.'' ''My Father's Place'' and ''I Fought the Law'' are also played in a 32-song set.
11/2/84 Los Angeles, Calif., Sports Arena
''Johnny Bye Bye'' and ''Stolen Car'' are played in a 30-song set.
11/4/84 Los Angeles, Calif., Sports Arena
Final night's 31-song set ends with ''Santa Claus.''
11/8/84 Tempe, Ariz., Arizona State University Activities Center
Thirty-song set includes ''Stolen Car.'' ''Shake'' and ''Sweet Soul Music'' make a last appearance in the ''Detroit Medley.''

Paris, France, June 18, 1988.

11/11-12/84 Denver, Colo., McNicholls Arena
Without "Rosalita," the second set now closes with "Racing in the Street." A 28-song set on 11/11/84 includes "State Trooper" and "Johnny Bye Bye."

11/15/84 St. Louis, Mo., St. Louis Arena
A 29-song set.

11/16/84 Ames, Iowa, Hilton Coliseum
A 30-song set includes the premiere of "Sugarland," a song written for possible inclusion on the *Born in the USA* album. The song deals with the plight of a farmer who, under economic strain, contemplates burning his grain field.

11/18/84 Lincoln, Neb., Bob Devaney Sports Center
"Sugarland" is played for the last time.

11/19/84 Kansas City, Mo., Kemper Arena
A 30-song set includes "Kansas City" in the "Detroit Medley."

11/23/84 Austin, Tex., Frank Erwin Center
A 29-song set includes "Stolen Car."

11/25-26/84 Dallas, Tex., Reunion Arena
A 29-song set on 11/25/84 includes "Atlantic City" and "Johnny Bye Bye." Unusual 28-song set on 11/26/84 includes the first *Born in the USA* tour performance of "Factory." Born in the USA/Out in the Street/Prove It All Night/Darkness/Factory/Johnny 99/Reason to Believe/Mansion on the Hill/I'm Goin' Down/Glory Days/Promised Land/My Hometown/Badlands/Thunder Road//Cover Me/Dancing in the Dark/Hungry Heart/Cadillac Ranch/No Surrender/Because the Night/Growin' Up/Bobby Jean/Racing in the Street/Jungleland/Born to Run/Detroit Medley (including "Travelin' Band" and "I Hear a Train")/Twist and Shout/Do You Love Me.

11/29-30/84 Houston, Tex., The Summit
"Factory" is played for the final time on 11/29/84. A 30-song set on

◀ *Philadelphia, Pa., September 19, 1988.*

11/30/84 includes "Because the Night" and "The River."

12/2/84 Baton Rouge, La., LSU Assembly Center
A 29-song set. "Mississippi Queen" is included in the "Detroit Medley."

12/6/84 Birmingham, Ala., Jefferson Civic Center
A 28-song set.

12/7/84 Tallahassee, Fla., Civic Center
A 30-song set again includes "Because the Night."

12/9/84 Murfreesboro, Tenn., James T. Murphy Center
A 28-song set.

12/11/84 Lexington, Ky., Rupp Arena
A 28-song set.

12/13-14/84 Memphis, Tenn., Mid-South Coliseum
A 27-song set is played the first night. Little Steven joins the band for the encores on 12/14/84, including "Drift Away" and "Two Hearts." A 30-song set.

12/16-17/84 Atlanta, Ga., The Omni
Little Steven again joins in encores that include "Two Hearts" and "Ramrod." A 29-song set on 12/16/84. The following night is the final show of the second leg of the tour. Miami Steve guests on "Two Hearts" and "Ramrod." Born in the USA/Badlands/Darlington County/Johnny 99/Darkness/Reason to Believe/Shut Out the Light/Johnny Bye Bye/Out in the Street/Glory Days/Promised Land/My Hometown/Prove It All Night/Thunder Road//Cover Me/Dancing in the Dark/Hungry Heart/Cadillac Ranch/Because the Night/I'm on Fire/Growin' Up/Bobby Jean/Racing in the Street/Two Hearts/Ramrod/Born to Run/Detroit Medley (including "Travelin' Band")/Twist and Shout/Do You Love Me/Santa Claus.

1/4-5/85 Hampton, Va., Hampton Roads Coliseum
Third leg of the tour opens with a 28-song set that ends with "Santa Claus." Soundcheck on 1/5/85 includes a rare performance of "Dual Moon Rising." "Because the Night" is played in the second set.

1/7-8/85 Indianapolis, Ind., Market Square Arena
A 27-song set is played on 1/7/85. Another 27-song set the following night includes "Growin' Up," "Shut Out the Light," and the first *Born in the USA* tour appearance of "I Can't Help Falling in Love."

1/10/85 Louisville, Ky., Freedom Hall Arena
"I Can't Help Falling in Love" is the first encore in a 29-song set.

1/13/85 Columbia, S.C., Carolina Coliseum
"Johnny 99" is introduced by Bruce, who makes reference to South Carolina's first legal execution in many years, which had occurred just days before.

1/15-16/85 Charlotte, N.C., Charlotte Coliseum
A 28-song set is played on 1/15/85. A 29-song set on 1/16/85 ends with "Ramrod."

1/18-19/85 Greensboro, N.C., Greensboro Coliseum
Bruce brings Gary U.S. Bonds and Robbin Thompson onstage on 1/18/85 for "Twist and Shout." A 29-song set again closes with "Ramrod." "Santa Claus" is back in the set on 1/19/85, 24 days after Christmas. The 29-song set includes "Darkness," "Trapped," and "Growin' Up."

1/23-24/85 Providence, R.I., Civic Center
A 28-song set on 1/23/85 includes "Shut Out the Light" and "I Can't Help Falling in Love." "Working on the Highway" finally reenters the set on 1/24/85, after not having been played since the first night of the tour. It will appear in the set consistently during the rest of the tour. The final two encores are played ten minutes after the taped music begins and the band has apparently left the stage for good. Probably the best show of the third leg. Born in the USA/Prove It All Night/Working on the Highway/Johnny 99/Reason to Believe/Mansion on the Hill/Johnny Bye Bye/Out in the Street/Glory Days/Promised Land/My Hometown/Trapped/Badlands//Cover Me/Dancing in the Dark/Hungry Heart/Cadillac Ranch/No Surrender/I'm on Fire/Growin' Up/Bobby Jean/Racing in the Street/I Can't Help Falling in Love/Born to Run/I'm a Rocker/Ramrod/Thunder Road/Wooly Bully/Santa Claus.

1/26-27/85 Syracuse, N.Y., Carrier Dome
Springsteen's first true stadium show is a 30-song set with "Thunder Road" in the encores on 1/26/85. Another 30-song set the following night closes the third leg of the tour. Born in the USA/Prove It All Night/Darlington County/Working on the Highway/Johnny 99/Darkness/Reason to Believe/The River/Trapped/Out in the Street/Glory Days/Promised Land/My Hometown/Badlands//Cover Me/Dancing in the Dark/Hungry Heart/Cadillac Ranch/Because the Night/I'm on Fire/Growin' Up/Bobby Jean/Racing in the Street/I Can't Help Falling in Love/Born to Run/I'm a Rocker/Ramrod/Thunder Road/Rockin' All Over the World.

3/21/85 Sydney, Australia, Entertainment Centre
Bruce's first show ever in Australia.

3/23-24/85 Sydney, Australia, Entertainment Centre
A 29-song set on 3/23/85 includes the return of "Rosalita" and a first set inclusion of "Darkness." A 28-song set on 3/24/85 includes "Point Blank."

3/27-28/85 Sydney, Australia, Entertainment Centre
"The River" is included in the first set on 3/27/85. A very unusual 32-song set on 3/28/85 as "Wreck on the Highway" makes its only appearance on the *Born in the USA* tour. Many songs this night have not been played since much earlier in the tour. Born in the USA/Darlington County/Out in the Street/Working on the Highway/Johnny 99/Atlantic City/My Father's House/The River/Prove It All Night/Glory Days/Promised Land/My Hometown/Badlands/Thunder Road//Cover Me/Dancing in the Dark/Hungry Heart/Cadillac Ranch/Wreck on the Highway/I'm on Fire/Pink Cadillac/Bobby Jean/Backstreets//Jungleland/I Can't Help Falling in Love/Born to Run/Ramrod/Twist and Shout/Do You Love Me/Santa Claus/Wooly Bully/Detroit Medley (including "I Hear a Train").

3/31/85 Brisbane, Australia, QE2 Stadium

4/3-4/85 Melbourne, Australia, Royal Melbourne Showgrounds
Final Australian show includes "Working on the Highway," "Open All Night," "Darkness," "Shut Out the Light," "Point Blank," "No Surrender," and "Rockin' All Over the World."

4/10-11/85 Tokyo, Japan, Yoyogi Olympic Pool

A 27-song set on 4/10/85 includes "Rockin' All Over the World" and "Ramrod." The Japanese shows are limited to under three hours by government regulation. "Darkness" and "Trapped" are included in the first set on 4/11/85, which begins with "Born in the USA" followed by "Darlington County."

4/13/85 Tokyo, Japan, Yoyogi Olympic Pool

4/15-16/85 Tokyo, Japan, Yoyogi Olympic Pool
A 26-song set on 4/15/85 includes "Point Blank" and "Rosalita." "Because the Night" and "No Surrender" are included in a 26-song set on 4/16/85.

4/19/85 Kyoto, Japan, Furitsu Taiikukan
"The River" is played in the first set.

4/22-23/85 Osaka, Japan, Castle Hall
A 25-song set ends the Japanese tour: Born in the USA/Out in the Street/Darlington County/Darkness/Point Blank/Working on the Highway/Prove It All Night/Glory Days/Promised Land/My Hometown/Badlands/Thunder Road//Cover Me/Dancing in the Dark/Hungry Heart/Cadillac Ranch/Sherry Darling/No Surrender/Backstreets/Rosalita/Bobby Jean/Born to Run/I Can't Help Falling in Love/Twist and Shout/Do You Love Me.

6/1/85 Dublin, Ireland, Slane Castle
Bruce's first European show in nearly four years. The 27-song set includes the only performances of the Beach Boys' "When I Grow Up to Be a Man." "Rosalita" closes the second set.

6/4-5/85 Newcastle, England, St. James Park
A 27-song set on 6/4/85 includes "Trapped," "The River," and "Bobby Jean," now in the encores. The set on 6/5/85 includes "Shut Out the Light," "Because the Night," and "Darkness."

6/8-9/85 Gothenburg, Sweden, Ullevi Stadium
"Sherry Darling" appears in the encores on 6/9/85.

6/12-13/85 Rotterdam, The Netherlands, Stadion Feynoord
The 28-song set on 6/12/85 is typical of most shows on the 1985 European tour: Born in the USA/Badlands/Out in the Street/Darlington County/Johnny 99/Atlantic City/The River/Trapped/Working on the Highway/Prove It All Night/Glory Days/The Promised Land/My Hometown/Thunder Road//Cover Me/Dancing in the Dark/Hungry Heart/Cadillac Ranch/Downbound Train/I'm on Fire/Because the Night/Rosalita/I Can't Help Falling in Love/Bobby Jean/Born to Run/Ramrod/Twist and Shout/Do You Love Me. The set on 6/13/85 includes "Darkness," "Shut Out the Light," and "Trapped."

6/15/85 Frankfurt, West Germany, Waldstadion
A 28-song set.

6/18/85 Munich, West Germany, Olympic Stadium

6/21/85 Milan, Italy, San Siro Stadium
One of the better shows on the European tour. A 29-song set includes "Backstreets" and closes with "Rockin' All Over the World."

6/23/85 Montpellier, France, Stade Richter

6/25/85 St. Etienne, France, Stade Geoffroy Guichard
"No Surrender" is included in a 28-song set.

6/29-30/85 Paris, France, La Courneuve
A 27-song set on 6/30/85 includes a rare European performance of "Point Blank."

7/3-4/85 London, England, Wembley Stadium
Bruce debuts a new song called "Seeds" in a 27-song set on 7/3/85. An exceptional 30-song July Fourth set opens with an acoustic version of "Independence Day." "Seeds" is again included in the first set, and Little Steven joins the band in the encores for "Two Hearts."

7/6/85 London, England, Wembley Stadium
Final night in London includes "Street Fightin' Man" in the encores. A 30-song set also includes "Highway Patrolman," "Because the Night," and "Two Hearts" with Little Steven.

7/7/85 Leeds, England, Roundhay Park
Final show of the European tour is a 30-song set that includes "Racing in the Street," "Follow That Dream," "Two Hearts" with Little Steven, and closes with "Rockin' All Over the World."

8/5/85 Washington, D.C., R.F.K. Stadium
Second performance ever of "Man at the Top," now with slightly

Dallas, Tex., November 8, 1980. ▶

different lyrics. The 29-song set list is very similar to the final English shows. Most of the shows of the 1985 stadium tour have nearly identical set lists, usually only varying by a song or two. The West Coast shows change a little more dramatically.

8/7/85 Cleveland, Ohio, Municipal Stadium
A 28-song set includes "This Land Is Your Land" and closes with "Sherry Darling." Born in the USA/Badlands/Out in the Street/ Johnny 99/Seeds/Atlantic City/The River/Working on the Highway/ Trapped/Darlington County/Glory Days/Promised Land/My Hometown/Thunder Road//Cover Me/Dancing in the Dark/Hungry Heart/ Cadillac Ranch/Downbound Train/I'm on Fire/Pink Cadillac/Bobby Jean/This Land Is Your Land/Born to Run/Ramrod/Twist and Shout/ Do You Love Me/Sherry Darling.

8/9/85 Chicago, Ill., Soldier Field
A 28-song standard set.

8/11/85 Pittsburgh, Pa., Three Rivers Stadium
Identical 28-song set.

8/14-15/85 Philadelphia, Pa., Veterans Stadium
Again, an identical 28-song set on 8/14/85. "Darkness," "I'm Goin' Down," and "Jersey Girl" are added to the set on 8/15/85.

8/18-19/85 East Rutherford, N.J., Giants Stadium
A 29-song set on 8/18/85 is the first of six New Jersey stadium shows; "Jersey Girl" is added to the standard set. "Darkness" replaces "Atlantic City," and "I'm Goin' Down" replaces "Darlington County" in a 29-song set on 8/19/85.

8/21-22/85 East Rutherford, N.J., Giants Stadium
"Growin' Up" replaces "Pink Cadillac" in a 27-song set on 8/21/85. Little Steven guests with the band on 8/22/85 for encores of "Two Hearts," "Ramrod," "Twist and Shout," and "Do You Love Me."

8/26-27/85 Toronto, Ontario, CNE Grandstand
"I Can't Help Falling in Love" replaces "This Land Is Your Land" on 8/26/85 in a 28-song set that also includes "I'm Goin' Down." A 28-song set on 8/27/85 includes "Growin' Up."

8/31-9/1/85 East Rutherford, N.J., Giants Stadium
"Growin' Up" is again included on 8/31/85 and Little Steven guests on a nine-song encore that includes the premiere of "Stand on It." The final night includes "Darkness," "I'm Goin' Down," and "This Land Is Your Land," and the only stadium tour performances of "Fire" and "Santa Claus."

9/4/85 Detroit, Mich., Silverdome
"Detroit Medley" makes its only appearance on the 1985 stadium tour.

9/6/85 Indianapolis, Ind., Hoosier Dome

9/9-10/85 Miami, Fla., Orange Bowl

9/13-14/85 Dallas, Tex., Cotton Bowl
"Travelin' Band" is played on 9/13/85 in response to a man in the second row who throws his artificial leg onstage during the encores. "Growin' Up" is added to a 29-song set on 9/14/85 that ends with "Travelin' Band."

The Main Point, Bryn Mawr, Pa., 1975.

9/18-19/85 Oakland, Calif., Oakland Stadium
"Stolen Car" is played on 9/18/85 for the only time on the 1985 stadium tour. The show on 9/19/85 includes rare performances of "Used Cars," with Roy Bittan on accordion, and "Highway Patrolman," featuring Clarence Clemons on harmonica.

9/23-24/85 Denver, Colo., Mile High Stadium
A 29-song set is played on 9/23/85. A very cold outdoor show. A 30-song set is played the following night, with "Because the Night" and a rare appearance of "High School Confidential" linked with "Travelin' Band" in the encores.

9/27/85 Los Angeles, Calif., Coliseum
A 31-song set includes the only performance of "Janey, Don't You Lose Heart." Edwin Starr's "War" is played for the first time, with Bruce reading the lyrics from a piece of paper strapped to his forearm.

9/29-30/85 Los Angeles, Calif., Coliseum
A 30-song set is played on 9/29/85, and a 32-song set the following night.

10/2/85 Los Angeles, Calif., Coliseum
The 33-song final show of the *Born in the USA* tour includes the first U.S. stadium performance of "Rosalita." Soundcheck includes "I Don't Wanna Go Home" and "Blinded by the Light." All four Los Angeles shows are professionally shot by Springsteen for potential future release. Videos of "War," "My Hometown," and "This Land Is Your Land" (shown on ABC's "20/20") are culled from this footage. Born in the USA/Badlands/Out in the Street/Johnny 99/Seeds/ Darkness/The River/War/Working on the Highway/Trapped/I'm Goin' Down/Prove It All Night/Promised Land/My Hometown/ Thunder Road//Cover Me/Dancing in the Dark/Hungry Heart/ Cadillac Ranch/No Surrender/I'm on Fire/Growin' Up/Rosalita/This Land Is Your Land/Born to Run/Bobby Jean/Ramrod/Twist and Shout/Do You Love Me/Stand on It/Travelin' Band/Rockin' All Over the World/Glory Days (with Jon Landau).

1/19/86 Asbury Park, N.J., Stone Pony
Bruce and the E Street Band minus Nils and Roy play at a benefit for workers at the 3M plant in Freehold, which is being closed down. Part of the 40-minute set is filmed by ABC, and airs the following week on "20/20": My Hometown/Promised Land/Badlands/Darkness/Stand on It/Ramrod/Twist and Shout.

3/2/86 Asbury Park, N.J., Stone Pony
Bruce calls this show "the E Street Band sneak attack." The band, minus Roy, tears through a loose nine-song set: Stand on It/Working on the Highway/Darlington County/Promised Land/Darkness/I'm Goin' Down/My Hometown/Cadillac Ranch/Glory Days.

10/13/86 Mountain View, Calif., Shoreline Amphitheater
Bruce, with help from Nils and Danny, turns in a magnificent acoustic set at Neil Young's Bridge Benefit Concert. The show is Springsteen's first all-acoustic set since the early 1970s. Bruce and Nils first appear onstage joining Neil Young on "Helpless." Bruce opens his own set with an a cappella version of "You Can Look," and is then joined by Nils and Danny on accordion. Helpless (with Neil Young)/You Can Look/Born in the USA/Seeds/Darlington County/Mansion on the Hill/Fire/Dancing in the Dark/Glory Days/Follow That Dream/ Hungry Heart (with Crosby, Stills, Nash, and Young)/Teach Your Children (all performers).

11/4/86 *Live 1975-85* is released in the U.S.

1/21/87 New York, N.Y., Waldorf-Astoria Hotel
Bruce gives the speech inducting Roy Orbison into the Rock 'n' Roll Hall of Fame. Bruce sings on "Stand By Me" and "Oh, Pretty Woman."

4/12/87 Asbury Park, N.J., Stone Pony
Bruce and an abbreviated E Street Band (Roy, Patti, Max, and Garry) make a surprise Pony appearance, their first in over a year. "Light of Day" debuts, opening the ten-song set. Jon Bon Jovi joins the band onstage for "Kansas City." Light of Day/Stand on It/Darlington County/My Hometown/Around and Around/Twist and Shout/Wooly Bully/Lucille/Cadillac Ranch/Kansas City.

7/29/87 Belmar, N.J., Key Largo
Bruce joins reggae band Jah Love onstage for reggae versions of

Tacoma, Wash., May 5, 1988. ▶

"Born in the USA" and "My Hometown." One of the most surprising live appearances Bruce has ever made. He will play three of the next four nights in Jersey clubs.

7/30/87 Neptune, N.J., Green Parrot
Bruce again joins Jah Love, this night for "One Love, One Heart," and again reggae versions of "Born in the USA" and "My Hometown."

7/31/87 Asbury Park, N.J., Stone Pony
After midnight, actually early the morning of 8/1/87, Bruce joins Marshall Crenshaw onstage for "You Can't Sit Down," a humorous "La Bamba," and "Twist and Shout."

8/2/87 Asbury Park, N.J., Stone Pony
Again, actually in the wee hours of 8/3/87, Bruce and the E Street Band (minus Nils) hit the stage for their longest show since the *Born in the USA* tour, a mix of Bruce's own material and some long-unplayed covers. Light of Day/I'm Bad, I'm Nationwide/Come On Let's Go/Gloria/I'm On Fire/Ruby Ruby/Sweet Little Sixteen/Proud Mary/Money/Jersey Girl/Around and Around/Glory Days/Havin' a Party/Twist and Shout.

8/9/87 Asbury Park, N.J., Stone Pony
Just after midnight, Bruce and the E Street Band are back for more, turning in another outstanding ten-song set to an overjoyed crowd. "I Don't Wanna Hang Up My Rock 'n' Roll Shoes" is played for the first time since 1978. Light of Day/Darlington County/I'm Bad, I'm Nationwide/Fortunate Son/Ruby Ruby/Stand By Me/I Don't Wanna Hang Up My Rock 'n' Roll Shoes/Glory Days/Havin' a Party/Twist and Shout.

8/14/87 Asbury Park, N.J., Stone Pony
Bruce joins former E Street Band member Ernest Carter and his new band, the Fairlanes. The set includes "Savin' Up," a Springsteen original given to Clarence Clemons for his first record with the Red Bank Rockers.

8/21/87 Asbury Park, N.J., Stone Pony
During Little Steven's show, Bruce comes onstage, and the two sing "Native American" and "Sun City."

8/22/87 Asbury Park, N.J., Stone Pony
Bruce joins Levon Helm's All Stars, including Max Weinberg, for "Lucille" and "Up on Cripple Creek."

8/26/87 Belmar, N.J., Key Largo
Bruce again joins Jah Love for three songs: "Jersey Girl," "My Hometown" and "Born in the USA." Later that same night, Bruce arrives at the Columns, in Avon, N.J., and joins the Cherubs on "Lucille" and "Stand By Me."

8/27/87 Sea Bright, N.J., The Tradewinds
Bruce joins Cats onstage for rousing versions of "Light of Day," "Proud Mary," "Fortunate Son," "I'll Be There," "Around and Around," and "Lucille."

9/25/87 Philadelphia, Pa., J.F.K. Stadium
Bruce joins U2 for "Stand By Me."

9/30/87 Los Angeles, Calif., Coconut Grove
Bruce becomes Roy Orbison's rhythm guitarist for the filming of the Cinemax special "Roy Orbison and Friends: A Black and White Night." Bruce is just one member of an all-star band that also includes Elvis Costello, Tom Waits, James Burton, k.d. lang, and Jackson Browne.

10/6/87 *Tunnel of Love* is released in the U.S.

10/8/87 New York, N.Y., The Ritz
Bruce again joins Little Steven for "Native American" and "Sun City."

10/22/87 New York, N.Y., St. Peter's Church
At the memorial service for John Hammond, Bruce performs an acoustic version of Bob Dylan's "Forever Young."

10/31/87 Sea Bright, N.J., McLoone's Rumrunner
Bruce and the E Street Band (minus Nils and Clarence) make a surprise Halloween appearance, dressed from head to toe in black, wearing hangman's masks, which they wear for the first song. The show includes the full-band debuts of "Brilliant Disguise," "Tougher Than the Rest," and "Two Faces," along with the first acoustic

◄ Philadelphia, Pa., May 26, 1978.

version of "Born to Run." Stand on It/Glory Days/Bad Moon Rising/Around and Around/Brilliant Disguise/Tougher Than the Rest/Light of Day/Born to Run/Fortunate Son/Two Faces/Lucille/Twist and Shout.

11/6/87 Rumson, N.J., Rumson County Day School
Bruce shows up for a benefit at the school across the street from his house in Rumson. He joins the Fabulous Grease Band for "Carol," "Lucille," "Twist and Shout," and "Stand By Me." At one point during the show, Bruce says, "Keep it down, my wife's asleep across the street."

11/20/87 Asbury Park, N.J., Stone Pony
Bruce joins Bobby Bandiera for "Little Latin Lupe Lu," "Stand by Me," and "Carol."

12/5/87 Asbury Park, N.J., Stone Pony
Bruce guests with Cats on "Carol," "Stand by Me," "Wooly Bully," "Around and Around," "Little Latin Lupe Lu," and "Twist and Shout."

12/7/87 New York, N.Y., Carnegie Hall
Bruce joins numerous other artists in a tribute to Harry Chapin. He gives a short speech and plays an acoustic version of Chapin's "Remember When the Music."

12/13/87 New York, N.Y., Madison Square Garden
At the request of Paul Simon, Bruce joins this all-star benefit show for New York's homeless. Bruce sings backup to Dion on "Teenager in Love," and performs three other songs: an acoustic version of "Born to Run," "Glory Days" (with David Letterman's band), and the finale of "Rock and Roll Music."

1/20/88 New York, N.Y., Waldorf-Astoria Hotel
Bruce gives the speech inducting Bob Dylan at the Rock and Roll Hall of Fame Awards. He also sings with others on "I Saw Her Standing There," "Born on the Bayou," and "Satisfaction." Max, Patti, Roy, Danny, and Garry are among the performers in the massed band.

· · · ·

TUNNEL OF LOVE EXPRESS TOUR

For song counts, "Detroit Medley" will be counted as one song. "Who Do You Love," "Ain't Got You" and "She's the One" have in past tours been counted as one song. In this tour these songs have become more distinct and stand on their own rather than being mere introductions, and therefore are counted as separate songs. "Land of 1000 Dances" and "Born to Be Wild," included in the midst of "Light of Day," will be counted as separate songs.

2/25/88 Worcester, MA, The Centrum
Bruce and the E Street Band, joined by the *Tunnel of Love* horns (Mario Cruz, Ed Manion, Mike Spengler, Mark Pender, and Richie "La Bamba" Rosenberg) return to the stage for their first tour in over two years. The 190-minute show includes eight songs from the *Tunnel of Love* LP and four other previously unplayed songs, not counting "Be True," which the band has played only once before (Landover, Md., 8/26/84). "Adam Raised a Cain" is played for the first time since September 1978, and "She's the One" is played for the first time since September 1981. "Born to Run" is played acoustically, a version that debuted at the surprise Halloween show 10/31/87. New songs include "Part Man, Part Monkey," a song about the evolution/creationism battle, and "I'm a Coward," a tune about the perils of love loosely based on Gino Washington's early sixties hit, "Gino is a Coward."

The basic set will remain through most of the tour, not changing significantly until the tour hits the West Coast in late April: Tunnel of Love/Be True/Adam Raised a Cain/Two Faces/All That Heaven Will Allow/Seeds/Roulette/Cover Me/Brilliant Disguise/Spare Parts/War/Born in the USA//Tougher Than the Rest/She's the One/You Can Look/I'm a Coward/I'm on Fire/One Step Up/Part Man, Part Monkey/Walk Like a Man/Dancing in the Dark/Light of Day/Born

to Run/Hungry Heart/Glory Days/I Can't Help Falling in Love/
Rosalita/Detroit Medley (including "Shake" and "Sweet Soul
Music").

2/28-29/88 Worcester, Mass., The Centrum
"Tenth Avenue Freeze-out" is added to the second encore on 2/28/88.
"Tenth Avenue Freeze-out" is not played on 2/29/88, but Presley's
"Love Me Tender" is premiered, replacing "I Can't Help Falling in
Love." The beautiful keyboard introduction to "Walk Like a Man" is
dropped following this show.

3/3-4/88 Chapel Hill, N.C., Dean Smith Center
"I Can't Help Falling in Love" replaces "Love Me Tender" on 3/4/88.
Soundchecks from the two shows include "I Shall Be Released," "Mr.
Tambourine Man," and "Just Like a Woman." Though the show set
list doesn't vary much from night to night, the soundchecks on the
tour are constantly changing and include numerous cover songs.
Toward the end of the U.S. dates, Springsteen begins to consistently
allow a few hundred fans in early to hear parts of these fascinating
soundchecks.

3/8-9/88 Philadelphia, Pa., The Spectrum
"Love Me Tender" replaces "I Can't Help Falling in Love" on 3/8/88.
Soundcheck includes "Stolen Car" and the only known live version
of "When You're Alone." "Raise Your Hand" is played on 3/9/88 for
the first time since the *River* tour. "Shake" is cut from the "Detroit
Medley."

3/13-14/88 Cleveland, Ohio, Richfield Coliseum

3/16-17/88 Chicago, Ill., Rosemont Horizon
The first notable changes in the set are made on 3/17/88 with "Dark-
ness" replacing "Seeds," and "Backstreets" replacing "Walk Like a
Man." Bruce does an Irish jig during "Rosalita" to celebrate St.
Patrick's Day.

3/20/88 Pittsburgh, Pa., Civic Arena
"Seeds" returns instead of "Darkness." Joe Grushecky, formerly of
the Iron City Houserockers, joins Bruce onstage for "Raise Your
Hand."

3/22-23/88 Atlanta, Ga., The Omni
"Darkness" replaces "Seeds"; "Walk Like a Man" returns for
"Backstreets" on 3/22/88. Bruce also adds part of "Who Do You
Love" as an intro to "She's the One." The standard set returns on
3/23/88, including both "Seeds" and "Walk Like a Man."
Spectacular soundchecks here include Ry Cooder's "Across the
Borderline," "Crazy Love," "Pretty Flamingo," and "Tupelo Honey"
among over fifteen other songs experimented with.

3/26/88 Lexington, Ky., Rupp Arena
Bruce adds one verse of "Ain't Got You" as an introduction to "She's
the One."

3/28-29/88 Detroit, Mich., Joe Louis Arena
MTV cameras are present to film footage for a half-hour special that
airs a month later. Bruce is interviewed for MTV by Kurt Loder.
"Ain't Got You" is expanded to two verses. The show is digitally
recorded, and a live version of "Be True" later appears on the
"Chimes"/"Tougher" live EPs. On 3/29/88 "Darkness" and "Backstreets" are both back in the set, for the last time until the West Coast.

4/1-2/88 Uniondale, N.Y., Nassau Coliseum
A standard set is played on 4/1/88 with "Seeds" and "Walk Like a
Man." This marks the first of ten shows with identical set lists, not
counting songs left out of the set and not replaced. This represents the
first time in Springsteen's career when the set stays the very same for
so long. "Ain't Got You" is deleted the following night. Bruce begins
adding the line "It's just a kiss away," from the Rolling Stones'
"Gimme Shelter," to "Cover Me."

4/4-5/88 Landover, Md., Capital Centre
"Ain't Got You" is back in on 4/4/88.

4/12-13/88 Houston, Tex., The Summit
"Love Me Tender" is taken out of the set from here on until Europe.
Tunnel of Love/Be True/Adam Raised a Cain/Two Faces/All That
Heaven Will Allow/Seeds/Roulette/Cover Me/Brilliant Disguise/
Spare Parts/War/Born in the USA//Tougher Than the Rest/Ain't Got
You/She's the One/You Can Look/I'm a Coward/I'm on Fire/One

Step Up/Part Man, Part Monkey/Walk Like a Man/Dancing in the
Dark/Light of Day/Born to Run/Hungry Heart/Glory Days/Rosa-
lita/Detroit Medley/Raise Your Hand.

4/15/88 Austin, Tex., Frank Erwin Center
Soundcheck includes "Follow That Dream."

4/17/88 St. Louis, Mo., St. Louis Arena
Enthusiastic crowd here produces perhaps the best of the standard-
out shows.

4/20/88 Denver, Colo., McNicholls Arena
"Sweet Soul Music" is played as a separate song from here on.

4/22-23/88 Los Angeles, Calif., Sports Arena
With Roy Orbison in attendance, celebrating his birthday on 4/23/88,
Bruce begins a series of small set changes that will continue through-
out the rest of the U.S. tour. "Backstreets" returns in place of "Walk
Like a Man." The encore begins with Bruce leading the crowd in
singing "Happy Birthday" to Orbison. Bruce had rehearsed Orbison's
"Crying" in the soundcheck, but unfortunately it is not played. The
"Detroit Medley" is given a much-needed rest and is replaced by
"Have Love, Will Travel," "Tenth Avenue Freeze-out," and "Sweet
Soul Music." "Have Love, Will Travel" is a cover of a song by the
Northwest band The Sonics. "Tenth Avenue Freeze-out" returns after
being played just once on the second date of the tour. Tunnel of Love/
Be True/Adam Raised a Cain/Two Faces/All That Heaven Will
Allow/Seeds/Roulette/Cover Me/Brilliant Disguise/Spare Parts/War/
Born in the USA//Tougher Than the Rest/Ain't Got You/She's the
One/You Can Look/I'm a Coward/I'm on Fire/One Step Up/She's
Man, Part Monkey/Backstreets/Dancing in the Dark/Light of Day/
Born to Run/Hungry Heart/Glory Days/Rosalita/Have Love, Will
Travel/Tenth Avenue Freeze-out/Sweet Soul Music/Raise Your Hand.

4/25/88 Los Angeles, Calif., Sports Arena
Same set as on 4/23/88.

4/27-28/88 Los Angeles, Calif., Sports Arena
Ry Cooder's "Across the Borderline," played in soundchecks for
weeks, is premiered on 4/27/88, replacing "Backstreets." This show
and the following night's are filmed for use in the "Tougher Than the
Rest" and "Born to Run (acoustic)" videos. The entire show is also
audio-recorded, and live versions of "Tougher Than the Rest" and
"Born to Run" later appear on the "Chimes"/"Tougher" live EPs.
The same set is played the following night.

5/2-3/88 Mountain View, Calif., Shoreline Amphitheater
On 5/2/88, "Walk Like a Man" replaces "Across the Borderline,"
and is dedicated by Bruce to his father, who is in attendance. For the
first time since the *River* tour, Bruce not only enters the crowd, but
climbs on top of a chair to sing "Hungry Heart" while the crowd
gently holds him up. During "Glory Days," Bruce, Nils, Patti,
Clarence, and the horn section all climb off the stage into the crowd,
dancing across the front row. First outdoor show of the tour. On
5/3/88, "Backstreets" replaces "Walk Like a Man." "Little Latin
Lupe Lu" is played with the band for the first time since 1977, after
"Raise Your Hand," and is followed by "Twist and Shout," played
for the first time in 1988. This is the longest show on the U.S. leg of the
Tunnel tour. These impromptu additions are clearly a surprise to the
band, who end "Twist and Shout" by themselves after Bruce leaves
the stage. The terrific show is highlighted by Bruce dancing with his
mother during "Dancing in the Dark." Perhaps the best show of the
entire U.S. tour. Soundcheck includes Roy playing part of "Jungleland" and Nils singing "Man at the Top." Bruce allows part of the
crowd in to hear "I'm So Lonesome I Could Cry" and "Crying."

5/5-6/88 Tacoma, Wash., Tacoma Dome
Same set as 5/2/88 is played on 5/5/88. Soundcheck includes "I'm So
Lonesome I Could Cry," "Crying," and Jackie Wilson's "Lonely
Teardrops." Steppenwolf's "Born to Be Wild" is played for the first
time on 5/6/88, with the E Street Band, in the middle of "Light of
Day." "Darkness" also returns for the first time since Detroit, this
time replacing "Roulette." "Backstreets" replaces "Walk Like a
Man," and "Twist and Shout" is again added after "Raise Your
Hand." Soundcheck includes "Big Boss Man," "Let It Be Me,"
"Cathy's Clown," "Crying in the Rain," "Rock 'n' Roll Music" and
"Sweet Little Sixteen." This is the first show in four years that doesn't
include "Dancing in the Dark." Second longest show of the tour, and

With Marshall Crenshaw, Asbury Park, N.J., July 31, 1987.

one of the best. Over 45,000 see both nights.

5/9-10/88 Bloomington, Minn., Met Center
Same set as 5/2/88 is played on 5/9/88. On 5/10/88, Bruce premieres John Lee Hooker's "Boom Boom," which will be included in the set from here on. "Cautious Man" is played for the first and only time, replacing the story before "Spare Parts." The song is rehearsed numerous times during the day's soundcheck. Tunnel of Love/Boom Boom/Adam Raised a Cain/Two Faces/All That Heaven Will Allow/Seeds/Cover Me/Brilliant Disguise/Cautious Man/Spare Parts/War/Born in the USA//Tougher Than the Rest/Ain't Got You/She's the One/You Can Look/I'm on Fire/One Step Up/Part Man, Part Monkey/Backstreets/Dancing in the Dark/Light of Day/Born to Run/Hungry Heart/Glory Days/Rosalita/Have Love, Will Travel/Tenth Avenue Freeze-out/Sweet Soul Music/Raise Your Hand/Twist and Shout.

5/13/88 Indianapolis, Ind., Market Square Arena
"Cautious Man" is out of the set. "Across the Borderline" replaces "Backstreets."

5/16/88 New York, N.Y., Madison Square Garden
"Crying" is added to the set after weeks of appearances in soundchecks. Tickets to the five New York shows were impossible to get as Bruce and the band make their first Madison Square Garden appearances since December 1980 with scalpers selling high-quality counterfeit tickets. The band closes the show with a brief snatch of "New York, New York." Tunnel of Love/Boom Boom/Be True/Adam Raised a Cain/Two Faces/All That Heaven Will Allow/Seeds/Roulette/Cover Me/Brilliant Disguise/Spare Parts/War/Born in the USA//Tougher Than the Rest/Ain't Got You/She's the One/You Can Look/I'm a Coward/I'm on Fire/One Step Up/Part Man, Part Monkey/Walk Like a Man/Dancing in the Dark/Light of Day/Born to Run/Hungry Heart/Glory Days/Crying/Have Love, Will Travel/Tenth Avenue Freeze-out/Sweet Soul Music/Raise Your Hand.

5/18-19/88 New York, N.Y., Madison Square Garden
Sets are the same as 5/16/88, but "Backstreets" replaces "Walk Like

◄ *Greensboro, N.C., January 19, 1985.*

a Man" on 5/18/88, and on 5/19/88 "Vigilante Man" is premiered and replaces "Roulette"; "Dancing in the Dark" is left out of the set.

5/22-23/88 New York, N.Y., Madison Square Garden
Set on 5/22/88 is the same as 5/19/88, but "Across the Borderline" replaces "Backstreets." "Born to Be Wild" is included in "Light of Day." Jackie Wilson's "Lonely Teardrops" is premiered, replacing "Crying." The final show of the U.S. tour is the same as the preceding night, but "Backstreets" replaces "Across the Borderline." Jon Landau joins the band onstage, strumming guitar during the encores, while Barbara Carr goes onstage for "You Can Look."

5/26/88 Irvine, Calif., Irvine Meadows
Bruce joins John Cougar Mellencamp onstage for "Like a Rolling Stone."

6/11/88 Turin, Italy, Stadio Comunale
Fifty-five thousand fans greet Bruce, the E Street Band, and the *Tunnel of Love* Horns for their first European show in nearly three years. Ticket sales across the European tour are varied; a second show here is canceled owing to poor ticket sales, but shows in Oslo and Copenhagen sell out immediately. This is the first stadium show on the *Tunnel* tour. "Because the Night" makes its *Tunnel* tour debut in the place of "Part Man, Part Monkey." Tunnel of Love/Boom Boom/Be True/Adam Raised a Cain/Two Faces/All That Heaven Will Allow/Seeds/Cover Me/Brilliant Disguise/Spare Parts/War/Born in the USA//Tougher Than the Rest/Ain't Got You/She's the One/You Can Look/I'm a Coward/I'm on Fire/One Step Up/Because the Night/Backstreets/Dancing in the Dark/Light of Day/Born to Be Wild/Born to Run/Hungry Heart/Glory Days/Have Love, Will Travel/Tenth Avenue Freeze-out/Sweet Soul Music/Raise Your Hand/Twist and Shout.

6/13/88 Rome, Italy, Piaza di Spagna
Bruce meets some street musicians and plays acoustic versions of "I'm on Fire" and "The River" on a borrowed guitar, for an audience of fifteen.

6/15-16/88 Rome, Italy, Stadio Flamminio
"Bobby Jean" is played on 6/15/88 for the first time on the *Tunnel* tour, in the place of "Have Love, Will Travel." The horns and Patti

do not play on the song. "The River" makes its first *Tunnel* tour appearance on 6/16/88, replacing "Two Faces" in a 30-song set that includes a handful of other set changes and adjustments. Tunnel of Love/Boom Boom/Adam Raised a Cain/The River/All That Heaven Will Allow/Seeds/Cover Me/Brilliant Disguise/Spare Parts/War/ Born in the USA//Tougher Than the Rest/Who Do You Love/She's the One/You Can Look/I'm a Coward/I'm on Fire/Because the Night/Backstreets/Dancing in the Dark/Light of Day/Born to Run/ Hungry Heart/Glory Days/Can't Help Falling in Love/Bobby Jean/Tenth Avenue Freeze-out/Sweet Soul Music/Raise Your Hand/Twist and Shout.

6/18/88 Paris, France, Chateau De Vincennes
Bruce and Clarence make a surprise appearance at the "SOS Racism" anti-racism benefit. The four-song acoustic set is broadcast live on French TV and includes Creedence's "Bad Moon Rising" and, for the first time, Dylan's "Blowin' in the Wind." Promised Land/My Hometown/Blowin' in the Wind/Bad Moon Rising.

6/19/88 Paris, France, Hippodromes De Vincennes
Same as 6/16/88, but "Born to Be Wild" is added to "Light of Day." Bruce begins adding lyrics from Muddy Waters's "Mannish Boy" to the end of "Adam Raised a Cain."

6/21-22/88 Birmingham, England, Aston Villa Football Ground
A 32-song set is played in 6/21/88, with more fine tuning. Tunnel of Love/Boom Boom/Adam Raised a Cain/Two Faces/All That Heaven Will Allow/The River/Seeds/Vigilante Man/Cover Me/Brilliant Disguise/Spare Parts/War/Born in the USA/Born to Run/Hungry Heart/Glory Days/Bobby Jean/Tenth Avenue Freeze-out/Sweet Soul Music/Raise Your Hand/Twist and Shout. The following night's set is the same, without "Vigilante Man." "Born to Be Wild" is added to "Light of Day," "Have Love, Will Travel" is added after "Sweet Soul Music," and "Who Do You Love" replaces "Ain't Got You." Bruce is joined on-stage by Edwin Starr for "War."

6/25/88 London, England, Wembley Stadium
Same as 6/22/88, but "Part Man, Part Monkey" replaces "One Step Up." Neither song will be played again on the European tour. "Ain't Got You" is back in for "Who Do You Love," and "Have Love, Will Travel" is now played before "Sweet Soul Music." Bruce adds "Love Me Tender" to the second encore as "something special for London." Edwin Starr again joins Bruce for "War."

6/28-29/88 Rotterdam, The Netherlands, Stadion Feynoord
The set on 6/28/88 is the same as 6/22/88, but "Have Love, Will Travel" follows "Sweet Soul Music." Jon Landau joins the band on-stage for "Glory Days." An outstanding second show, on 6/29/88, includes many surprises and changes. The park-bench story before "All That Heaven Will Allow" is dropped completely, and there is no introduction before "Spare Parts." After "Born in the USA," the band remains onstage and instead closes the set with Dylan's "Chimes of Freedom," played only once before, in Detroit on 9/1/78. During the intermission, new set lists are placed onstage. The second set opens with the long-lost instrumental "Paradise by the C," played for the first time since mid-*Darkness* tour. The *Tunnel* tour, as a whole, shares a lot of similarities with the *Darkness* tour, adding "Paradise" to the set further cements the comparison. This show also premieres the "Don't You Touch That Thing" song/story that introduces "You Can Look." The story is really a song in itself and sounds not unlike "From Small Things. . . ."

7/2-3/88 Stockholm, Sweden, Stockholms Stadion
The 7/22/88 set is the same as 6/29/88, but "All that Heaven Will Allow" and "The River" switch places. "I Can't Help Falling in Love" and "Have Love, Will Travel" are not played, but "Cadillac Ranch" is added after "Bobby Jean" for the first time on the *Tunnel* tour. The first set on 7/3/88 is broadcast live via satellite to 15 countries around the world; it is Bruce's first live radio broadcast since the *Darkness* tour. The entire 35-song set is one of the longest ever. Bruce rearranges the first set to make it a full 90 minutes, and announces that he will be

◄ *Chicago, Ill., July 17, 1984.*

joining the Amnesty International Human Rights Now! tour, before he sings "Chimes of Freedom." "Roulette" is played for the first time on the European tour. "Downbound Train" also makes its *Tunnel* tour debut. Over the next four weeks, nearly all of the *Born in the USA* tour staples will reenter the set for at least one show. "Quarter to Three" makes a surprise appearance for the first time since 8/81. One of the best shows on the 1988 tour, though patients at a hospital next to the stadium don't see it that way and are issued ear plugs. Tunnel of Love/Boom Boom/Adam Raised a Cain/The River/All That Heaven Will Allow/Seeds/Roulette/Cover Me/Brilliant Disguise/Tougher Than the Rest/Spare Parts/War/ Born in the USA/Chimes of Free-dom//Paradise by the C/Who Do You Love/She's the One/You Can Look/I'm a Coward/I'm on Fire/Downbound Train/Because the Night/Dancing in the Dark/Light of Day/Born to Be Wild/Born to Run/Hungry Heart/Glory Days/I Can't Help Falling in Love/Bobby Jean/Cadillac Ranch/Tenth Avenue Freeze-out/Sweet Soul Music/ Raise Your Hand/Quarter to Three/Twist and Shout.

7/7/88 Dublin, Ireland, RDS Jumping Enclosure
Same as 7/3/88, but "Downbound Train" is moved up to the first set, replacing "Roulette." Both "Quarter to Three" and "I Can't Help Falling in Love" are not included. "Seeds" and "All That Heaven Will Allow" switch places, and Wilson Pickett's "Land of 1,000 Dances" is included for the first time in the middle of "Light of Day."

7/9-10/88 Sheffield, England, Bramall Lane Stadium
A 33-song set is played on 7/9/88, same set list as Dublin, but the order is rearranged. This show is recorded, and "Spare Parts" is later issued as a live B-side. On 7/10/88, Jackie Wilson's "Lonely Tear-drops" is played for the first time on the European tour, during a superb 11-song encore. Bruce continues to rearrange the set order, as he did the previous night. Tunnel of Love/Boom Boom/Adam Raised a Cain/Downbound Train/All That Heaven Will Allow/The River/Seeds/Roulette/Cover Me/Brilliant Disguise/War/Born in the USA/Chimes of Freedom//Tougher Than the Rest/Who Do You Love/She's the One/You Can Look/I'm a Coward/I'm on Fire/Spare Parts/Because the Night/Dancing in the Dark/Light of Day/Land of 1,000 Dances/Born to Run/Hungry Heart/Glory Days/I Can't Help Falling in Love/Bobby Jean/Cadillac Ranch/Tenth Avenue Freeze-out/Sweet Soul Music/Raise Your Hand/Lonely Teardrops/Twist and Shout.

7/12/88 Frankfurt, West Germany, Waldstadion
Still more rearranging in a 33-song set: Tunnel of Love/Boom Boom/ Adam Raised a Cain/Downbound Train/All That Heaven Will Allow/The River/Seeds/Cover Me/Brilliant Disguise/Spare Parts/ War/Born in the USA/Chimes of Freedom//Paradise by the C/Who Do You Love/She's the One/You Can Look/I'm a Coward/I'm on Fire/Tougher Than the Rest/Because the Night/Dancing in the Dark/ Light of Day/Land of 1,000 Dances/Born to Run/Hungry Heart/ Glory Days/Bobby Jean/Cadillac Ranch/Tenth Avenue Freeze-out/Sweet Soul Music/Raise Your Hand/Twist and Shout.

7/14/88 Basel, Switzerland, St. Jakob Stadion
"Follow That Dream" is played for the first and only time on the *Tunnel* tour, following "Glory Days." "Roulette" is also played instead of "Seeds" in an excellent 34-song set.

7/17/18 Munich, West Germany, Olympia Riding Stadium
"Badlands" replaces "Roulette," as it will for the rest of the European tour. Also added here and remaining for the rest of the tour is "Havin' a Party" following "Twist and Shout." Bruce also throws in a verse and chorus from "Do You Love Me," for its only *Tunnel* tour appearance. Onstage set lists confirm that "Badlands" and "Havin' a Party" were planned additions, but "Do You Love Me" was called out by Bruce to the band. "Havin' a Party" is played for the first time in years outside of club dates.

7/19/88 East Berlin, East Germany, Weissensee Cycling Track
The largest show ever held in East Germany draws more than 160,000 people, and is also the largest show Bruce has ever played, and one of the largest rock concerts ever. DT64, the East German radio station, broadcasts most of the show on a two-hour delay. The East German television network broadcasts the entire show minus six songs later the same night and in a further-edited version the next day. This is the only show on the tour that does not include "Tunnel of

Love" in the set, and is the first show so far not to open with this song. "Badlands" opens a show for the first time in four years. "Out in the Street" is played for the first and only time on the *Tunnel* tour, and "Promised Land" also makes its 1988 tour premiere. For the first time on the *Tunnel* tour, "Born to Run" is not played acoustically, but with the full band. Bruce is inspired, and he shows it in an excellent, government-sanctioned, 180-minute show. Badlands/Out in the Street/ Boom Boom/Adam Raised a Cain/All That Heaven Will Allow/The River/Cover Me/Brilliant Disguise/Promised Land/Spare Parts/ War/Born in the USA/Chimes of Freedom//Paradise by the C//Who Do You Love/She's the One/You Can Look/I'm a Coward/I'm on Fire/Downbound Train/Because the Night/Dancing in the Dark/ Light of Day/Land of 1,000 Dances/Born to Run/Hungry Heart/ Glory Days/I Can't Help Falling in Love/Bobby Jean/Cadillac Ranch/Tenth Avenue Freeze-out/Sweet Soul Music/Twist and Shout/Havin' a Party.

7/22/88 West Berlin, West Germany, Walbuehne Ampitheater
Show opens with "Badlands." "Tunnel of Love" is the second song in another inspired 35-song set. During the next shows Springsteen includes lyrics from "Tears of a Clown" in the end of "Tunnel of Love." Badlands/Tunnel of Love/Boom Boom/Adam Raised a Cain/ All That Heaven Will Allow/The River/Promised Land/Cover Me/ Brilliant Disguise/Spare Parts/War/Born in the USA/Chimes of Freedom//Tougher Than the Rest/Who Do You Love/She's the One/ You Can Look/I'm a Coward/I'm on Fire/Downbound Train/Because the Night/Dancing in the Dark/Light of Day/Land of 1,000 Dances/Born to Run (acoustic)/Hungry Heart/Glory Days/I Can't Help Falling in Love/Bobby Jean/Cadillac Ranch/Tenth Avenue Freeze-out/Sweet Soul Music/Raise Your Hand/Twist and Shout/ Havin' a Party.

7/23/88 Copenhagen, Denmark
Bruce joins street musician John Magnusson on acoustic guitar for a three-song set before a gathered crowd of around 100 on the streets of Copenhagen. I'm on Fire/The River/Dancing in the Dark. The performance is filmed by a tourist with a camcorder, and part of the footage is shown later on Danish TV.

7/25/88 Copenhagen, Denmark, Idraetspark
Same as 7/12/88, but "Badlands" replaces "Seeds," "Tenth Avenue Freeze-out" is left out, and "Havin' a Party" closes the show.

7/27/88 Oslo, Norway, Valle Hovin Stadion
Same as 7/25/88, but "Thunder Road" makes its first *Tunnel* tour appearance, replacing "Paradise by the C."

7/31/88 Bremen, West Germany, Weser Stadion
Same as 7/25/88, but "Working on the Highway" replaces "Because the Night," its first *Tunnel* tour appearance. "Can't Help Falling in Love" is added before "Bobby Jean." "Born to Run" is played with the full band, as it will be for the rest of the tour.

8/2/88 Madrid, Spain, Viecente Calderon Stadium
Same as 7/25/88, but "Born to Run" is played with the full band.

8/3/88 Barcelona, Spain, Camp Nou Stadium
Over 80,000 people are in attendance at this final show of the *Tunnel of Love Express* tour. Springsteen had started the tour off in Worcester, Massachusetts, playing eight tunes from *Tunnel of Love* and five from *Born in the USA*. By Barcelona, those numbers were reversed. Tunnel of Love/Boom Boom/Adam Raised a Cain/Downbound Train/All That Heaven Will Allow/The River/Badlands/Cover Me/Brilliant Disguise/Spare Parts/War/Born in the USA/Chimes of Freedom// Thunder Road/Who Do You Love/She's the One/You Can Look/I'm a Coward/I'm on Fire/Tougher Than the Rest/Working on the Highway/Dancing in the Dark/Light of Day/Land of 1,000 Dances/Born to Run/Hungry Heart/Glory Days/I Can't Help Falling in Love/ Bobby Jean/Cadillac Ranch/Sweet Soul Music/Raise Your Hand/ Twist and Shout/Havin' a Party.

8/21/88 Asbury Park, N.J., Stone Pony
Bruce guests with Cats on "Stand by Me" and "Around and Around."

8/25/88 New York City, N.Y., Madison Square Garden
Just a week before the start of the Amnesty tour, Bruce joins Sting on-

◄ *Worcester, Mass., February 28, 1988.*

◄ *Seattle, Wash., October 24, 1980.*

stage for an acoustic version of "The River" and "Message in a Bottle."

·   ·   ·   ·

HUMAN RIGHTS NOW! TOUR

9/2/88 London, England, Wembley Stadium
First show of the Amnesty Human Rights Now! tour, a multi-artist concert that will tour the entire world during the next three months. Springsteen and the E Street Band are joined on the tour by Youssou N'Dour, Tracy Chapman, Sting, Peter Gabriel, and indigenous artists in each country. Ticket prices vary across the globe according to the average income of each region, ranging from over $35.00 in Japan to less than $5.00 in Harare and San Jose. Press conferences are held before most shows, involving Springsteen with the press on an everyday basis for the first time in many years. Springsteen and the E Street Band close the shows in most cities.

The concerts begin with all five performers onstage singing Bob Marley's "Get Up, Stand Up." After Springsteen's set, all five performers regroup for "Chimes of Freedom" and a reprise of "Get Up, Stand Up," this time backed by the E Street Band. Springsteen's set at a majority of the shows consists mostly of greatest hits, with few introductions and most songs segueing one into the next with no break between them. The result is a hasty, but satisfying set, which varies slightly over the course of the tour. All the artists on the tour give exemplary performances throughout, but in most cities (outside the Southern Hemisphere) the crowd is there primarily to see Springsteen. Born in the USA/Promised Land/Cover Me/Cadillac Ranch/The River/Spare Parts/War/My Hometown/Thunder Road/She's the One/Glory Days/Light of Day/Land of 1,000 Dances/Born to Run/Chimes of Freedom/Get Up, Stand Up.

9/4-5/88 Paris, France, Palais Omnisports Bercy
One of only two cities on this tour to host arena-sized shows. For the first time on the tour, Sting joins Springsteen for a duet on "The River." They will sing it together at every show on the tour in which they both perform. There were enthusiastic crowds of 16,500 each night. Born in the USA/Promised Land/Cover Me/Brilliant Disguise/The River/Cadillac Ranch/War/My Hometown/Thunder Road/Bobby Jean/Glory Days/Born to Run/Raise Your Hand/Chimes of Freedom/Get Up, Stand Up. On 9/5/88 Springsteen performs the same set as the previous night, but replaces "Bobby Jean" with "Because the Night."

9/6/88 Budapest, Hungary, Nepstadion
Springsteen's second concert in an Eastern-Bloc country and the first Western group of artists allowed to perform together in Hungary. The show's only restriction is a ban on the sale of souvenir T-shirts and programs. Amnesty officials hope that this show will pave the way for a performance in Moscow, but it cannot be arranged. During both "Thunder Road" and "Hungry Heart," Springsteen urges the crowd to sing along in the places that are usually familiar to fans, but the crowd in Budapest does not know the lyrics and is silent. Born in the USA/Promised Land/Cover Me/Working on the Highway/The River/Cadillac Ranch/War/My Hometown/Thunder Road/Hungry Heart/Glory Days/Raise Your Hand/Chimes of Freedom/Get Up, Stand Up.

9/8/88 Turin, Italy, Stadio Comunale
A very vocal crowd of 60,000 turns out to see Springsteen, singing along from the very first notes of "Born in the USA." The set is the same as on 9/6/88.

9/10/88 Barcelona, Spain, Camp Nou Stadium
The set is the same as 9/5/88. Branford Marsalis lends his saxophone talent to "Raise Your Hand."

Tacoma, Wash., May 5, 1988.

9/13/88 San Jose, Costa Rica, Estadio Nacional
Again the set is the one of 9/5/88 but played during a heavy rainstorm. Church and parent groups in this country that see few rock 'n' roll programs are worried that the show will have ill effects on the nation's youth. One parent group issues a statement calling rock 'n' roll music "subversive energy with erotic overtones, in an environment of base passions and evil." Bruce's first-ever show in Central America.

9/15/88 Toronto, Canada, Maple Leaf Gardens
The same set as 9/4/88, except that "War" is not played and "Dancing in the Dark" replaces "Bobby Jean." The final arena show of the tour will always be memorable if only for "Dancing in the Dark," during which Springsteen chose, and danced spiritedly with, a male partner. This was Springsteen's first indoor show in Toronto since 1981 and his first show there of any kind since 1985, as the *Tunnel* tour did not include Canada.

9/17/88 Montreal, Quebec, Olympic Stadium
For the first time Bruce joins Sting for a duet of "Every Breath You Take," with which the two continue to close Sting's set throughout the remainder of the tour. Born in the USA/Promised Land/Cover Me/Brilliant Disguise/The River/Cadillac Ranch/War/My Hometown/Thunder Road/Glory Days/Born to Run/Twist and Shout/Chimes of Freedom/Get Up, Stand Up.

9/19/80 Philadelphia, Pa., J.F.K. Stadium
The same set as 9/17/88, except for the addition of "Jungleland" after "My Hometown." This first U.S. show of the tour also brings a big surprise in Springsteen's set. "Jungleland" returns to the set for the first time since 1985, in a superb version that highlights Clarence Clemons on saxophone, as much of the tour abroad has done. Gabriel's violin player, L. Shankar, adds strings to "The River."

Another surprise of this performance was the guest appearance of David Sancious on keyboards in "Glory Days." Bruce introduced him as "E Street Alumni." Sancious, who currently plays in Gabriel's band, hadn't sat in with the E Street Band in more than ten years. The band was also joined by the *Tunnel of Love* horn players on "Cover Me," "War," "Glory Days," and "Raise Your Hand."

9/21/88 Los Angeles, Calif., Coliseum
The same set as 9/19/88. Joan Baez opens the show, as she does at all three U.S. performances of the tour. U2's Bono joins the artists in encores of "Chimes of Freedom" and "Get Up, Stand Up," and receives a warm welcome from the crowd.

9/23/88 Oakland, Calif., Oakland Stadium
Bruce's 39th birthday means a special show. Roy Orbison flies in to surprise Bruce backstage, something Bruce did for Roy a few months earlier. To open the show Joan Baez leads the crowd in singing "Happy Birthday" to Bruce, who then joins her onstage for a duet of "Blowin' in the Wind." Because Sting does not perform in either this or the Tokyo show, Gabriel's and Bruce's sets are extended. Gabriel introduces Bruce by leading the crowd once again in "Happy Birthday." Bruce and the band turn in a 14-song set that includes the only Amnesty tour performance of "Tunnel of Love." The arrangement of the song is slightly different, opening directly into the verse and leaving out the familiar introduction of the *Tunnel* tour performances. Bruce also plays a superb acoustic version of "I Ain't Got No Home" for the first time in concert. Because of the length of the show and the special occasion, this is probably the best show of the Amnesty tour. War/Born in the USA/Promised Land/Tunnel of Love/Brilliant Disguise/The River/I Ain't Got No Home/Cover Me/Cadillac Ranch/My Hometown/Thunder Road/Glory Days/Born to Run/Raise Your Hand/Chimes of Freedom/Get Up, Stand Up.

9/27/88 Tokyo, Japan, Tokyo Dome (The Big Egg)
Strangely this show does not receive much attention in Japan, and as a result it does not come close to selling out. "I'm on Fire" is performed for the first time in the Amnesty tour. This concert is Bruce's first in Japan since his triumphant shows there in March and April of 1985. Fifteen-song set includes "I'm on Fire."

9/30/88 New Delhi, India, Jawaharlal Nehru Stadium
This show is somewhat shrouded in controversy owing to the downplaying of the concert's human rights aspect by the show's sponsor, the newspaper, *The Times of India*. "Working on the Highway" and "Dancing in the Dark" are included in a 15-song set. Gabriel's violinist L. Shankar opens the show and Springsteen joins him on harmonica for one song.

10/3/88 Athens, Greece, New Olympic Stadium
Fourteen-song set without "Thunder Road." The Athens show is added in place of performances planned for Moscow which could not be arranged.

10/7/88 Harare, Zimbabwe, National Sports Stadium
Bruce's first-ever performance in Africa. This show is attended by approximately 20,000 South Africans, and the subject of Apartheid is present in the sets of all the artists. Portions of "War" and "My Hometown," along with Gabriel's "Biko" are broadcast to South Africa via the independent Capitol Radio. Born in the USA/Promised Land/Cover Me/I'm on Fire/The River/Cadillac Ranch/War/My Hometown/Dancing in the Dark/Glory Days/Born to Run/Twist and Shout/Chimes of Freedom/Get Up, Stand Up.

10/9/88 Abidjan, Cote D'Ivoire, Houphouet-Boigny Stadium
The same set as 10/7/88. This is the first show of the tour in which Bruce is not the final performer. All artists on the tour relinquish the closing spot to the immensely popular African artist Johnny Clegg.

10/12/88 Sao Paulo, Brazil, Palmeiras Stadium
The set for this concert is the same as 10/7/88.

10/14/88 Mendoza, Argentina, Estadio Mundialista Mendoza
The crowd includes thousands of people who cross the nearby border from Chile. As in Zimbabwe, part of the show is broadcast to neighboring Chile.

10/15/88 Buenos Aires, Argentina, River Plate Stadium
The final night of the world tour is broadcast on radio around the world and in the U.S. with highly questionable results — fans felt the broadcast did not feature enough music. The show is also filmed and is televised worldwide on December 10th, the 40th anniversary of the United Nations Declaration of Human Rights. All four other artists join Bruce for "Twist and Shout," and David Sancious again sits in on "Cadillac Ranch." Sting and Gabriel are decked out in matching Jersey attire. Born in the USA/Promised Land/Cover Me/I'm on Fire/The River/Cadillac Ranch/War/My Hometown/Dancing in the Dark/Glory Days/Raise Your Hand/Twist and Shout/Chimes of Freedom/Get Up, Stand Up.

All totaled, the Amnesty tour covered 20 cities, many of which had never before been visited by Springsteen and the E Street Band, nor by any other Western musicians of any kind.

11/12/88 Tarrytown, N.J., Music Hall
Bruce joins John Prine onstage for a performance of Prine's "Paradise." Patti Scialfa attends the show but does not play. Bruce, Patti and Prine pose for photographers backstage.

11/26/88 San Francisco, Calif., The Stone
For the first time in many years Bruce joins Southside Johnny and the Jukes for a rollicking four-song set that starts at 1:40 A.M. In the Midnight Hour/Hearts of Stone/Keep a Knockin'/Little Queenie.

1/18/89 New York, N.Y., Waldorf-Astoria Hotel
Bruce honors the late Roy Orbison by performing "Crying" at the fourth annual Rock and Roll Hall of Fame induction dinner. Bruce is joined at the dinner by Patti Scialfa, George Theiss and Vini Lopez, who also joins Bruce onstage.

3/10/89 Los Angeles, Calif., Rubber
Bruce joins the Mighty Hornets on "C.C. Rider" after spending the early evening at a party for Ray "Boom Boom" Mancini.

4/25/89 Los Angeles, Calif., Rubber
Bruce climbs on stage at Mickey Rourke's club, performing "Stand By Me" and a few other tunes.

6/2/89 Asbury Park, N.J., Stone Pony
Bruce, Patti, Roy, Max and the horns join members of Killer Joe for a four-song set which includes "You Never Can Tell," "Lucille," "Boom Boom" and "Travelin' Band."

6/9/89 Asbury Park, N.J., Stone Pony
Bruce and Max join Nils Lofgren on stage for "Not Fade Away," "In the Midnight Hour," "Lean on Me" and an extra long version of "Glory Days."

6/14/89 Jones Beach, N.Y., Jones Beach
Bruce joins Neil Young for a final encore of "Down By the River."

Asbury Park, N.J., August 21, 1988. ►

RESOURCES
· · · · · · · · · ·

Hiding on the Backstreets

BRUCE SPRINGSTEEN: You can write Bruce Springsteen care of CBS Records, 51 West 52nd Street, New York, N.Y. 10019.

ASBURY PARK: If you travel to Asbury Park be sure to visit the Asbury Park Rock 'n' Roll Museum. They are currently without a site but you can write them at P.O. Box 296, Allenhurst, N.J. 07711 for information on their new location.

THUNDER ROAD: *Thunder Road* was the original Bruce Springsteen fanzine and the one that provided the idea and inspiration for *Backstreets*. Both Ken Viola and Lou Cohan helped provide some of the spark for *Backstreets*. Though *Thunder Road* stopped publishing in 1982 some back issues are still available and can be obtained by writing Backstreet Records, P.O. Box 51219, Seattle, Wash., 98115-9966.

BRUCE TRAMPS: If you have any corrections or additions to any of the material listed in this book, please write us and let us know. If you write us and enclose a self-addressed-stamped-envelope, we'll send you a list of all currently published fanzines for Bruce Springsteen, Little Steven and Southside Johnny.

BACKSTREETS MAGAZINES: If you'd like more information on subscribing to *Backstreets* magazine, rates are currently $15 a year in the U.S. Rates are $20 (in U.S. funds) a year for overseas airmail service. Over 30 issues are in print. Some back issues are available and if you send a self-addressed-stamped-envelope we'll send you a current list. *Backstreets'* address is P.O. Box 51225, Department B, Seattle, Wash. 98115-9966.

PHOTO CREDITS
· · · · · · · · · ·

Walking in the Sights

Thanks to diligent work by all contributing photographers and researchers, we've attempted to indicate date and location on all photographs. Special thanks for their research efforts go to Phil and Bernadette Ceccola, Ken Viola, Erik Flannigan, and the Asbury Park Rock 'n' Roll Museum. Jeff Albertson/Stock, Boston (64); Steven Allan (105); Asbury Park Rock 'n' Roll Museum (33,37,38); Kenny Barr (101); Joel Bernstein/LGI (76); Watt M. Casey, Jr., (78,126,158-159,182,183,203,224); Phil Ceccola (24,30,31,60,61,66,70,74,90,103,128,129,146,151,153,155,163, 178,181,185,204,220); B. Struye (110); Mike D'Adamo (127,164); Ron Delany (190); David Denenberg (19,85,91,95,112,156,196,200,212); John C. DeSantis/Asbury Park Rock 'n' Roll Museum (22); David DuBois (8,40,43,94,166,187,197,205,217); David Gahr (5,20,27,82, 106-107,115,130,148); Mark Greenberg (169); Lynn Goldsmith/LGI (13,54,172); Chuck Jackson/LGI (118,119); Joanne Jefferson (199); Todd Kaplan/ Starfile (front cover); Brooks Kraft (2,186,210); Kathie Maniaci (45,47,48); Eric Meola/Contact Press (63); Robert Minkin (81); Jim O'Loughlin (170); A.J. Pantsios/Starfile (back cover); A.J. Pantsios (44,193); Marty Perez (161); Barbara Y.E. Pyle/Contact Press (56,69,72, 175); Ellen Reed (98); Debra L. Rothenberg (49,51,52,86,108,124,179,208,211,214,219); Rex Rystedt (endpaper, 10,14,58,79,92,96,117,189,195,216); Robert Santelli (53); James Shive (59,73,120,122,176,206); Franck Stromme/Starfile (201); Bob Zimmerman (89,132,222); Steve Zuckerman (61); Vinnie Zuffante/ Starfile (145).

◄ *Bryn Mawr, Pa., February 5, 1975.*

Remember all the Movies: Washington, D.C., 1985.

ACKNOWLEDGMENTS
· · · · · · · · · · · · · · · · ·

Tramps Like Us . . .

Literally thousands of Bruce Tramps worldwide have contributed to this effort both by their support of *Backstreets* magazine and by their help with this book. It would be impossible to list everyone who has lent an ear, sent a set list in, or bought us beers over the past ten years, but for all who have believed in what we've been doing, and for all who believed in our magazine back when we put out 200 copies from my basement, this book is for you. And for all those who've believed in me personally, even when they didn't understand just what the hell I saw in Bruce Springsteen — especially Kathleen, Herb, Cathy, Jill, Betty, Sis, Francis, and the matriarch of my family Virginia Cross — I consider myself blessed to have known such love. A special thanks to Bob Cornfield and Michael Pietsch for their help in putting this whole effort together. This book is dedicated to all those who took the message of Bruce Springsteen's music and used it to make their own lives and the world a better place. Very special thanks must go to Erik Flannigan, who deserved to be born earlier so he could have been sitting next to me in 1974 when Bruce danced on my table at the Bottom Line, Mary Schuh, Barbie Herbert, Robert Santelli, Art Masciocchi, David DuBois, Rex Rystedt, Debra L. Rothenberg, Steve Bumball, Billy Smith, Eason Jordan, Arlen Schumer, Cathy Cross, Steve Smollen, Andy Reid, Phil Ceccola, Jimmy Guterman, Dale Yarger, John Fontana, Kate Blacklock, Bob Zimmerman, Mark Stricherz, Phil A. Delphia, David Denenberg, Watt M. Casey, Jr., Paul Williams, James Shive, Robert Hilburn, David Gahr, Lynn Goldsmith, Star File, Marcello Villella, Kathie Maniaci, Mike Appel, Curtis Minato, Art Chantry, Grant Alden, Vera Denke, Lara Williamson, Lisa Peranzi, Johan Bjernick, David Dingle, Alan Glaser, Ralf Dissmann, Joe Crawford, and Ed Kosinski. And special thanks also go to the thousands of Bruce Tramps whose support through the years has made this effort part of the ties that bind, folks like Michael Dougan, Chuck Bauerlein, Michael MacCambridge, Noel Brooks Ebner, Robert Allen, Debbie Mayer, Robert Newman, Dale Martin, Janet Wainwright, Cathy Bell, Ernie Hinterder, Vini Lopez, Mitch McGeary, John Lyon, Bill Nesnay, Brad Peaslee, Marietta Phillips, Jim Ragsdale, Don Rasmussen, Ed Sciaky, Jeff Tamarkin, Barry Elliot, Dan French, Paul Johnson, Karen Fox, Paul Natkin, Marty Perez, Sarah Erwin, Les Kippel, Jacquie Scheer, Wendy Dunlap, Larry Canale, Wendy King, Mike Wentzel, Linda Conner, Jesse Reyes, Steve Zuckerman, Jim O'Loughlin, Max Vlahovich, Cathy Elton, Caius Charnell, Ken Deranleau, David Johnson, John Kohl, Stu Reid, Bernie Ranellone, Max Weinberg, Rick Rodarte, Martin Venturo, Ruth Atherley, Dan Benson, Constant Chantal, Paul Bradshaw, Yvonne Schuur, Jon Pont, Larry Bausch, Steven Allan, Randy Cepuch, Vicky Gill, John Koeing, George Hill, Robert Minkin, Terry McGibbon, Cary Judd, Kevin Addis, Brian Magid, Rob Roth, Andrea Klein, John Mackie, Patrick McDonald, Sil Pepe, Bosse Nerbe, Allen Schery, Lee Mrowicki, The Stone Pony, Chris Hunt, Linda Segall, Rene Slegers, Chris Higgens, Gretchen Lauber, Mary Ann Savo, Mike Blackwell, Peter Callaghan, John Keister, Chuck Yopp, Lou Cohan, Lee Gammon, Cindy May, Tom Collicott, Cori Chacon, Karen Moskowitz, Cam Garrett, Lisa Orth, Scott Bannatyne, Bernadette Ceccola, London Features, Linda Tartaglione, Holly Cara, Diane Brookshire, Suzanne Talbot, Michelle Unger, Edna Gunderson, David Peltz, Jared Houser, Steve and Phil Jump, Joe Kivak, Dave Marsh, whose first book *Born to Run* inspired so many Bruce Tramps, Victoria Scott, Daniel Funkhouse, Sean Curry, Pat Curry, Sharon Carlos, Doreen Wood, Cheryl Pawelski, Kathy Sinnott, Tony Shramko, Betty Button, Randi Ferst, Michelle Weiss, John Bandrowski, Bunky Cochran, Shaun Stuart, Frank Arbanas.

And Paul Malyn, Jeff Harrow, Robin Serfass, Mari Taliaferro, Ruth Brady, Flower Shaffstall, Darren Scarpa, Maggie Haselswerdt, Jean Dobson, Kathi Smith, Judy Anderson, Joe Bonnet, Suzanne Sturgill, Susan Yamaguchi, Joan Smith, Tamara Squire, Yoji Shimizu, the guy that wrote "Rosalita" back in 1973, Loren K. Shupe, Bob Brewster, Mrs. Adele Springsteen, Mary Lou Simko, Dot Mahaffcy, Bob Brewster, Shannon Daugherty, Anthony D'Angelo, Lorece Newton-Moore, Joan Van Gorp, Gerald Muldowney, Bill Shaw, Lisa Grinnel, Frank Robitaille, Diane Green, Judi Retter, Sean Cronin, Ginger Masse, Sandy Andsejewski, Lee Ackerley, Christine Corson, Michelle Maiatico, Ruth Kelly, Suzanne Oliver, Joanne Norris, Glen Boyd, Lewis Bloom, Kenny Barr, Billy Chinnock, Brooks Kraft, Wayne King, Thom Ross, Alyse Liebowitz, Laura Levine, 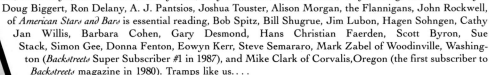 Doug Biggert, Ron Delany, A. J. Pantsios, Joshua Touster, Alison Morgan, the Flannigans, John Rockwell, whose review of *American Stars and Bars* is essential reading, Bob Spitz, Bill Shugrue, Jim Lubon, Hagen Sohngen, Cathy Maesk, Jan Willis, Barbara Cohen, Gary Desmond, Hans Christian Faerden, Scott Byron, Sue Stack, Simon Gee, Donna Fenton, Eowyn Kerr, Steve Semararo, Mark Zabel of Woodinville, Washington (*Backstreets* Super Subscriber #1 in 1987), and Mike Clark of Corvalis, Oregon (the first subscriber to *Backstreets* magazine in 1980). Tramps like us. . . .

                                                    —Charles R. Cross

Austin, Tex., November 9, 1980. ▶

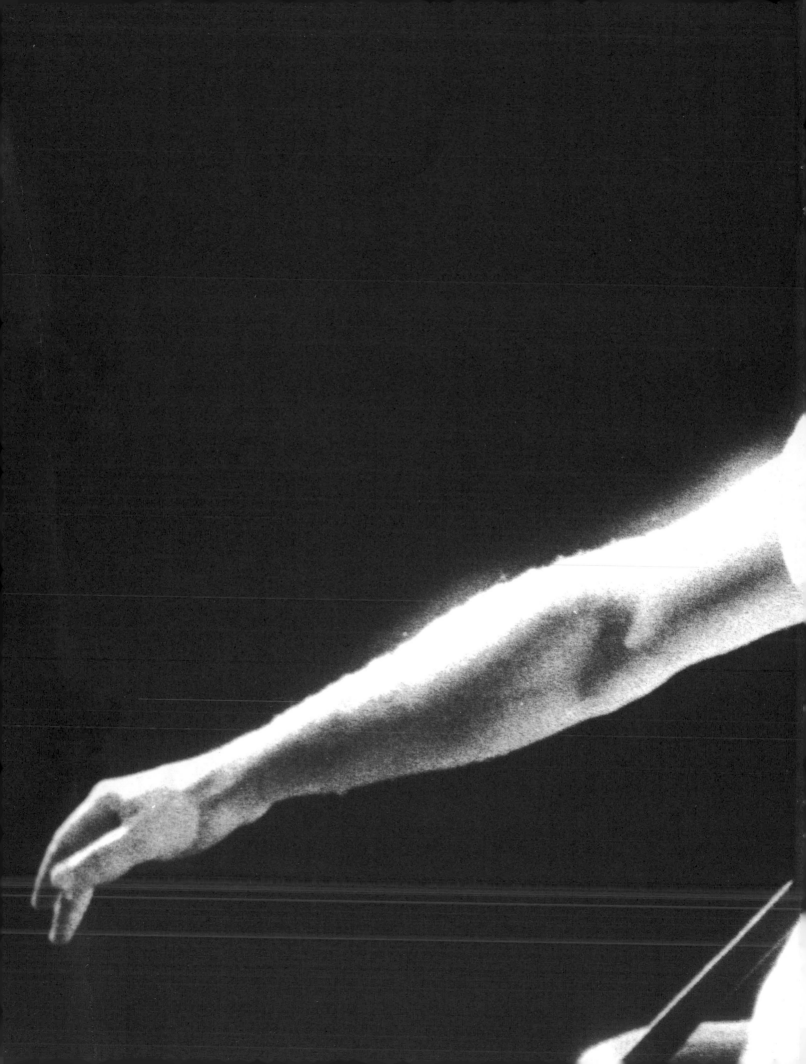